KOREAN WOK COOKBOOK

2 BOOKS IN 1: MERGE TRADITIONAL KOREAN FLAVORS WITH THE ART OF WOK COOKING

EMMA YANG

© Copyright 2024 by Emma Yang - All rights reserved.

Without the prior written permission of the Publisher, no part of this publication may be stored in a retrieval system, replicated, or transferred in any form or medium, digital, scanning, recording, printing, mechanical, or otherwise, except as permitted under 1976 United States Copyright Act, section 107 or 108. Permission concerns should be directed to the publisher's permission department.
Legal Notice

This book is copyright-protected. It is only to be used for personal purposes. Without the author's or publisher's permission, you cannot paraphrase, quote, copy, distribute, sell, or change any part of the information in this book.
Disclaimer Notice

This book is written and published independently. Please keep in mind that the material in this publication is solely for educational and entertaining purposes. All efforts have provided authentic, up-to-date, trustworthy, and comprehensive information. There are no express or implied assurances. The purpose of this book's material is to assist readers in having a better understanding of the subject matter. The activities, information, and exercises are provided solely for self-help information. This book is not intended to replace expert psychologists, legal, financial, or other guidance. If you require counseling, please get in touch with a qualified professional.

By reading this text, the reader accepts that the author will not be held liable for any damages, indirectly or directly, experienced due to the use of the information included herein, particularly, but not limited to, omissions, errors, or inaccuracies. You are accountable for your decisions, actions, and consequences as a reader.

PREFACE

Welcome to a celebration of wok craftsmanship, where sizzle meets serenity, and where the ancient practice of stir-frying is elevated into an art form that dances across nations and tastebuds. This cookbook is not only a vessel traversing the great culinary expanse of Asia but also a passport to the vibrant street markets, the tranquil countryside, and the bustling cities where these flavors were born and nurtured.

In the following pages, we embark on a voyage that is as much cultural as it is culinary. Like the well-seasoned wok—a companion that lovingly carries the tale of a thousand meals—each recipe in this collection is charged with a story, a history, and a soul. A narrative not just of delectable fare, but of communities and connections formed around the quick toss of a spatula and the mesmerizing flame under the wok.

Our journey commences in the aromatic kitchens of China, honoring the tried and true classics like the ever-comforting Stir-Fried Tomatoes and Eggs, and ventures through the fiery passion of a Sichuan Pepper Chicken Stir-Fry. We pay homage to the traditional "wok hei," the breath of the wok, as we present timeless Chinese favorites alongside dishes that illustrate the rich tapestry of flavors unique to this vast culinary empire.

From there, we are whisked into the bustling bylanes of Southeast Asia, where the wok is central to daily life and storytelling. Here, we unveil the secrets of Indonesian Mee Goreng Mamak and explore thrilling Malaysian street eats like Wok-Seared Char Siew. With influences from Malay, Chinese, and Indian cuisines, this section of our cookbook is a heady mix of the old and new, the tangy and the fiery.

Continuing our exploration, we witness the wok's versatility yet again. From the Thai Basil Beef Bliss, which ignites the palate with its balance of sweet, spicy and aromatic herbs, to the Filipino Pancit Canton, which brings together a bountiful assortment of textures and flavors in an intricate noodle dance.

The universal appeal of a good stir fry breaks geographical barriers, and so we also venture into the unique flavors of Nepal, Korea, and Japan. Each dish, like the Sandheko or the Spicy Korean Squid Stir-Fry, is an invitation to experience a new tradition, a new festival of the senses.

This collection of recipes not only aims to teach the art of the stir fry but also embodies a respect for the produce, an understanding of the delicate interplay between ingredients, and the pursuit of harmony on the palate. With each turn of the page, cooks from all walks of life are encouraged to take their woks and create magic—one that is suffused with their own experiences, nourished by their creativity, and ready to gather round a table of eager storytellers.

At the heart of this cuisine lies a simple truth: that the best memories are often forged with the clanging of a wok, the fragrance of spices in the air, and shared plates amongst friends and family.

And so, dear reader, we urge you to light the flame, pick up your spatula, and join us in the ancient, yet ever-new symphony of flavors. May your kitchen be filled with the laughter and joy that is the essence of wok stir fry cooking. Welcome to your sumptuous and sizzling adventure—zhù nǐ yǒu yī gè měiwèi de lǚchéng, wishing you a delicious journey!

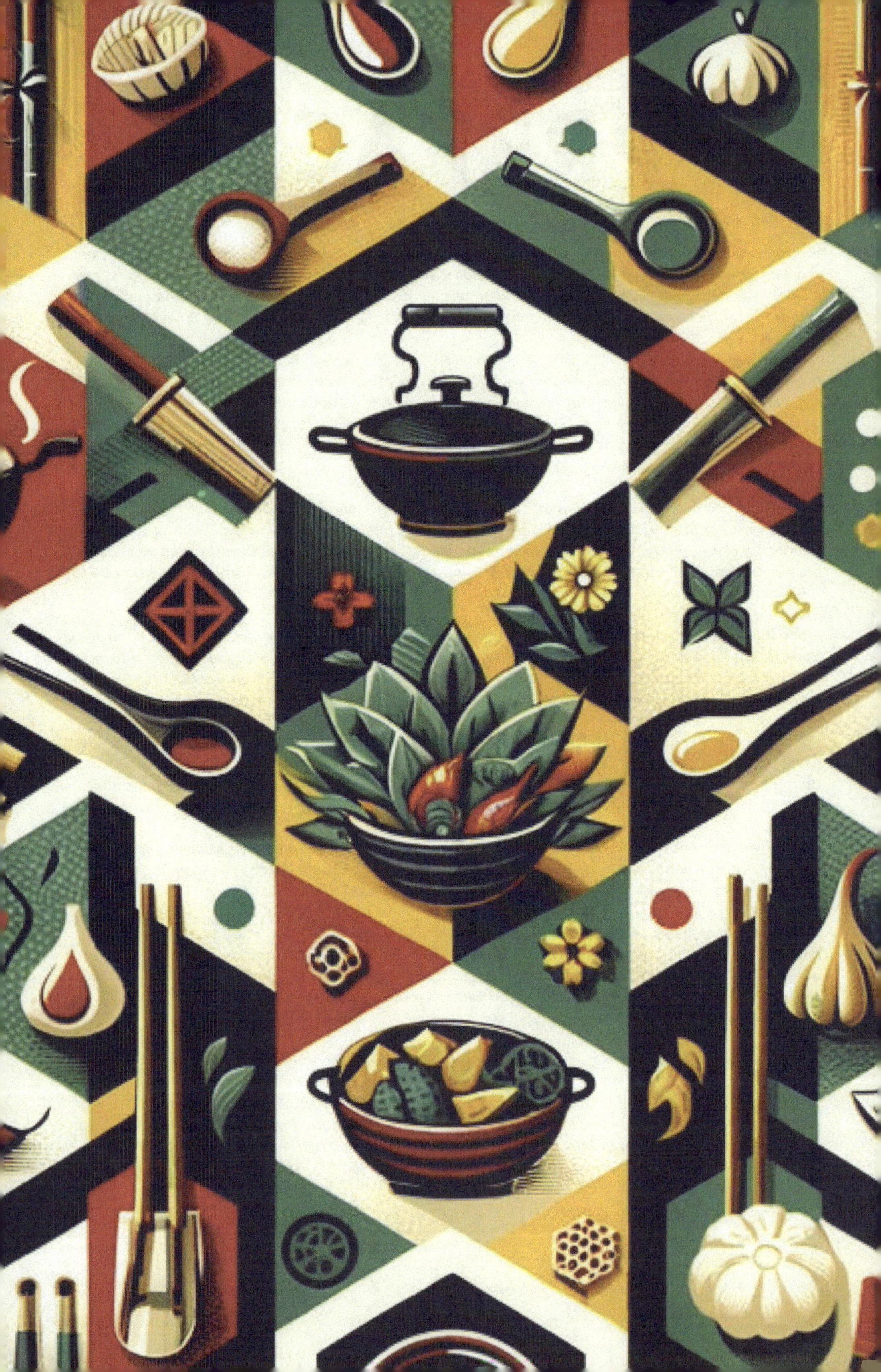

AUTHENTIC WOK RECIPES

BOK CHOY WITH GARLIC

Stir-Frying is a fundamental technique in Chinese cuisine, prized for its ability to cook ingredients quickly while retaining their texture and nutrients. Bok choy, a type of Chinese cabbage, is a beloved vegetable across Asia, known for its tender leaves and crisp stalks. This simple, yet delicious dish showcases the fresh, mild sweetness of bok choy contrasted with the aromatic punch of garlic. It is a common side dish often found accompanying a multitude of meals, providing a healthy and flavorful balance to richer main courses.

INGREDIENTS

- 1 lb bok choy, washed and cut into bite-sized pieces
- 4 large garlic cloves, finely minced
- 2 tablespoons vegetable oil
- 1 teaspoon sesame oil
- 2 tablespoons soy sauce
- 1 tablespoon oyster sauce (optional)
- ½ teaspoon sugar
- Salt to taste
- A pinch of white pepper
- 1 teaspoon cornstarch dissolved in 2 tablespoons water (optional, for thickening)

DIRECTIONS

1. Start by preparing your bok choy: trim off the base, then chop the stalks into similar-sized pieces to ensure even cooking. Separate the leaves from the stalks, as the stalks will take longer to cook.
2. Heat the vegetable oil in a large skillet or wok over high heat until it just starts smoking.
3. Add the minced garlic and stir quickly for about 10 seconds or until fragrant—be careful not to let it burn.
4. Place the bok choy stalks in the pan first and stir-fry for about 2 minutes.
5. Add the leaves and continue to stir-fry for another minute until the leaves start to wilt.
6. Pour in the soy sauce, sesame oil, oyster sauce (if using), and sugar, then sprinkle a pinch of salt and white pepper. Stir everything well to combine.
7. If you desire a slightly thickened sauce, add the cornstarch slurry and stir quickly to coat the bok choy evenly.
8. Once the bok choy is cooked to a tender-crisp texture, remove from heat.
9. Taste and adjust seasoning if needed, then serve immediately as a side dish with your choice of protein or enjoy it on its own with steamed rice.

DIETARY MODIFICATIONS

Vegetarian: Simply omit the oyster sauce or substitute with vegetarian stir-fry sauce or hoisin sauce.

Vegan: In addition to removing the oyster sauce as mentioned above, ensure that the soy sauce is a variety that does not contain any animal products, as some may use bone char in the process.

Gluten-Free: Substitute the soy sauce with tamari or another gluten-free soy sauce alternative and ensure the oyster sauce and sesame oil are labeled gluten-free if used.

INGREDIENT SPOTLIGHT: BOK CHOY

Bok choy is the star of this recipe. Also known as pak choi or Chinese cabbage, its origins can be traced back to China, where it has been cultivated for over 5,000 years. It's a member of the Brassica family, which includes broccoli, kale, and brussels sprouts. Bok choy is rich in vitamins A, C, and K and has high calcium content. In a stir-fry, its leaves wilt beautifully while the stalks maintain a satisfying crunch, providing an excellent textural contrast. This vegetable is crucial for this dish due to its ability to absorb flavors while contributing its own subtle, earthy notes.

CHEF'S TIPS

- Always rinse and dry bok choy thoroughly to remove any dirt trapped in the stems.
- Preheat the wok before adding the oil to prevent the garlic from sticking and ensure instant searing of the bok choy.
- Cut bok choy stems into uniform sizes for even cooking and aesthetic appeal.
- Add garlic first to infuse the oil, but keep the heat high and moving to avoid burning it.
- Use a cornstarch slurry to create a glossy sauce that clings to the bok choy without making it soggy.

POSSIBLE VARIATIONS OF THE RECIPE

- **Spicy Kick:** Add a teaspoon or more of chili flakes with the garlic to introduce some heat to the dish.
- **Mushroom Medley:** Alongside the bok choy, stir-fry a combination of sliced mushrooms such as shiitake, oyster, or cremini for added umami and texture.
- **Protein-Boosted:** For a more filling dish, add slices of firm tofu or chicken breast at the beginning and stir-fry until cooked before adding the bok choy.

HEALTH NOTE & CALORIC INFORMATION

This dish is low in calories and high in nutrients. Bok choy is particularly a good source of vitamin C, vitamin K, and vitamin A, as well as minerals like calcium and iron. Depending on the serving size, one portion of this stir-fry is typically around 50-70 calories, with the majority of the calories coming from the vegetable oils used in cooking. It's low in carbs and fats but packs a good fiber punch due to the bok choy.

KUNG PAO TOFU

Kung Pao Tofu is a vegetarian twist on the classic Sichuan dish, Kung Pao Chicken. The original dish dates back to the Qing Dynasty and is believed to be named after Ding Baozhen, a governor of Sichuan province, whose title was "Kung Pao." The dish is known for its complex flavor profile—spicy, slightly sweet, and umami-rich.

INGREDIENTS

- 14 oz. firm tofu, pressed and cubed
- 2 tablespoons soy sauce, divided
- 1 tablespoon cornstarch
- 3 tablespoons peanut oil or vegetable oil, divided
- 1 teaspoon Sichuan peppercorns
- 2 cloves garlic, minced
- 1 inch ginger, minced
- 2 green onions, chopped, whites and greens separated
- 8 dried red chili peppers, chopped (adjust to taste)
- 1/2 cup roasted unsalted peanuts
- 1 red bell pepper, diced
- 1 green bell pepper, diced
- 1 zucchini, cut into half-moons

For the Sauce:

- 2 tablespoons Chinkiang vinegar (or balsamic vinegar)
- 1 tablespoon hoisin sauce
- 1 tablespoon sesame oil
- 2 teaspoons sugar
- 1 teaspoon cornstarch

DIRECTIONS

1. Start by pressing the tofu to remove excess moisture. Wrap the tofu block in a kitchen towel and place a heavy object on top. Let it sit for at least 20 minutes.
2. Cut the tofu into 1-inch cubes and place them in a bowl. Drizzle with 1 tablespoon of soy sauce and gently toss to coat.
3. Sprinkle 1 tablespoon of cornstarch over the tofu cubes and toss until evenly coated.
4. In a small bowl, whisk together the ingredients for the sauce: Chinkiang vinegar, hoisin sauce, sesame oil, sugar, the remaining 1 tablespoon of soy sauce, and 1 teaspoon of cornstarch. Set aside.
5. Heat 2 tablespoons of oil in a wok or large frying pan over medium-high heat. Add the tofu cubes and fry until golden brown on all sides. Remove the tofu from the wok and set aside.
6. Add the remaining 1 tablespoon of oil to the wok, reduce the heat to medium, and add Sichuan peppercorns. Fry for about 30 seconds, or until fragrant.
7. Add the minced garlic, ginger, white parts of green onions, and dried chili peppers to the oil, stirring frequently for 1-2 minutes.
8. Increase heat to medium-high and add the bell peppers and zucchini, stir-frying until the vegetables start to soften, about 3-4 minutes.
9. Return the fried tofu to the wok and pour the sauce over everything. Toss well to ensure the tofu and vegetables are evenly coated with the sauce.
10. Stir in the roasted peanuts and cook for an additional 1-2 minutes.
11. Serve hot, garnished with the green parts of the green onions.

DIETARY MODIFICATIONS

Gluten-Free: Replace traditional soy sauce with tamari to ensure the dish is gluten-free. Many hoisin sauces contain wheat, so look for a certified gluten-free hoisin sauce.

Nut-Free: Substitute the peanuts with sunflower seeds or pumpkin seeds to maintain the crunch without using nuts.

Low-Carb: For a lower carbohydrate version, replace the sugar with a lower-carb sweetener such as erythritol, and use less cornstarch or substitute it with xanthan gum.

INGREDIENT SPOTLIGHT: SICHUAN PEPPERCORNS

Sichuan peppercorns are the featured ingredient in this dish. Unlike black peppercorns, Sichuan peppercorns aren't particularly hot. Instead, they have a unique aroma and flavor with citrus notes and create a tingling sensation on the tongue. Native to China, these peppercorns are a key component in Sichuan cuisine and are responsible for its distinctive ma (numbing) quality, which balances the la (spicy) heat from chili peppers. This ingredient is integral to Kung Pao Tofu, providing the authentic flavor profile that defines the dish.

CHEF'S TIPS

- For best results, press the tofu thoroughly to remove excess water; this ensures a better texture and absorption of flavors.
- Toasting the Sichuan peppercorns before use can enhance their flavor. Just be careful not to burn them.
- Adjust the number of dried chili peppers according to your spice preference. The heat level can vary, so it's better to start with less and add more if needed.
- Stir the sauce before adding it to the wok to recombine any settled cornstarch.
- Serve the dish immediately after cooking to enjoy the contrast of textures from the crispy tofu and the crunch of the peanuts.

POSSIBLE VARIATIONS OF THE RECIPE

- **Thai-Inspired Kung Pao:** Add a splash of coconut milk and replace the dried chilies with Thai bird chilies. Serve with lime wedges and fresh basil leaves.
- **Orange Kung Pao Tofu:** Introduce some grated orange zest and a splash of orange juice to the sauce for a citrusy twist.
- **Mushroom Medley Kung Pao:** Replace the zucchini with a variety of mushrooms like shiitake, button, and oyster for an earthy flavor profile.

HEALTH NOTE & CALORIC INFORMATION

This dish is high in protein and contains beneficial nutrients from the vegetables, such as vitamins A and C. The tofu provides a good source of iron and calcium. However, the dish also contains oil and peanuts, which add to the calorie content. A single serving typically has around 400 to 500 calories, along with 20-30 grams of fat, 30-40 grams of carbohydrates, and 20-25 grams of protein. Remember, these values can vary based on the exact measurements and substitutions used in the recipe.

SIZZLING BEEF HO FUN

Originating from the south of China, especially famous in Guangdong province, Beef Ho Fun is a staple dish in Cantonese cuisine. It is profoundly loved for its intriguing blend of textures, from the silky rice noodles to the tender bite of marinated beef—each stir fry creates an aromatic symphony. The flames of the wok lend a smoky taste known as "wok hei," which is the spirit of this dish, encapsulating centuries of culinary tradition.

INGREDIENTS

- 300g flat rice noodles (ho fun)
- 200g beef sirloin, thinly sliced
- 3 tablespoons light soy sauce
- 2 tablespoons oyster sauce
- 1 tablespoon dark soy sauce (for color)
- 1 tablespoon rice wine (Shaoxing wine)
- 1 teaspoon cornstarch
- 2 cloves garlic, minced
- 1 medium onion, thinly sliced
- 1 bell pepper, julienned
- 4 stalks spring onions, cut into 2-inch lengths
- 1 teaspoon sugar
- 2 tablespoons peanut oil
- 1 tablespoon sesame oil
- Salt and ground white pepper, to taste

DIRECTIONS

1. Slice the beef sirloin against the grain into thin strips. In a bowl, mix 1 tablespoon light soy sauce, rice wine, cornstarch, and a dash of white pepper. Add the beef and marinate for at least 15 minutes.
2. While the beef is marinating, separate the rice noodles with your hands to loosen them, being careful not to break them.
3. Preheat a wok or a large skillet over high heat. Add 1 tablespoon of peanut oil and swirl to coat the base and sides.
4. Add the marinated beef to the wok. Quickly stir fry until the beef is about 70% cooked. Remove and set aside.
5. Add the remaining peanut oil to the wok. Add garlic and onion, stir-frying until fragrant.
6. Toss in the bell pepper and stir fry for about 1 minute.
7. Add the rice noodles and the rest of the light soy sauce, dark soy sauce, and oyster sauce. Stir gently to combine everything, being careful not to break the noodles.
8. Return the beef to the wok, sprinkle in sugar and drizzle sesame oil. Mix well.
9. Toss in the spring onions, season with salt to taste, and stir fry for another minute to ensure everything is heated through and mixed well.
10. Serve immediately to enjoy the noodles with the best texture and the iconic 'wok hei'.

DIETARY MODIFICATIONS

For **vegetarians:** Replace beef with extra-firm tofu or seitan. Marinate and cook using the same steps as for the beef.
For a **vegan option:** Use tofu as suggested for vegetarians and substitute oyster sauce with mushroom sauce or vegan oyster sauce.
For **gluten intolerance:** Ensure the soy sauce is gluten-free and replace Shaoxing wine with a gluten-free option. Checking the rice noodles' package for gluten content is also essential.

INGREDIENT SPOTLIGHT: FLAT RICE NOODLES

The star of Beef Ho Fun is the flat rice noodles, known as "ho fun." This staple ingredient originated in China, is noted for its smooth, wide shape, and has been pivotal in numerous Asian dishes. Made from rice flour and water, it's a gluten-free alternative to wheat noodles. They are perfect for soaking up flavors and adding a chewy texture that's central to the experience of enjoying Beef Ho Fun.

CHEF'S TIPS

- Ensure the wok is very hot before adding your ingredients to achieve the characteristic 'wok hei'.
- Cut your beef thinly and against the grain for maximum tenderness.
- Stir fry ingredients quickly and in batches if necessary to avoid overcrowding and steaming the food instead.
- Handle the rice noodles gently to keep them from breaking and becoming mushy.
- If the noodles stick together, a quick rinse with cold water before cooking can help separate them without additional oil.

POSSIBLE VARIATIONS OF THE RECIPE

- **Spicy Kick:** Add a tablespoon of chili paste or sliced fresh chili peppers when stir-frying the vegetables for a fiery twist.
- **Seafood Delight:** Swap the beef for a mix of seafood like shrimp, squid, and scallops, adjusting the cooking time accordingly.
- **Eggstra Flavor:** Scramble an egg in the wok before adding the noodles for an additional layer of flavor and protein.

HEALTH NOTE & CALORIC INFORMATION

A typical serving of Beef Ho Fun is high in carbohydrates due to the rice noodles and provides protein from the beef. It's also relatively high in sodium from the soy and oyster sauces and may contain moderate amounts of fat, depending on the cut of beef and amount of oil used. The dish can range from 400 to 600 calories per serving. Always be cautious of portion sizes and consider incorporating vegetables to boost the meal's nutritional profile.

SCALLION FISH FILLET

Hailing from the fusion of Chinese culinary traditions, the Ginger Scallion Fish Fillet is a testament to the subtlety and freshness that defines many dishes from East Asia. Often served during family gatherings, this dish has made its way onto restaurant tables, showcasing the delicate balance of the warmth of ginger and the bright, sharp taste of scallion over a perfectly cooked piece of fish.

INGREDIENTS

- 4 fish fillets (such as tilapia, cod, or halibut), about 6 oz each
- 2 tablespoons soy sauce
- 1 tablespoon Shaoxing wine (or dry sherry as a substitute)
- 1 teaspoon sesame oil
- 1 teaspoon sugar
- 1/4 teaspoon white pepper
- 2 tablespoons cornstarch
- 3 tablespoons vegetable oil
- 4 scallions, julienned
- 2-inch piece of ginger, julienned
- 2 cloves of garlic, minced
- Salt to taste

DIRECTIONS

1. Start by patting the fish fillets dry with paper towels. This helps to remove excess moisture, ensuring a better sear in the pan.
2. In a shallow bowl, combine soy sauce, Shaoxing wine, sesame oil, sugar, white pepper, and a pinch of salt to taste. Stir until the sugar dissolves.
3. Place the fish fillets in the marinade, ensuring they are well-coated. Allow them to marinate for 15 to 20 minutes at room temperature.
4. Remove the fish from the marinade and dust each fillet with cornstarch, making sure both sides have a light, even coating. This will help create a slightly crispy exterior.
5. Heat a large skillet over medium-high heat with the vegetable oil. When the oil is hot, gently lay the fish fillets in the skillet and cook for about 3 to 4 minutes on each side or until golden brown and the fish flakes easily with a fork. Cook in batches if necessary to avoid overcrowding.
6. Once the fish is cooked, transfer it to a serving platter and keep it warm.
7. In the same skillet with the remaining oil, add the julienned ginger and scallions, along with minced garlic. Sauté for about 1 to 2 minutes, or until aromatic but not browned.
8. Spoon the ginger and scallion mixture over the fish fillets.
9. Serve immediately with steamed rice or your choice of side.

DIETARY MODIFICATIONS

Gluten-Free: Use tamari or a gluten-free soy sauce to ensure this dish is gluten-free while maintaining its umami richness.

Low-FODMAP: Omit the garlic and use only the green parts of the scallions to keep this dish within low-FODMAP guidelines. This provides the flavor without the fructans that can cause distress.

Keto-Friendly: Eliminate the sugar and cornstarch from the recipe. Instead, cook the fish with a sear in the oil and garnish with the aromatics as directed. This will reduce carbohydrates while maintaining the essence of the dish.

INGREDIENT SPOTLIGHT: GINGER

Ginger is the spotlight ingredient in this recipe. With its origin dating back over 5,000 years in Southeast Asia, ginger is now a widely used spice around the world. Its pungent, spicy flavor and aromatic qualities make it a cornerstone in many Asian cuisines. Medically, ginger has been acclaimed for its anti-inflammatory and digestive properties. In this dish, ginger imparts warmth and a burst of flavor that complements the mild taste of the fish.

CHEF'S TIPS

- To prevent sticking, ensure the skillet is well-heated before adding the fish, and do not flip the fillets too early; wait until they naturally release from the pan.
- Keep the marinade time brief to ensure the fish remains delicate and does not become overly salty.
- Use a non-stick or well-seasoned cast-iron skillet for an easier fish flip and to achieve a beautiful golden crust.
- Julienned ginger and scallions should be cut uniformly for even cooking and optimal texture.
- Be cautious of the fish's cook time. Overcooking can cause it to become tough and dry.

POSSIBLE VARIATIONS OF THE RECIPE

- **Spicy Kick:** Add a teaspoon of chili flakes to the ginger and scallion sauté for those who enjoy a bit of heat.
- **Citrusy Zest:** Squeeze fresh lemon juice over the finished dish to add a bright, refreshing twist.
- **Heartier Sauce:** Deglaze the pan with a splash of stock after cooking the aromatics and reduce it to create a flavorful sauce to pour over the fish.

HEALTH NOTE & CALORIC INFORMATION

This Ginger Scallion Fish Fillet dish is high in protein and low in carbohydrates. It contains healthy fats, particularly if prepared with fish rich in omega-3 fatty acids like halibut. Depending on the type of fish and the amount of oil used for cooking, a single serving can range from 200 to 300 calories. It is relatively low in calories but watch for sodium content due to the soy sauce.

MEE GORENG MAMAK

Mee Goreng Mamak is a savory, spicy, and slightly sweet dish commonly savored in Indonesia and Malaysia. With roots in Indian Muslim cuisine, this street food favorite exemplifies the melting pot of culinary traditions in Southeast Asia. Vendors, known as "mamak," prepare this dish with flourish in woks over blazing-hot flames, creating an enticing smoky flavor. The "mee" means noodles, while "goreng" means fried, describing the essence of the dish.

INGREDIENTS

- 200g yellow wheat noodles or Hokkien noodles
- 100g boneless chicken breast, thinly sliced
- 2 cloves garlic, minced
- 1 shallot, thinly sliced
- 1 red chili, deseeded and sliced (optional for heat)
- 100g firm tofu, cut into small cubes
- 50g choy sum or bok choy, cut into 2-inch pieces
- 2 tablespoons cooking oil
- 1 egg
- 1 tomato, cut into wedges
- 2 tablespoons sweet soy sauce (kecap manis)
- 1 tablespoon oyster sauce
- 1 tablespoon soy sauce
- 1 teaspoon tomato ketchup
- 1 tablespoon sambal oelek (chili paste)
- Salt to taste
- Fresh lime wedges, for serving
- Sliced green onions and fried shallots, for garnish

DIRECTIONS

1. Prepare the noodles according to the package instructions, usually by soaking or boiling until they are just tender. Avoid overcooking. Drain and set aside.
2. Heat the cooking oil in a large wok or frying pan over medium-high heat.
3. Add garlic, shallot, and red chili. Fry until aromatic, taking care not to burn them, around 1 minute.
4. Increase the heat to high, and add the chicken slices. Stir-fry until they are just cooked through, approximately 2-3 minutes.
5. Push the ingredients to the side of the wok, crack the egg into the center, and scramble until just set before mixing with the other ingredients.
6. Add the cubes of tofu and stir-fry for another minute.
7. Introduce the choy sum or bok choy, stir-frying until slightly wilted.
8. Toss in the cooked noodles and tomato wedges. Stir everything to combine.
9. Pour in sweet soy sauce, oyster sauce, soy sauce, tomato ketchup, and sambal oelek. Toss and stir fry until the noodles are evenly coated with the sauces and heated through, about 2 minutes.
10. Season with salt to taste and adjust the spice level if necessary.
11. Serve hot, garnished with lime wedges, sliced green onions, and fried shallots.

DIETARY MODIFICATIONS

Vegetarian: Substitute chicken with additional vegetables such as bell peppers and mushrooms or paneer. Replace oyster sauce with mushroom sauce or a vegetarian stir-fry sauce.

Vegan: Follow the vegetarian modifications and omit the egg. Use a vegan-friendly sweet soy sauce or make your own by reducing soy sauce with brown sugar.

Gluten-Free: Use gluten-free noodles, gluten-free tamari sauce instead of soy sauce, and ensure that the sweet soy sauce and oyster sauce are also gluten-free variants.

INGREDIENT SPOTLIGHT: KECAP MANIS

Sweet soy sauce, or kecap manis, is the soul of Indonesian dishes like Mee Goreng. This thick, molasses-like sauce is traditionally made by simmering soy sauce with palm sugar and spices such as star anise, galangal, and garlic until it reduces to a syrupy consistency. Kecap manis adds a complex sweetness and depth of flavor unique to Indonesian cuisine, and its sticky glaze coats the noodles beautifully, giving Mee Goreng its characteristic appearance and taste.

CHEF'S TIPS

- Preheat your wok until it's really hot to get the iconic 'wok hei'—a smoky aroma imparted from a very hot wok.
- Have all your ingredients prepped and ready to toss in quickly, as this dish cooks fast.
- If you can't handle too much heat, adjust the amount of sambal oelek or omit the fresh chili.
- Use a spatula to move and toss the ingredients vigorously to ensure they get a nice char and are cooked evenly.
- If the noodles start sticking to the wok, add a splash of water to help deglaze the pan and distribute the heat.

POSSIBLE VARIATIONS OF THE RECIPE

- **Seafood Mee Goreng:** Replace chicken with a combination of shrimp and squid for a seafood twist.
- **Spicy Beef Mee Goreng:** Use thinly sliced beef instead of chicken and add extra sambal oelek for a spicier kick.
- **Tofu and Mushroom Mee Goreng:** A vegetarian option substituting chicken with extra tofu and a variety of mushrooms, like shiitake or oyster.

HEALTH NOTE & CALORIC INFORMATION

Mee Goreng Mamak is high in carbohydrates due to the noodles. The dish also contains protein from the chicken and tofu and a moderate amount of vegetables, providing vitamins and fiber. The sauces contribute to the sodium content. A typical serving may have approximately 500-600 calories, depending on the amount of oil and type of noodles used. It is advisable to use lean chicken, limit the oil, and increase the vegetable serving for a healthier version of this dish.

GAN BIAN SI JI DOU

This dish hails from the fiery heart of Sichuan cuisine, an emblematic example of how simple ingredients can be elevated into a complex, mouth-numbing experience. Sichuan Dry-Fried Green Beans, or Gan Bian Si Ji Dou, typically feature the famous Sichuan peppercorn that delivers its signature tingling sensation. The dry-frying technique used here intensifies the flavor and texture of the green beans, contrasting the crispness of the vegetables with the umami-rich notes of the preserved ingredients.

INGREDIENTS

- 1 lb fresh green beans, trimmed
- 2 tbsp vegetable oil
- 3 cloves garlic, minced
- 1 inch ginger, minced
- 4 oz ground pork (optional)
- 1 tbsp Sichuan peppercorns
- 2 tbsp soy sauce
- 1 tbsp Shaoxing wine
- 1 tsp sugar
- 2 tbsp preserved mustard greens, finely chopped (optional)
- 1 tsp sesame oil
- Salt to taste
- Red chili flakes (optional, for extra heat)

DIRECTIONS

1. Dry the green beans thoroughly after washing to prevent splattering during frying.
2. Heat a wok or large frying pan over high heat. Add the vegetable oil and swirl to coat the surface.
3. Add the green beans in a single layer and let them fry for about 4-5 minutes, stirring occasionally, until they blister and start to brown. Remove and drain on paper towels.
4. Lower the heat to medium and add the Sichuan peppercorns to the leftover oil. Fry them for about 1 minute until fragrant, then remove and discard, leaving the flavored oil behind.
5. In the same oil, add the minced garlic and ginger, frying until aromatic, about 30 seconds.
6. If using ground pork, add it now and cook until no longer pink, breaking it up into small bits.
7. Stir in the soy sauce, Shaoxing wine, sugar, and the preserved mustard greens if using, and cook for another minute.
8. Return the green beans to the pan and toss with the other ingredients to coat and heat through.
9. Season with salt and red chili flakes if additional heat is desired.
10. Drizzle with sesame oil before taking off the heat.
11. Serve immediately as a side dish or with rice for a complete meal.

DIETARY MODIFICATIONS

Vegetarian: Skip the ground pork and add a mix of mushrooms (like shiitake or oyster) sautéed along with the garlic and ginger for a meaty texture.

Vegan: Follow the vegetarian modifications and ensure the soy sauce and other condiments used are vegan; substitute the Shaoxing wine with vegetable stock if necessary.

Gluten-Free: Use tamari or a certified gluten-free soy sauce instead of traditional soy sauce and make sure all other condiments are gluten-free.

INGREDIENT SPOTLIGHT: SICHUAN PEPPERCORNS

Sichuan peppercorns are the dried berries of the Chinese prickly ash tree. Noted for their unique aroma and the peculiar tingling numbness they produce on the palate, they are a hallmark of Sichuan cuisine. The peppercorns aren't spicy in the heat sense but instead add a complex, citrus-like flavor that complements many ingredients. Introduced to Chinese cooking more than two centuries ago, these peppercorns are essential for creating the authentic flavor profile Sichuan cooking is known for.

CHEF'S TIPS

- Ensure the green beans are completely dry before frying to prevent oil splatters and help them crisp up.
- Get the wok very hot before adding ingredients to achieve the characteristic "wok hei" flavor.
- Avoid overcrowding the pan to ensure the green beans blister properly.
- Fry the Sichuan peppercorns separately to infuse the oil but remove them before continuing, as the husks can be unpleasant to bite into.
- If the dish is too dry, add a splash of water to the wok to create a bit of steam that helps cook the beans evenly.

POSSIBLE VARIATIONS OF THE RECIPE

- **Chicken or Shrimp:** Substitute ground pork with ground chicken or small shrimp for a different protein if desired.
- **Nutty Crunch:** Top with toasted sesame seeds or crushed peanuts for additional texture and flavor.
- **Fiery Delight:** Incorporate more heat with sliced fresh chilies or increase the amount of chili flakes to your preference.

HEALTH NOTE & CALORIC INFORMATION

A typical serving of Sichuan Dry-Fried Green Beans is rich in vitamins and minerals from the green beans and contains moderate calories. The addition of pork adds protein but also contributes to the fat content. The dish is relatively low in carbohydrates unless sugar is used liberally. For a serving without pork, expect around 100-150 calories, with negligible fat unless extra oil is used for frying.

MONGOLIAN CHICKEN

Originating from the nomadic tribes of Mongolia, Mongolian cuisine primarily revolves around dairy products, meat, and animal fats, due to the harsh winters and limited agricultural land. Mongolian Chicken, while not a traditional dish from Mongolia itself, is a delightful fusion that embodies the bold flavors appreciated in Mongolian cooking. This dish, popular in Westernized Chinese restaurants, captures the balance of savory and sweet with its rich sauce and tender chicken pieces, usually served over a bed of crispy fried noodles or rice.

INGREDIENTS

- 1 pound chicken breast, thinly sliced
- 2 tablespoons vegetable oil
- 2 teaspoons cornstarch

For the sauce:

- 1/2 cup soy sauce
- 1/4 cup brown sugar
- 1 tablespoon hoisin sauce
- 2 teaspoons sesame oil
- 1 teaspoon minced ginger
- 2 cloves garlic, minced
- 1/2 teaspoon crushed red pepper flakes (adjust to taste)

For the stir-fry:

- 1 cup sliced green onions (scallions)
- 1/2 cup julienned carrots
- 1/2 cup sliced mushrooms
- 1/2 cup sliced bell peppers

DIRECTIONS

1. Tenderize the chicken slices by placing them between two sheets of plastic wrap and pounding gently with a mallet. Then, sprinkle the cornstarch over the chicken and toss to coat evenly.
2. In a bowl, whisk together all the ingredients for the sauce until the brown sugar dissolves.
3. Heat the vegetable oil in a wok or large pan over medium-high heat. When oil is hot, add the chicken and stir-fry until browned and nearly cooked through. Remove chicken from the pan and set aside.
4. In the same pan, add a touch more oil if needed, and stir-fry the carrots, mushrooms, and bell peppers until they begin to soften.
5. Return the chicken to the pan with the vegetables and pour the sauce over the top. Simmer for a few minutes until the chicken is cooked through and the sauce has thickened slightly.
6. Stir in the green onions and red pepper flakes, cooking for another minute.
7. Serve hot over steamed rice, crispy fried noodles, or your choice of side.

DIETARY MODIFICATIONS

Vegetarian: Swap the chicken for tofu or tempeh. Press the tofu to remove excess moisture before slicing and coating with cornstarch. Tempeh can be sliced and used directly. Follow the same cooking instructions.

Vegan: Use the vegetarian modification and ensure that the hoisin sauce used is vegan, as some brands contain fish sauce or other animal products. Replace it with a mixture of miso paste and maple syrup if unavailable.

Gluten-Free: Use tamari or a gluten-free soy sauce instead of regular soy sauce and ensure the hoisin sauce is gluten-free. Some brands make a specifically gluten-free hoisin sauce.

INGREDIENT SPOTLIGHT: HOISIN SAUCE

Hoisin sauce is a thick, fragrant sauce commonly used in Chinese cuisine. The name "hoisin" is derived from the Chinese word for seafood, but the sauce does not contain any seafood ingredients. Its primary components include fermented soybean paste, garlic, vinegar, and usually chili and sweetener. Hoisin sauce adds a sweet and salty taste that is essential for the depth of flavor in many Asian dishes, particularly this Mongolian Chicken.

CHEF'S TIPS

- Velvet the chicken: To ensure tender chicken, marinate slices in a mixture of soy sauce, cornstarch, and a little water for 30 minutes before cooking.
- Get your pan hot: A hot wok or pan ensures a good sear on the meat and vegetables, locking in flavor.
- Prep ingredients: Have all sauce ingredients and vegetables prepared and within reach before starting to cook, as the process goes quickly.
- Adjust sweetness: Tailor the sweetness of the sauce to your taste by adding or reducing brown sugar.
- Crisp vegetables: Stir-fry vegetables only until they're brightly colored and tender-crisp to keep texture in the dish.

POSSIBLE VARIATIONS OF THE RECIPE

- Spicy Orange Mongolian Chicken: Incorporate 1/4 cup of fresh orange juice and 1 tablespoon of grated orange zest into the sauce mixture for a citrusy, tangy twist.
- Cashew Mongolian Chicken: Add 1/2 cup of roasted cashews in the final minutes of cooking for a delightful crunch and nutty flavor.
- Mongolian Chicken Stir-Fry with Noodles: Cook and drain noodles of your choice (e.g., udon, rice noodles) and add them into the wok with the chicken and sauce, toss to combine well for a hearty one-pan meal.

HEALTH NOTE & CALORIC INFORMATION

The nutritional content for this Mongolian Chicken recipe (assuming four servings) per serving would be approximately:

- Calories: 300-350
- Protein: 25-30g
- Carbohydrates: 20-25g
- Fats: 10-15g
- Sugars: 10-15g
- Sodium: Moderate to high (due to soy sauce, adjust for low sodium diets)

CHINESE BROCCOLI

Chinese Broccoli with Oyster Sauce is a classic Cantonese dish steeped in simplicity and elegance, known in China as 'Gai Lan'. The star of the dish is the Chinese broccoli itself, a leafy green that is slightly bitter yet full-bodied. Married with the savory and sweet flavors of the oyster sauce, this dish is a staple at Dim Sum and often enjoyed during the Chinese New Year for its symbolic representation of longevity and vitality. Its roots reach deep into the traditions of Southeast Asia, where it has been savored for generations as a beloved side dish.

INGREDIENTS

- 1 pound Chinese broccoli (Gai Lan)
- 2 tablespoons oyster sauce
- 2 tablespoons soy sauce
- 1 tablespoon vegetable oil
- 2 garlic cloves, minced
- 1 teaspoon sugar
- 1/2 teaspoon sesame oil
- Water, for blanching
- Optional: Toasted sesame seeds for garnish

DIRECTIONS

1. Wash the Chinese broccoli thoroughly in cold water to remove any dirt or grit. Trim off the bottom ends of the stalks.
2. Fill a large pot with enough water to cover the broccoli and bring it to a boil. Add a pinch of salt to the water.
3. Drop the broccoli into the boiling water and blanch for about 2 minutes or until the stems are just tender but still crisp.
4. Immediately transfer the broccoli to an ice water bath to stop the cooking process and preserve its bright green color.
5. In a small bowl, mix together the oyster sauce, soy sauce, sugar, and sesame oil. Set aside.
6. Heat the vegetable oil in a pan over medium heat. Add the minced garlic and sauté until it's fragrant but not browned, about 30 seconds.
7. Add the blanched broccoli to the pan and stir for a minute to heat it through.
8. Pour the oyster sauce mixture over the broccoli and toss to coat evenly.
9. Cook for another 1-2 minutes until the sauce is heated through and the broccoli is well coated.
10. Serve the broccoli hot, garnished with toasted sesame seeds if desired.

DIETARY MODIFICATIONS

Vegetarian: Replace the oyster sauce with a vegetarian oyster sauce, made from mushrooms, to maintain a similar umami-rich flavor profile without the need for seafood.

Vegan: Alongside using vegetarian oyster sauce, ensure that the soy sauce is vegan (some brands use animal products), and substitute the sugar with an alternative like maple syrup if avoiding processed sugars.

Gluten-Free: Opt for gluten-free soy sauce and ensure the oyster sauce is also certified gluten-free. As wheat and other gluten-containing ingredients are sometimes hidden in sauces, always read labels carefully.

INGREDIENT SPOTLIGHT: OYSTER SAUCE

Oyster sauce, a key component in this dish, is a thick, dark, rich condiment made by caramelizing oyster juices, salt, sugar, and sometimes soy sauce. Introduced during the late 19th century in Guangdong province of China by a chef named Lee Kam Sheung who fortuitously reduced oyster broth into a deliciously thick sauce. It is essential to many Cantonese dishes, providing a complex mixture of sweetness, saltiness, and umami, and has become a staple in not just Chinese, but also Thai, Vietnamese, and Khmer cuisines.

CHEF'S TIPS

- To maintain the vibrant green of the broccoli, do not skimp on the ice bath step. It is crucial for setting the color.
- When blanching, cook in batches to ensure that the water temperature doesn't drop too much, which can lead to unevenly cooked stems.
- Use a pinch of baking soda in the blanching water to enhance the green color if desired.
- Adjust the sweetness and saltiness of the sauce by adding more or less sugar or soy sauce according to your taste.
- Garlic burns easily and can turn bitter, so keep an eye on it when sautéing and remove it from the heat if necessary.

POSSIBLE VARIATIONS OF THE RECIPE

- **Spicy Kick:** Add a teaspoon of chili flakes or a dollop of chili paste to the oyster sauce mixture to imbue a warm heat that contrasts the savory flavor.
- **Ginger Infusion:** Introduce thin slices of fresh ginger during the sautéing step for an additional zesty aroma that complements the green note of the broccoli.
- **Nut Crumble:** Sprinkle crushed peanuts or cashews on top of the finished dish for a crunchy texture and a nutty flavor that adds another dimension to the dish.

HEALTH NOTE & CALORIC INFORMATION

Chinese Broccoli with Oyster Sauce is relatively low in calories, with each serving containing approximately 90-120 calories. The dish is also rich in Vitamin C, Vitamin K, and contains iron, along with dietary fiber from the Chinese broccoli. The sauce, however, does add sodium, so those watching their salt intake should consume in moderation.

TEMPEH VEGETABLES

Inspired by the principles of stir-frying in Chinese cuisine, this dish showcases the harmonious blend of crunch and savor that comes from quickly cooking fresh vegetables and protein-packed tempeh in a blazing hot wok. Originating in Indonesia, tempeh is a soy product that's become popular worldwide as a versatile and nutrient-rich meat alternative. This recipe allows for a variety of vegetables, making it a perfect seasonal dish that respects the Chinese culinary philosophy of eating according to the environment.

INGREDIENTS

- 1 block of tempeh (about 8 oz), cut into bite-size pieces
- 2 tablespoons soy sauce
- 1 tablespoon sesame oil
- 2 tablespoons vegetable oil
- 1 red bell pepper, sliced into thin strips
- 1 yellow bell pepper, sliced into thin strips
- 2 medium carrots, julienned
- 1 small head of broccoli, cut into florets
- 2 cloves garlic, minced
- 1 inch piece ginger, minced
- 1 tablespoon hoisin sauce
- 1 tablespoon rice vinegar
- 1 teaspoon cornstarch
- 3 tablespoons water
- Salt to taste
- Freshly ground black pepper to taste
- Optional: sesame seeds and sliced green onions for garnish

DIRECTIONS

1. Begin by prepping your vegetables and tempeh. Ensure all ingredients are cut uniformly for even cooking.
2. In a small bowl, whisk together the soy sauce, sesame oil, hoisin sauce, rice vinegar, and cornstarch with the water to make the sauce. Set aside.
3. Heat a wok or large frying pan over high heat. Once hot, add 1 tablespoon of vegetable oil and swirl to coat the surface.
4. Add the tempeh pieces and season with a little salt and pepper. Stir-fry for about 4-5 minutes until golden brown on all sides. Remove the tempeh from the wok and set aside on a plate.
5. In the same wok, add the remaining tablespoon of vegetable oil, garlic, and ginger. Stir-fry for about 30 seconds until fragrant.
6. Add the bell peppers, carrots, and broccoli to the wok. Toss and stir-fry for about 2-3 minutes until the vegetables are brightly colored but still crisp.
7. Return the tempeh to the wok and pour the sauce over the mixture. Toss all the ingredients together and stir-fry for an additional 1-2 minutes, or until the sauce thickens and coats the vegetables and tempeh evenly.
8. Taste and adjust seasoning if necessary. Serve immediately, garnished with sesame seeds and sliced green onions if desired.

DIETARY MODIFICATIONS

Gluten-Free: Swap traditional soy sauce for tamari, which is a gluten-free soy sauce alternative. Ensure that the hoisin sauce is also gluten-free, or substitute with another gluten-free sauce such as a gluten-free oyster sauce.

Vegan: This recipe is already vegan-friendly. Make sure to use vegan hoisin sauce since some brands may contain honey or other animal-derived ingredients.

Low-Calorie: To reduce the calorie content, use a low-calorie cooking spray instead of vegetable oil for stir-frying the tempeh and vegetables. Opt for a light soy sauce and skip the sesame seeds garnish.

INGREDIENT SPOTLIGHT: TEMPEH

Tempeh is a traditional Indonesian food made from fermented soybeans that are pressed into a compact cake. It has a firm texture and a nutty, earthy flavor profile, very different from tofu. The fermentation process not only enriches the flavor but also increases its nutritional value by producing natural antibiotics and enhancing the body's absorption of minerals. It's a fantastic source of protein, dietary fiber, and vitamins. In this recipe, tempeh absorbs the flavors of the sauce and adds a satisfying chew to the dish, complementing the textures of the seared vegetables.

CHEF'S TIPS

- Keep all ingredients ready before starting to cook as the stir-frying process is quick.
- Cutting vegetables uniformly ensures they cook evenly.
- Use a well-seasoned wok to prevent sticking and to imbue the dish with a subtle smokiness.
- High heat is critical in stir-frying; it sears the food, locks in flavors, and retains the nutrients in veggies.
- Add a small amount of water to the wok when stir-frying tougher vegetables like broccoli to help them steam and cook faster.

POSSIBLE VARIATIONS OF THE RECIPE

- **Protein Swap:** You can replace tempeh with tofu or for a non-vegetarian option, try chicken or shrimp. Adjust cooking times accordingly.
- **Spice It Up:** For a spicy variation, include a teaspoon of chili flakes or a few dashes of hot sauce when adding the vegetables.
- **Seasonal Twist:** Use seasonal vegetables like snow peas in spring, eggplant in summer, butternut squash in fall, or bok choy in winter to mix things up and enjoy produce at its peak.

HEALTH NOTE & CALORIC INFORMATION

This dish is rich in plant-based protein, fiber, vitamins, and minerals while remaining relatively low in calories. Tempeh itself is cholesterol-free and high in soy protein, which can contribute to heart health. The various vegetables add antioxidants and dietary fiber. A serving size (1/4 of recipe) roughly contains 250-300 calories, 14-18 grams of protein, and significant amounts of iron, calcium, and potassium.

THAI BASIL BEEF BLISS

Thai Basil Beef, a twist on the traditional Pad Kra Pao Gai, swaps chicken for beef to cater to beef lovers. Hailing from the bustling streets of Thailand, this dish is a testament to Thai cuisine's explosive flavor. Thai Basil Beef inherits the balance of hot, sweet, sour, and salty that captivates taste buds worldwide, while introducing a robust beefy dimension that makes it a heavy hitter in the taste arena.

INGREDIENTS

- 400g flank steak, thinly sliced against the grain
- 2 cups Thai basil leaves, loosely packed
- 2 tablespoons vegetable oil
- 3 cloves garlic, minced
- 2 small red chilies, finely sliced (adjust to taste)
- 1 red bell pepper, thinly sliced
- 1 medium-sized yellow onion, thinly sliced
- 3 tablespoons oyster sauce
- 2 tablespoons soy sauce
- 1 tablespoon fish sauce
- 1 tablespoon dark soy sauce (for color, optional)
- 1 teaspoon sugar
- 1 tablespoon water

DIRECTIONS

1. Begin by prepping your ingredients: Peel and mince the garlic, thinly slice the chilies, onion, bell pepper, and the flank steak.
2. Heat the vegetable oil in a large wok or skillet over medium-high heat.
3. Add the garlic and chilies to the wok. Stir-fry for about 30 seconds, or until aromatic.
4. Increase the heat to high and add the sliced beef to the wok. Spread it out and let it sear for a minute before stirring to brown all sides.
5. Toss in the sliced onion and bell pepper. Continue stir-frying for another 2-3 minutes. The vegetables should soften slightly but remain crisp.
6. In a small bowl, mix together the oyster sauce, soy sauce, fish sauce, dark soy sauce, sugar, and water.
7. Pour the sauce mixture over the beef and vegetables in the wok. Stir well to ensure everything is evenly coated and the sauce begins to caramelize, about 1-2 minutes.
8. Add the Thai basil leaves, stirring them through just until they wilt.
9. Remove from heat immediately once the basil is incorporated to avoid overcooking the basil and beef.
10. Serve your Thai Basil Beef Bliss hot with a side of steamed jasmine rice for an authentic experience.

DIETARY MODIFICATIONS

Vegetarian: Replace beef with firm tofu slices. Use mushroom oyster sauce instead of regular oyster sauce and replace fish sauce with soy sauce or a vegan fish sauce substitute.

Vegan: In addition to the vegetarian alterations, ensure your soy sauce is without any animal products and that your sugar is vegan-certified (not processed with bone char).

Gluten-Free: Substitute regular soy sauce with tamari and ensure that the oyster sauce is gluten-free. Use only gluten-free products and skip the dark soy sauce unless you have a gluten-free version.

INGREDIENT SPOTLIGHT: THAI BASIL

Thai basil, also known as holy basil or 'krapow' in Thai, is the key ingredient that gives this dish its name and its unique anise-like aroma and slightly spicy flavor. Native to Southeast Asia, it's widely used in Thai cuisine and is considered a staple in many Thai dishes, such as curries and stir-fries. It's different from the sweet basil used in Italian cooking; its robustness withstands high cooking temperatures, releasing flavor that becomes the backbone of dishes like Thai Basil Beef.

CHEF'S TIPS

- Slicing the beef against the grain ensures tenderness, as it shortens the muscle fibers, making it easier to chew.
- Pay attention to the heat; a hot wok is crucial for achieving the characteristic char and flavor that stir-frying offers.
- Do not overcrowd the wok – cook in batches if necessary. Overcrowding may lead to steaming the ingredients rather than frying them.
- If Thai basil is hard to find, try using holy basil or even a combination of sweet basil and mint as a substitute, though the flavor will be altered.
- Ensure the basil is added at the very end to maintain its vibrant color and fresh taste.

POSSIBLE VARIATIONS OF THE RECIPE

- **Spicy Lemongrass Beef:** Incorporate finely chopped lemongrass into the oil with garlic and chilies for a zesty twist.
- **Thai Basil Beef Rice Bowl:** Layer the beef over a bowl of rice, add a fried egg on top, and drizzle with a bit of Sriracha for a complete meal in a bowl.
- **Stir-Fried Beef with Cashew Nuts:** Add a handful of roasted cashews in the final minute of stir-frying for an added crunch and nutty flavor.

HEALTH NOTE & CALORIC INFORMATION

Calories: Approximately 350-400 per serving (without rice)
High in protein, iron, and vitamins from the beef and vegetables
Contains healthy fats and is a source of antioxidant-rich herbs
Can be adapted to lower calorie content by using leaner cuts of beef or reducing oil used in cooking.

YU XIANG EGGPLANT

This dish originates from Sichuan cuisine, known for its bold flavors—spicy, pungent, and garlicky. "Yu Xiang" translates to "fish fragrance," which refers to a common seasoning mixture in Sichuan cooking, showcasing flavors traditionally used in fish dishes but paradoxically contains no seafood. It's a beloved technique applied to a variety of ingredients, including eggplant and pork, which absorb the robust sauce beautifully.

INGREDIENTS

- 2 medium eggplants (Chinese or globe), cut into 3-inch strips
- 200 grams pork loin, thinly sliced
- 2 tablespoons soy sauce (divided)
- 2 teaspoons cornstarch (divided)
- 4 tablespoons vegetable oil (divided)
- 3 cloves garlic, minced
- 1 tablespoon ginger, minced
- 2 green onions, sliced diagonally
- 1 tablespoon doubanjiang (fermented broad bean paste)
- 1 tablespoon Shaoxing wine
- 1 teaspoon sugar
- 1/2 cup chicken stock or water
- 1 teaspoon sesame oil
- Red chili flakes to taste (optional)

DIRECTIONS

1. Prep the pork by marinating it in a mixture of 1 tablespoon soy sauce and 1 teaspoon cornstarch. Set aside for 15-20 minutes.
2. While the pork marinates, prep the eggplant by tossing the strips with the remaining 1 teaspoon cornstarch. This will help the eggplant to crisp up while cooking.
3. Heat up 2 tablespoons of vegetable oil in a large skillet or wok over medium-high heat. Add the eggplant strips and stir-fry until they are brown and soft, about 5-7 minutes. Remove and set them aside.
4. Add the remaining 2 tablespoons of oil to the skillet. Stir-fry the pork slices until they are no longer pink, roughly 3-4 minutes.
5. Push the pork to the side of the skillet. In the empty space, add the garlic and ginger and fry until aromatic, about 1 minute.
6. Mix in the doubanjiang paste, and stir everything together for a minute.
7. Pour the Shaoxing wine around the edges of the skillet to deglaze, then incorporate the sugar, remaining soy sauce, and red chili flakes if using.
8. Return the eggplant to the skillet, add green onions, and pour in the chicken stock or water. Allow everything to come to a simmer and let the sauce thicken slightly.
9. Drizzle with sesame oil, give everything a final stir and transfer to a serving dish.
10. Best served hot with a side of steamed rice.

DIETARY MODIFICATIONS

Vegetarian: Replace pork with firm tofu, pressed and cut into thin strips. For the chicken stock, use vegetable stock or water.

Gluten-Free: Use tamari or a gluten-free soy sauce alternative and ensure that the doubanjiang and any other flavor enhancers are certified gluten-free.

Low-Fat Diet: Reduce the vegetable oil to 2 tablespoons in total and use a non-stick skillet to prevent sticking. You can also opt for leaner cuts of pork or replace it with lean chicken breast.

INGREDIENT SPOTLIGHT: DOUBANJIANG

Doubanjiang, or fermented broad bean paste, is a quintessential Sichuan ingredient with over a millennium of history. Made with fava beans, chili peppers, salt, and wheat flour, it is aged like a fine wine to develop its complex flavors. This paste lends a unique spicy, salty, and slightly sour taste that is fundamental to authentic Sichuan cooking and vital in a Yu Xiang sauce.

CHEF'S TIPS

- Salt the eggplant prior to cooking to draw out moisture, which will help prevent it from absorbing too much oil.
- Use a high smoking point oil, like peanut or canola, for the stir-fry to withstand the high heat.
- Avoid over-stirring the ingredients to give them the chance to sear and develop more flavor.
- Slice ingredients consistently to ensure even cooking.
- Prep all your ingredients beforehand, as stir-frying is a quick cooking process.

POSSIBLE VARIATIONS OF THE RECIPE

- **Spicy Lover's Delight:** Amp up the heat by adding Sichuan peppercorns and more chili flakes for that numbing spiciness.
- **Seafood Twist:** Substitute pork with shrimp or firm white fish for a pescatarian-friendly version that maintains the Sichuan essence.
- **Tofu Infusion:** Add cubed silken tofu in the last few minutes of cooking for a soft contrast to the other textures.

HEALTH NOTE & CALORIC INFORMATION

A typical serving of Yu Xiang Eggplant and Pork Stir-Fry contains a rich mix of vitamins from the eggplant, protein from the pork, and beneficial fats from the oils used in cooking. The use of fermented ingredients like doubanjiang also adds a small amount of probiotics. A standard portion may have approximately 350-400 calories, contingent upon the exact quantity of ingredients and cooking oils used.

TOMATOES AND EGGS

This humble yet beloved dish is a staple across China, found both in high-end restaurants and home kitchens. Touted for its simplicity and comfort, it reflects the Chinese culinary philosophy of harmony between colors, flavors, and textures. The dish, with its bright red tomatoes and soft yellow eggs, not only offers a colorful presentation but also a balance between the acidity of the tomatoes and the creaminess of the eggs. It holds a special place in many hearts as a taste of childhood and a touchstone of home cooking.

INGREDIENTS

- 4 large eggs
- 3 medium ripe tomatoes, cut into wedges
- 2 green onions, finely chopped
- 3 tablespoons vegetable oil
- 1 teaspoon salt, or to taste
- 1 teaspoon sugar
- 1 teaspoon soy sauce
- 1/2 teaspoon white pepper (optional)
- Fresh cilantro, chopped, for garnish (optional)

DIRECTIONS

1. Crack the eggs into a bowl and beat them lightly with a fork or whisk until just blended. Season with a pinch of salt and white pepper.
2. Heat 1 tablespoon of vegetable oil in a non-stick skillet or wok over medium-high heat. Add the beaten eggs and quickly scramble until just set but still slightly runny. Remove the eggs from the skillet and set aside.
3. Add the remaining 2 tablespoons of vegetable oil to the skillet. Once hot, add the chopped green onions and stir-fry for about 30 seconds until fragrant.
4. Add the tomato wedges to the skillet. Sprinkle with salt and sugar to help the tomatoes release their juices. Stir-fry for about 2-3 minutes until the tomatoes are softened but still hold their shape.
5. Return the eggs to the skillet with the tomatoes. Add soy sauce and gently toss to combine, being careful not to break up the tomatoes too much.
6. Cook for an additional minute until everything is heated through. Adjust the seasoning if needed.
7. Transfer to a serving plate and garnish with chopped cilantro if desired. Serve hot with steamed rice or as desired.

DIETARY MODIFICATIONS

Vegetarian: Use a vegetarian soy sauce and ensure that all other ingredients are vegetarian-friendly. The eggs are already vegetarian, so no substitution is needed there.

Vegan: Replace the eggs with a soft tofu scramble. Crumble firm tofu and stir-fry with turmeric, black salt (kala namak), and nutritional yeast to mimic the taste and texture of eggs.

Lactose Intolerance: This recipe is naturally lactose-free, so no modifications are necessary. However, for a richer, creamier texture without dairy, you can stir in a bit of lactose-free cream or coconut cream before serving.

INGREDIENT SPOTLIGHT: TOMATO

The tomato is the star of this dish, and its use in Chinese cuisine dates back to the 19th century, following the Columbian Exchange. Considered both a fruit and a vegetable, tomatoes are praised for their rich flavor, nutritional benefits, and versatility in cooking. They provide the dish with moisture, acidity, and a vibrant color. In this recipe, the balance of sweetness and a hint of savory depth is key to creating the perfect sauce that coats the eggs.

CHEF'S TIPS

- Select ripe but firm tomatoes to ensure they add sweetness and remain intact after stir-frying.
- Avoid over-beating the eggs – a light mix will give you softer, fluffier curds in the final dish.
- Heat control is essential – do not let the tomatoes cook down into a sauce; they should be soft yet retain their structure.
- For an extra layer of flavor, a splash of Chinese rice wine or Shaoxing wine can be added to the tomatoes before the eggs are returned to the skillet.
- Serve immediately for the best texture, as the eggs will continue to cook in the residual heat and may become rubbery if left too long.

POSSIBLE VARIATIONS OF THE RECIPE

- **Spicy Kick:** Add a diced hot chili pepper or a spoonful of chili sauce when you add the tomatoes for a bit of heat.
- **Protein Boost:** Include cooked, shredded chicken or small cubes of tofu for added protein.
- **Seafood Version:** Stir in some shrimp or crabmeat with the eggs for a seafood twist on this classic dish.

HEALTH NOTE & CALORIC INFORMATION

A serving of Chinese stir-fried tomatoes and eggs is relatively low in calories, providing a good balance of protein and vitamins, particularly from the eggs and tomatoes. The dish is also low in carbohydrates, making it a suitable option for those on low-carb diets. A typical serving has around 200 calories, 12 grams of protein, and 10 grams of fat. The tomatoes contribute antioxidants like lycopene and vitamin C. It's advisable to watch the oil and soy sauce to manage fat and sodium intake.

BLACK PEPPER CHICKEN

Black Pepper Chicken has its roots in Asian cuisine, with variations found in Chinese, Indian, and Southeast Asian cooking. It's known for its simple yet potent blend of ingredients that complement the key player—the black pepper. This recipe is inspired by Chinese stir-fries where the balance of savory sauces and spices creates a heartwarming dish that's both comforting and invigorating.

INGREDIENTS

- 500g boneless, skinless chicken thighs, cut into bite-sized pieces
- 2 tablespoons soy sauce
- 1 tablespoon Shaoxing wine (or dry sherry)
- 2 teaspoons cornstarch
- 3 tablespoons vegetable oil
- 1 tablespoon freshly ground black pepper, to taste
- 1 onion, sliced
- 1 red bell pepper, cut into squares
- 1 green bell pepper, cut into squares
- 4 cloves garlic, minced
- 1 tablespoon ginger, minced
- 3 tablespoons oyster sauce
- 1 tablespoon dark soy sauce
- 1 teaspoon sugar
- 1/2 cup chicken broth
- 2 scallions, chopped
- Salt, to taste

DIRECTIONS

1. In a bowl, mix chicken pieces with soy sauce, Shaoxing wine, and cornstarch. Let it marinate for at least 15 minutes.
2. Heat 2 tablespoons vegetable oil in a large pan or wok over high heat. Add the marinated chicken in a single layer and sear until browned and cooked through. Remove chicken and set aside.
3. Reduce the heat to medium and add the remaining tablespoon of oil to the pan. Add the ground black pepper and stir frequently for about 30 seconds to release its fragrance.
4. Toss in the onion, red and green bell peppers, and stir-fry for 2 minutes, or until the vegetables start to soften.
5. Add the garlic and ginger and stir-fry for another minute until fragrant.
6. Mix in the oyster sauce, dark soy sauce, sugar, and chicken broth. Bring the sauce to a simmer.
7. Return the chicken to the pan and stir well to coat with the sauce. Cook for another 2-3 minutes.
8. Taste and adjust seasoning with salt and more black pepper, if needed.
9. Garnish with chopped scallions and serve hot with steamed rice or noodles.

DIETARY MODIFICATIONS

Vegetarian: Replace chicken with firm tofu cubes or seitan and use mushroom sauce instead of oyster sauce. Be sure to press the tofu well to remove excess moisture, which allows it to sear better and absorb the flavors.
Vegan: Follow the vegetarian modifications and also ensure that the soy sauces used are vegan, as some may contain traces of animal products.
Gluten-Free: Use gluten-free soy sauce and oyster sauce, and ensure the Shaoxing wine or dry sherry is gluten-free. Cornstarch is naturally gluten-free and is suitable for thickening the sauce.

INGREDIENT SPOTLIGHT: BLACK PEPPER

The key ingredient in this recipe is undoubtedly the black pepper. With a history that dates back thousands of years, black pepper was once considered so valuable that it was used as currency. Originating from South India, it's now a global kitchen staple. Black pepper doesn't just add a spicy kick to dishes; it also has a subtle earthiness and can aid digestion. In this recipe, it defines the flavor profile and offers a spicy contrast to the umami-rich sauces.

CHEF'S TIPS

- Toasting the black pepper before adding other ingredients intensifies its flavor.
- Use freshly ground black pepper rather than pre-ground for a fresher and more pungent spice.
- Searing the chicken over high heat locks in juices resulting in tender, flavorful pieces.
- Cut vegetables into uniform sizes for even cooking.
- Resting the marinated chicken for at least 15 minutes allows the flavors to penetrate the meat and tenderizes it with the cornstarch.

POSSIBLE VARIATIONS OF THE RECIPE

- **With Nuts:** Add a crunchy texture by including a handful of toasted cashews or almonds with the vegetables.
- **Spicy Kick:** If you like your dish with more heat, add a teaspoon of crushed red pepper flakes when stir-frying the vegetables.
- **Sweet and Sour:** For a tangy twist, add a tablespoon of vinegar or add pineapple chunks with the peppers.

HEALTH NOTE & CALORIC INFORMATION

Black Pepper Chicken Stir-Fry is high in protein and low in carbohydrates, making it an excellent choice for a balanced meal. The use of fresh vegetables adds vitamins and fiber. However, the sodium content can be high due to the soy and oyster sauces, so it's advisable to use low-sodium options or adjust to taste. Depending on portion size and exact ingredients used, a serving typically contains around 250-350 calories.

CUMIN LAMB STIR-FRY

Often found dancing on the hot stovetops of street-side vendors in China's northwestern provinces, cumin lamb stir-fry echoes the historic Silk Road influences on Chinese cuisine. This dish melds the warmth of cumin with the robust flavors of lamb in a symphony of aromatics and quick-fire cooking.

INGREDIENTS

- 500g (1 lb) lamb tenderloin, thinly sliced
- 2 teaspoons cumin seeds
- 1 teaspoon Sichuan peppercorns (optional)
- 3 tablespoons soy sauce
- 2 tablespoons Chinese cooking wine (Shaoxing wine)
- 1 tablespoon cornstarch
- 1 teaspoon sugar
- 4 cloves garlic, minced
- 1 inch ginger, minced
- 3 green onions, cut into 2-inch pieces
- 2 medium green bell peppers, deseeded and sliced
- 1 medium red onion, sliced
- 4 tablespoons vegetable oil
- 1 teaspoon red chili flakes (adjust to taste)
- Salt to taste

DIRECTIONS

1. Start by toasting the cumin seeds in a dry wok or frying pan over medium heat for about 2 minutes or until fragrant. Transfer to a mortar and crush lightly with a pestle to release flavors. If using, also toast Sichuan peppercorns and crush them.
2. Place sliced lamb into a bowl and season with half the crushed cumin, 1 tablespoon of soy sauce, Chinese cooking wine, cornstarch, and sugar. Mix well to coat and marinate for at least 15 minutes.
3. Heat 2 tablespoons of vegetable oil in the wok over high heat until just smoking. Add the lamb in batches, being careful not to overcrowd the wok. Stir-fry until the lamb is just browned, then remove and set aside.
4. Lower the heat to medium-high, then add the remaining vegetable oil. Sauté garlic and ginger until aromatic, about 30 seconds.
5. Increase the heat back to high, add the green onion, bell peppers, and red onion. Stir-fry for about 2 minutes until the vegetables are tender yet crisp.
6. Return the lamb to the wok and add the remaining soy sauce, crushed cumin, Sichuan peppercorns (if using), red chili flakes, and salt to taste. Stir-fry everything together for a final 2 minutes.
7. Taste and adjust the seasoning if necessary. Serve immediately, garnished with additional green onion if desired.

DIETARY MODIFICATIONS

Vegetarian: Substitute lamb for thick slices of king oyster mushrooms or extra-firm tofu. Ensure to press out any extra moisture from the tofu before marinating.

Vegan: Follow the vegetarian modifications and swap soy sauce with a vegan alternative if regular soy sauce isn't suitable. Use maple syrup or agave nectar instead of sugar.

Gluten-Free: Use gluten-free soy sauce and ensure that the Chinese cooking wine is gluten-free. Alternatively, use dry sherry as a substitute.

INGREDIENT SPOTLIGHT: CUMIN

Cumin is an ancient spice, originally cultivated in Iran and the Mediterranean region. It's been used for thousands of years, both as a culinary spice and for medicinal purposes. In this dish, cumin is the soul of the flavor profile, providing earthy, pungent notes that complement the gamey taste of lamb spectacularly. Without cumin, the dish would lose its signature aroma and depth.

CHEF'S TIPS

- For the most tender results, slice the lamb across the grain.
- Freezing the lamb for 20 minutes prior to slicing can make it easier to cut thin, even strips.
- Don't skip the marination time; it tenderizes the lamb and infuses it with flavor.
- Keep the wok very hot to sear the meat and vegetables quickly, preserving their texture and flavor.
- Prep all ingredients before heating the wok, as stir-frying is a fast process that leaves no time for chopping.

POSSIBLE VARIATIONS OF THE RECIPE

- **Spicy Orange:** Add zest of one orange to the marinade and a splash of orange juice during the final stir-fry for a citrusy twist.
- **Cumin Beef:** Substitute lamb with thinly sliced beef, adjusting the cooking time as necessary depending on the cut of beef.
- **Sweet and Crunchy:** Introduce dry-roasted peanuts or cashews in the final minute of stir-frying for a sweet nutty flavor and extra crunch.

HEALTH NOTE & CALORIC INFORMATION

Each serving of Sizzling Cumin Lamb Stir-Fry contains approximately 310 calories, with 18g of fat, 23g of protein, and 13g of carbohydrates. This energy-packed dish is high in protein and can be a part of a balanced diet when served with whole grain or steamed rice and a side of vegetables. Keep in mind that the sodium content can be high due to soy sauce, adjust intake accordingly if on a low-sodium diet.

SANDHEKO

Sandheko is a beloved appetizer originating from the vibrant streets of Nepal. A testament to the culinary depth of this Himalayan nation, Sandheko is known for its fiery kick and rich blend of spices. Typically enjoyed with drinks at local eateries called "bhattis," it's a dish that brings people together, often shared among friends and family. It's not just the taste but the shared experience that makes Sandheko a cornerstone of Nepalese hospitality.

INGREDIENTS

- 500g boneless meat (chicken, pork, or mutton), cut into bite-sized pieces
- 1 tablespoon mustard oil
- 2 tablespoons lemon juice
- 1 teaspoon fenugreek seeds
- 4 cloves of garlic, minced
- 1-inch ginger, minced
- 1/2 teaspoon turmeric powder
- 1/2 teaspoon cumin powder
- 1 tablespoon red chili powder (adjust to taste)
- 1/2 red onion, finely chopped
- 2 green chilies, finely chopped
- A handful of fresh cilantro, chopped
- Salt to taste
- 2 Sichuan pepper (Timur, optional for authentic flavor)

DIRECTIONS

1. Boil the meat in water with a pinch of salt until fully cooked. Drain and set aside to cool.
2. Heat a pan over medium heat. Toast the fenugreek seeds for about 30 seconds or until they are fragrant and darkened, being careful not to burn them.
3. Add the toasted fenugreek seeds to a mortar and pestle along with the Sichuan pepper (if using) and grind to a coarse powder.
4. In a large mixing bowl, combine the cooled meat, ground spices, dry spice powders (turmeric, cumin, and red chili), mustard oil, lemon juice, minced garlic, and ginger. Mix well, ensuring each piece of meat is coated evenly.
5. Add the chopped red onion, green chilies, and fresh cilantro to the meat mixture. Season with salt to taste and mix thoroughly.
6. Allow the mixture to marinate for at least 30 minutes at room temperature to let the flavors meld together.
7. Serve your Sandheko as a spicy and flavorful starter or side dish with a staple such as rice or beaten rice (Chiura).

DIETARY MODIFICATIONS

Vegetarian: Replace the meat with paneer (Indian cottage cheese) or tofu for a vegetarian version. Make sure to pan-fry the paneer or tofu until slightly brown before marinating.

Vegan: For a vegan alternative, use firm tofu and follow the same instructions as for paneer in the vegetarian modification. Additionally, use vegetable oil instead of mustard oil if the pungency is a concern.

Gluten-Free: This recipe is naturally gluten-free. Just ensure that all spices and condiments used are certified gluten-free to avoid cross-contamination.

INGREDIENT SPOTLIGHT: MUSTARD OIL

Mustard oil, with its distinct pungent and spicy flavor profile, is the spotlight ingredient for Sandheko. A staple in Nepalese and other South Asian cuisines, mustard oil is extracted from mustard seeds and contains a compound called allyl isothiocyanate, giving it its characteristic kick. It holds antimicrobial properties and has been traditionally used for its presumed health benefits. It's key to this recipe as it infuses the meat with a depth of flavor that is uniquely South Asian.

CHEF'S TIPS

- Always toast the fenugreek seeds to release their maximum flavor before grinding.
- Let the cooked meat cool down before marinating to prevent the garlic and spices from cooking further and losing potency.
- For an authentic flavor, try to find and use Sichuan pepper, known as 'Timur' in Nepalese, which adds a unique lemony zing and slight numbing effect.
- If mustard oil is not available, it can be substituted with oil that can withstand high heat like canola or vegetable oil, but the authentic taste will be slightly altered.
- The marination time is crucial—let the flavors blend for at least 30 minutes, but for richer flavor, marinate longer, even overnight in the refrigerator.

POSSIBLE VARIATIONS OF THE RECIPE

- **Seafood Variation:** Substitute the meat with shrimp or fish fillets cut into pieces. Adjust the cooking time as seafood cooks faster than meats.
- **Spicy Peanut Sandheko:** Add roasted, crushed peanuts to the meat once it has cooled, for a crunchy texture and nutty flavor.
- **Sandheko Salad:** Incorporate chopped tomatoes, cucumber, and roasted sesame seeds for a refreshing salad variation, perfect for warmer days.

HEALTH NOTE & CALORIC INFORMATION

Sandheko is a high-protein dish that can be tailored to one's preference for spice levels. It is relatively low in carbohydrates, especially when served without a grain accompaniment. Mustard oil used in the recipe contains monounsaturated and polyunsaturated fats, which may contribute to good heart health. The calorie count for a serving size of 100g is approximately 200-250 calories, although this can vary depending on the type of meat used and the quantity of oil added.

PAD PAK BOONG

Stir-Fried Morning Glory, also known as Pad Pak Boong, is a staple dish in Thai cuisine. Its origins date back to the integration of Chinese cooking techniques into Thai food culture. Morning glory, a semi-aquatic tropical plant, is revered in Asia for its tender shoots and leaves. It's often found in waterways and marsh environments. In the culinary world, it's celebrated for its crunchy texture and its ability to absorb flavors, making it perfect for a quick stir-fry.

INGREDIENTS

- 2 bunches of fresh morning glory (water spinach), approximately 400 grams
- 4 cloves of garlic, smashed
- 2-3 bird's eye chilies (adjust to preferred spiciness), crushed
- 2 tablespoons of vegetable oil
- 1 tablespoon of oyster sauce
- 1 tablespoon of light soy sauce
- 1 teaspoon of sugar
- 1 tablespoon of fermented bean paste (tao jiao)
- 2 tablespoons of water
- 1 teaspoon of fish sauce (optional)
- A pinch of ground white pepper

DIRECTIONS

1. Start by thoroughly washing the morning glory to remove any sediment or debris. Shake off excess water and then cut it into 3-inch long pieces, separating the stems from the leaves.
2. In a mortar and pestle, crush the garlic and bird's eye chilies into a rough paste.
3. Heat the vegetable oil in a wok or a large frying pan over high heat until it's hot but not smoking.
4. Add the garlic and chili paste to the wok, stirring constantly, and sauté until aromatic (about 30 seconds).
5. Quickly add the morning glory stems, stir-frying them for about a minute since they take longer to cook than the leaves.
6. Add the morning glory leaves, and continue to stir-fry for another minute or until the leaves start to wilt.
7. Push the morning glory to the side of the wok, and pour in the water, oyster sauce, light soy sauce, sugar, and fermented bean paste to the center of the wok.
8. Stir to combine the sauces with the morning glory, mixing everything well for another minute.
9. For an optional umami boost, stir in the fish sauce.
10. Sprinkle with a pinch of ground white pepper before taking the wok off the heat.
11. Serve immediately, either on its own or with steamed rice.

DIETARY MODIFICATIONS

Vegetarian: Omit the fish sauce and use mushroom sauce or soy sauce as a substitute for oyster sauce to maintain umami flavors.

Vegan: Follow the vegetarian modifications and ensure the fermented bean paste does not contain any shrimp or other non-vegan ingredients.

Gluten-Free: Replace the soy sauce with tamari and ensure to use a gluten-free oyster sauce or replace it with a gluten-free mushroom sauce.

INGREDIENT SPOTLIGHT: MORNING GLORY

The star of this dish, Morning Glory (scientifically named Ipomoea aquatica), holds historical significance as both a medicinal herb and a nutritious vegetable in Southeast Asian cultures. Its rapid growth along waterways makes it a readily available food source. Culinary usage of morning glory dates back centuries, and it's key to this recipe for its unique texture and the way it soaks up flavors while retaining a satisfying crunch.

CHEF'S TIPS

- Ensure the wok is very hot before adding ingredients; this is key to a flavorful stir-fry without overcooking the greens.
- Maintain a vigorous stir-fry motion to cook evenly and prevent the garlic and chilies from burning.
- Cutting the stems and leaves separately accounts for their different cooking times.
- Do not overcook the morning glory as it should retain a crisp texture; it will continue to cook with residual heat once off the stove.
- Use a mortar and pestle for the garlic and chilies to release all their essential oils, which contribute significantly to the dish's aroma.

POSSIBLE VARIATIONS OF THE RECIPE

- **Spicy Lemongrass Morning Glory:** Add two stalks of finely chopped lemongrass to the mortar and pestle mixture for a fragrant, zesty twist.
- **Seafood Delight:** Toss in a handful of prawns or squid rings in the wok with the morning glory stems, for a protein-packed version.
- **Tofu Crunch:** For added protein and texture, include firm tofu cubes that have been fried or baked until golden brown and toss them in with the morning glory leaves.

HEALTH NOTE & CALORIC INFORMATION

Morning glory is low in calories but high in vitamins A and C, as well as iron. It's also rich in dietary fiber, making it an excellent choice for digestive health. A serving of this stir-fried dish is approximately 100-120 calories, depending on the use of sauces and oil. The inclusion of oyster sauce and fermented bean paste contributes small amounts of sodium.

HUNAN BEEF

Hunan cuisine, also known as Xiang cuisine, hails from the Hunan region of China and is known for its hot spicy flavor, fresh aroma, and deep colors. Hunan Beef with Peppers is a vibrant dish that reflects the fiery passion of the region's culinary tradition. With a history of bold flavors and an emphasis on the chili pepper's heat, it is said that this dish evolved from the hearty diets of ancient warriors. Today, Hunan Beef with Peppers graces tables worldwide, reminding diners of the robust and spirited flavors of Hunan.

INGREDIENTS

- 1 lb beef sirloin, thinly sliced against the grain
- 2 bell peppers, one red and one green, cut into bite-size pieces
- 4 Thai bird's eye chilies, finely chopped
- 3 cloves garlic, minced
- 2 tbsp ginger, minced
- 1/4 cup soy sauce
- 2 tbsp Chinese rice wine or dry sherry
- 1 tbsp Chinese black vinegar or balsamic vinegar
- 1 tsp cornstarch
- 2 tsp sugar
- 1 tbsp ferments black beans, rinsed and coarsely chopped
- 3 tbsp vegetable oil
- Salt to taste
- 1 green onion, chopped, for garnish
- Steamed white rice, for serving

DIRECTIONS

1. In a small bowl, whisk together soy sauce, rice wine, vinegar, cornstarch, and sugar until well combined. This will be your marinade and sauce.
2. Place the sliced beef in a bowl and pour half of the marinade over it. Ensure the beef is well coated. Let the beef marinate for at least 30 minutes at room temperature.
3. Heat two tablespoons of vegetable oil in a wok or large skillet over high heat until shimmering. Add the beef in a single layer, allowing it to sear and brown without moving for about 1 minute.
4. Stir-fry the beef for another 2 minutes until it is just cooked through. Remove the beef from the wok and set aside.
5. Reduce the heat to medium-high and add the remaining tablespoon of oil to the wok. Sauté garlic, ginger, bird's eye chilies, and fermented black beans for about 30 seconds until fragrant.
6. Add the bell peppers to the wok and stir fry for about 3-4 minutes, until they start to soften but retain some crunch.
7. Return the beef to the wok and pour over the remaining marinade. Stir well to combine, cooking for about 2 minutes until everything is heated through and the sauce thickens slightly.
8. Season with salt to taste and garnish with chopped green onions.
9. Serve hot with steamed white rice.

DIETARY MODIFICATIONS

Vegetarian: Substitute beef with firm tofu slices or seitan. Press and drain the tofu to remove excess moisture before marinating. Tofu can absorb flavors well and offers a substantial texture.

Vegan: Follow the vegetarian alternative, and ensure to use a vegan black bean sauce that does not contain any animal byproducts often present in fermented condiments.

Gluten-free: Use tamari or a certified gluten-free soy sauce. Ensure that all other sauces and condiments are labeled gluten-free, as well as the cornstarch.

INGREDIENT SPOTLIGHT: BIRD'S EYE CHILIES

Bird's Eye Chilies—often overlooked outside of Asian and African cuisines, these tiny yet fierce chilies add a fiery kick to any dish. Originating from Ethiopia, they were spread throughout the world, notably in Southeast Asia, becoming a staple in Thai, Malaysian, and Vietnamese cuisines. They pack high heat level and a slightly fruity flavor when used fresh. In this recipe, they're integral to achieving the characteristic Hunan spiciness.

CHEF'S TIPS

- Slicing Beef: Freeze the beef for about 30 minutes before slicing to get thin, clean cuts.
- High Heat Cooking: Keep your wok or skillet on high heat to sear the beef quickly without overcooking, preserving its tenderness.
- Batch Cooking: If doubling the recipe, cook the beef in batches to avoid overcrowding the wok and steaming the meat.
- Freshness Counts: Use fresh bird's eye chilies for the best flavor, though dried can be used in a pinch.
- Resting the Meat: Allow the beef to rest after cooking and before adding back into the wok to maintain juiciness.

POSSIBLE VARIATIONS OF THE RECIPE

- **Szechuan-style Twists:** Incorporate Szechuan peppercorns for a numbing heat that contrasts the spiciness, emphasizing the characteristic 'ma la' flavor.
- **Sweet and Sour Adjustments:** Add pineapple chunks and a splash of pineapple juice for a sweet and tangy variation, reducing the vinegar to balance the flavors.
- **Meat Alternatives:** Try the recipe with sliced chicken thighs or pork loin for a different protein base that complements the robust sauce.

HEALTH NOTE & CALORIC INFORMATION

A serving of Hunan Beef with Peppers is high in protein and contains vitamins A and C from the bell peppers. However, it is also moderately high in sodium due to soy sauce and black beans. One serving is typically around 250 to 400 calories when served without rice, depending on the cut of beef and amount of oil used.

SALT AND PEPPER SQUID

Chinese Salt and Pepper Squid is a classic dish known for its crispy texture and aromatic flavors, often served in Chinese restaurants and at street food stalls. Its origins can be traced back to the coastal regions of China where seafood is plentiful. A favorite among locals and tourists alike, it has also gained popularity in Western countries. This dish is simple, quick to prepare, and showcases the perfect blend of salt, pepper, and subtle spice.

INGREDIENTS

- 500g squid tubes, cleaned and cut into rings
- 1/2 cup cornstarch
- 2 teaspoons sea salt
- 1 teaspoon black pepper, freshly ground
- 1 teaspoon five-spice powder
- 1/2 teaspoon red chili flakes (optional for extra heat)
- 4 cups vegetable oil, for deep frying
- 2 garlic cloves, finely minced
- 1 fresh red chili, sliced thinly (optional for garnish)
- 2 spring onions, sliced thinly
- 1/2 lemon, cut into wedges for serving

DIRECTIONS

1. In a large bowl, combine cornstarch, sea salt, black pepper, five-spice powder, and red chili flakes if using. Mix well to create the coating for the squid.
2. Add the squid rings into the bowl with the cornstarch mixture and toss to coat evenly. Shake off any excess coating.
3. Heat the vegetable oil in a deep fryer or a large wok to 180°C (350°F). It's ready when a small amount of the flour mixture sizzles upon contact with the oil.
4. Carefully add the coated squid rings in batches to the hot oil. Do not overcrowd the wok.
5. Fry for 2-3 minutes or until the squid is golden brown and crispy. Remove with a slotted spoon and drain on paper towels.
6. In another pan over medium heat, quickly sauté the minced garlic until fragrant, for about 30 seconds.
7. Add the fried squid to the pan with garlic and toss to coat.
8. Serve immediately, garnished with fresh red chili slices, spring onions, and lemon wedges on the side.

DIETARY MODIFICATIONS

Gluten-Free: Replace cornstarch with a gluten-free flour mix to cater to those with gluten intolerances or celiac disease.

Low-Carb/Keto: Omit cornstarch altogether and use a blend of almond flour and grated parmesan cheese for a low-carb, keto-friendly breading.

Paleo-Friendly: Use arrowroot powder or tapioca starch instead of cornstarch for a paleo diet and ensure all other ingredients are paleo-approved.

INGREDIENT SPOTLIGHT: FIVE-SPICE POWDER

Five-spice powder is the spotlight ingredient. A staple in Chinese cuisine, five-spice powder typically includes star anise, cloves, Chinese cinnamon, Sichuan pepper, and fennel seeds — although compositions can vary. Its history dates back to ancient China, intended to incorporate the five elements (wood, fire, earth, metal, and water) through flavor. Unique and aromatic, it imparts a warm, complex flavor to the squid, making it an indispensable element of this recipe.

CHEF'S TIPS

- Ensure the oil temperature is correct for a crispy coating without overcooking the squid. Use a cooking thermometer if possible.
- Pat squid dry before coating to help the cornstarch mixture adhere better.
- Remove as much excess coating as possible to prevent the oil from becoming clumpy.
- Avoid overcooking the squid as it can become tough and chewy. It cooks very quickly in hot oil.
- Use fresh squid for optimal taste and texture, although frozen and thawed squid can suffice in a pinch.

POSSIBLE VARIATIONS OF THE RECIPE

- **Spicy Salt and Pepper Squid:** Add extra red chili flakes into the cornstarch mixture for a spicier kick.
- **Lemon Pepper Squid:** Focus on the citrus elements by adding grated lemon zest to the cornstarch mixture and serving with extra lemon wedges.
- **Herbal Salt and Pepper Squid:** Incorporate dried herbs such as thyme, rosemary, or oregano into the cornstarch mixture for a different aromatic profile.

HEALTH NOTE & CALORIC INFORMATION

Salt and Pepper Squid is relatively high in protein due to the squid and contains some essential micronutrients, such as selenium and vitamin B12. However, it is also high in sodium and, because it is fried, has a significant amount of fat. An average serving of this dish contains approximately 300-400 calories, with variation depending on the size of the serving and the exact preparation method. For those watching their calorie intake, moderation is key.

BABY CORN MUSHROOMS

This dish brings together the earthy depth of mushrooms with the sweet crunch of baby corn, a combination often found in Asian cuisine, particularly influenced by Chinese stir-fries. Stir-frying is a cooking technique that's been used for over a thousand years, originating from China, it allows for a quick, healthy, and flavorful way of cooking fresh ingredients. This stir-fried mushrooms and baby corn dish is a modern take on a classic technique, perfect for a quick weeknight dinner or as a side dish in a larger Asian-inspired feast.

INGREDIENTS

- 300g mixed mushrooms (shiitake, oyster, button), sliced
- 200g baby corn, halved lengthwise
- 3 tablespoons vegetable oil
- 2 cloves garlic, minced
- 1 inch piece ginger, finely chopped
- 1 medium red bell pepper, sliced
- 1 medium yellow bell pepper, sliced
- 2 tablespoons soy sauce
- 1 tablespoon oyster sauce
- 1 teaspoon sugar
- Salt to taste
- Freshly ground black pepper to taste
- 1 tablespoon cornstarch, dissolved in 2 tablespoons water
- 2 scallions, sliced, for garnish
- 1 teaspoon sesame seeds, for garnish
- 1 teaspoon sesame oil, for final drizzle

DIRECTIONS

1. Clean the mushrooms with a damp cloth and slice them.
2. Halve the baby corn lengthwise and set aside.
3. Heat a wok or large frying pan over high heat. Once hot, add the vegetable oil.
4. Toss in the minced garlic and chopped ginger, and stir-fry for about 30 seconds or until fragrant.
5. Add the sliced mushrooms to the wok. Stir-fry for 3-4 minutes until they begin to soften.
6. Introduce the baby corn and bell peppers to the wok, and continue to stir-fry for another 3-4 minutes.
7. While vegetables are cooking, in a small bowl, combine soy sauce, oyster sauce, sugar, salt, and black pepper, then set aside.
8. Once the vegetables are tender but still crisp, stir in the soy sauce mixture to coat the vegetables evenly.
9. Pour the dissolved cornstarch into the wok and stir quickly as the sauce thickens.
10. Cook for an additional minute, then turn off the heat.
11. Drizzle with sesame oil, and garnish with scallions and sesame seeds.
12. Serve immediately with steamed rice or noodles.

DIETARY MODIFICATIONS

Vegetarian: Replace oyster sauce with a vegetarian stir-fry sauce or vegetarian oyster sauce made from mushrooms.

Vegan: Along with the vegetarian modifications, substitute any honey in the recipe with maple syrup or agave nectar.

Gluten-Free: Use tamari or a gluten-free soy sauce instead of regular soy sauce and ensure the oyster sauce (or its vegetarian alternative) is gluten-free.

INGREDIENT SPOTLIGHT: MUSHROOMS

Mushrooms are a culinary delight and a source of fascinating history and nutrition. They have been enjoyed and utilized medicinally in various cultures for centuries. With a range of textures and flavors, mushrooms can absorb and enhance the flavors in the dishes, making them a key ingredient in stir-fries for their umami quality. Shiitake mushrooms, in particular, introduce a meaty texture and a smoky flavor, while oyster and button mushrooms bring tenderness and a delicate taste to the dish, respectively.

CHEF'S TIPS

- Preheat your wok or pan to ensure quick cooking and that smoky 'wok hei' flavor.
- Don't wash mushrooms with water; they'll absorb it and become soggy. Wipe them clean instead.
- Cut vegetables uniformly for even cooking.
- Prepare all ingredients before you start cooking—stir-frying is a fast process.
- To preserve crunch, don't overcook the vegetables; they should be tender yet crisp.

POSSIBLE VARIATIONS OF THE RECIPE

- **Spicy Kick:** Add a tablespoon of chili sauce or a sprinkle of red pepper flakes to the soy sauce mixture for some heat.
- **Nutty Crunch:** Toss in a handful of toasted cashews or almonds in the final minute of stir-frying for added texture.
- **Meaty Version:** Include sliced chicken breast or beef strips with the mushrooms for a protein-rich dish. Cook meat first, remove, and then follow the rest of the recipe.

HEALTH NOTE & CALORIC INFORMATION

This dish is a good source of vitamins and minerals, particularly vitamin D from the mushrooms. It's also high in fiber due to the vegetables and provides antioxidants. Depending on the size of the portions, a single serving without rice or noodles typically contains approximately 150-200 calories. It is relatively low in carbohydrates and can be incorporated into a low-carbohydrate diet. However, the sodium content might be high due to soy and oyster sauces, so those monitoring sodium intake should adjust accordingly.

PANCIT CANTON

Pancit Canton is a beloved dish in the Philippines, tracing its roots to the influence of Chinese immigrants on Filipino cuisine. The term "pancit" is derived from the Hokkien phrase "pian e sit" which means "something conveniently cooked fast." Often served at birthday celebrations and family gatherings, it symbolizes long life and good health due to its long noodle strands. This particular version, Pancit Canton, is known for its savory flavor and bountiful mix of meat, seafood, and vegetables.

INGREDIENTS

- 400g Pancit Canton noodles (Filipino-style wheat noodles)
- 2 tablespoons vegetable oil
- 4 cloves garlic, minced
- 1 onion, sliced
- 200g chicken breast, thinly sliced
- 100g pork belly, thinly sliced
- 100g shrimp, peeled and deveined
- 2 pieces Chinese sausage, thinly sliced
- 2 cups chicken broth
- 2 tablespoons soy sauce
- 1 tablespoon oyster sauce
- 1/2 cup carrot, julienned
- 1/2 cup snow peas, trimmed
- 1 cup cabbage, sliced
- 1/2 cup bell pepper, julienned
- 1/2 cup celery, sliced diagonally
- Salt and pepper to taste
- 1/2 cup green onions, chopped
- Lemon or calamansi wedges, for serving

DIRECTIONS

1. Soak Pancit Canton noodles in warm water for about 5 minutes to soften. Drain and set aside.
2. Heat vegetable oil in a large wok or skillet over medium-high heat.
3. Sauté garlic and onion until aromatic and slightly translucid, about 2 minutes.
4. Add the chicken and pork belly and cook until lightly browned, approximately 5 minutes.
5. Stir in the shrimp and Chinese sausage, and cook for another 2 minutes or until shrimp turns pink.
6. Pour in chicken broth, followed by soy sauce and oyster sauce. Bring the mixture to a boil.
7. Add the carrots, snow peas, cabbage, bell pepper, and celery to the wok. Cook for about 2 minutes, or until the vegetables are tender-crisp.
8. Season the broth with salt and pepper to taste.
9. Add the softened Pancit Canton noodles to the wok. Toss everything together, ensuring the noodles are evenly coated with the sauce and mixed with the meat and vegetables.
10. Continue to cook, stirring occasionally, until most of the liquid is absorbed and the noodles are cooked through, about 5 minutes.
11. Garnish with chopped green onions and serve with lemon or calamansi wedges on the side. Squeeze the lemon or calamansi over the noodles before eating for added zest.

DIETARY MODIFICATIONS

Vegetarian: Substitute chicken and pork with tofu, and shrimp with additional vegetables such as snap peas or zucchini. Use vegetable broth instead of chicken broth.

Vegan: Follow the vegetarian modifications and replace the oyster sauce with a vegan mushroom-flavored sauce. Omit the Chinese sausage or use a suitable vegan alternative.

Gluten-Free: Use gluten-free soy sauce and gluten-free oyster sauce. Ensure that your choice of Pancit Canton noodles is gluten-free or substitute with rice noodles.

INGREDIENT SPOTLIGHT: PANCIT CANTON NOODLES

The Pancit Canton noodles are the star of this dish. Unlike typical Chinese lo mein noodles, these Filipino wheat noodles have a distinct texture and capacity to absorb flavors. Originating from the Chinese culinary influence on Filipino food culture, these noodles are typically pre-cooked or dried and require only a short soaking or boiling time before stir-frying, which helps them maintain their unique springy texture throughout the cooking process.

CHEF'S TIPS

- Prep all the ingredients ahead of time; this dish cooks quickly once you start.
- Cook meats and shrimp just until done to prevent overcooking, as they'll continue to cook with the noodles.
- Don't over-soak the noodles; just soften enough to separate them, as they'll cook further in the wok.
- Keep the vegetables crisp by not overcooking them, adding a nice contrast to the noodles.
- Adjust seasoning as you go; the broth's evaporation will concentrate flavors.

POSSIBLE VARIATIONS OF THE RECIPE

- **Seafood Delight:** Swap out the chicken and pork for a variety of seafood such as squid, mussels, and scallops for a seafood lover's feast.
- **Spicy Kick:** Add a tablespoon of chili garlic sauce or sliced fresh chili peppers while stir-frying the vegetables for some heat.
- **Meatless Monday:** Make it vegetarian-friendly using tofu and an assortment of mushrooms like shiitake or oyster mushrooms for a savory umami flavor.

HEALTH NOTE & CALORIC INFORMATION

A serving of Filipino Pancit Canton is rich in carbohydrates due to the noodles. It also contains protein from the mixture of meat and seafood, as well as vitamins and minerals from the medley of vegetables used. However, it can be high in sodium from the soy sauce and oyster sauce. A typical serving size may contain around 400-500 calories, but this can vary significantly based on the proportions of ingredients used and serving sizes. To reduce calories or sodium content, adjust the amounts and types of meat and sauces, use low-sodium broth, or increase the vegetable ratio.

SPICY CLAMS

Wok-Tossed Spicy Clams draw inspiration from the hearty and flavorsome coastal cuisines found across Asia, where the wok's intense heat sears in the freshness of seafood while the spices awaken the palate. The dish exudes a rustic charm that balances the simplicity of seafood with the complexity of fiery seasonings, a testament to the traditional cooking methods that have spanned generations.

INGREDIENTS

- 1 kg (2.2 pounds) fresh clams, cleaned and scrubbed
- 2 tablespoons vegetable oil
- 5 cloves garlic, finely minced
- 2 fresh red chilies, sliced (or to taste)
- 1 green bell pepper, sliced
- 1 red bell pepper, sliced
- 3 green onions, sliced into 1-inch pieces
- 2 tablespoons oyster sauce
- 1 tablespoon soy sauce
- 1 tablespoon fish sauce
- 1 teaspoon sugar
- 1/2 teaspoon black pepper
- 1/4 cup fresh Thai basil leaves
- 1/4 cup chicken or vegetable broth
- Lemon wedges for serving

DIRECTIONS

1. Begin by preparing your ingredients. Ensure the clams are thoroughly cleaned, the garlic is minced, the chilies and bell peppers are sliced, and the green onions are cut into 1-inch pieces. Keep the Thai basil leaves and lemon wedges on the side.
2. Heat the vegetable oil in a large wok over high heat. Once the oil is hot, add the garlic and chilies, stirring quickly for about 30 seconds or until fragrant.
3. Add the sliced bell peppers to the wok and stir-fry for another 1-2 minutes until they begin to soften.
4. Carefully place the clams into the wok and toss them with the other ingredients.
5. Pour in the oyster sauce, soy sauce, fish sauce, sugar, and black pepper. Stir everything to ensure the clams are well-coated with the sauce.
6. Add the chicken or vegetable broth and cover the wok with a lid. Allow the clams to steam for 5-7 minutes, or until they are fully opened. Discard any clams that do not open.
7. Remove the lid and add the Thai basil leaves and the green onions, tossing everything together for another minute.
8. Transfer the clams to a serving dish, making sure to pour over the delicious sauce from the wok.
9. Serve immediately with lemon wedges on the side.

DIETARY MODIFICATIONS

Vegetarian: Replace clams with oyster mushrooms sliced to mimic the texture of clams. Use a vegetarian oyster sauce and a vegan fish sauce alternative to maintain similar flavors.

Vegan: Follow the vegetarian substitutions and additionally, ensure soy sauce is vegan. Garnish with extra green onions instead of Thai basil if desired.

Gluten-Free: Ensure all sauce preparations (oyster sauce, soy sauce, fish sauce) are gluten-free variants, and avoid cross-contamination with gluten-containing ingredients.

INGREDIENT SPOTLIGHT: THAI BASIL

Thai basil is a quintessential herb in Southeast Asian cuisine, identifiable by its distinct anise-like fragrance and slight spiciness which differentiate it from its Western counterpart, sweet basil. Native to Southeast Asia, it is a key ingredient in many Thai dishes, notably in spicy stir-fries and as a garnish for soups. Thai basil is central to this recipe as it infuses an exotic aroma and elevates the overall flavor profile with its unique taste.

CHEF'S TIPS

- Fresh clams should smell like the ocean; any strong, unpleasant odor indicates they are not fresh.
- Do not overcook the clams, as they will become rubbery. They are done as soon as their shells open.
- Use a high smoke point oil for stir-frying, such as vegetable or peanut oil, to withstand the high temperatures of the wok.
- The wok must be very hot before adding ingredients. This ensures a good sear and helps to release the natural flavors.
- Adjust the heat of the dish by controlling the amount of fresh red chilies and black pepper according to your preference.

POSSIBLE VARIATIONS OF THE RECIPE

- **Asian Fusion Clams:** Add a teaspoon of Sambal Oelek or Sriracha sauce for an extra spicy kick and a dash of coconut milk for a creamy texture.
- **Mediterranean Twist:** Use olive oil instead of vegetable oil, replace the oyster and fish sauces with white wine, and garnish with parsley instead of Thai basil.
- **Sweet and Sour Clams:** Introduce pineapple chunks and a tablespoon of honey to the stir-fry, balancing the heat with sweetness and tang.

HEALTH NOTE & CALORIC INFORMATION

A serving of Wok-Tossed Spicy Clams is rich in protein and contains beneficial minerals such as zinc and iron from the clams. However, it is important to be aware of the sodium content contributed by the fish sauce and oyster sauce. Approximate calorie content would be around 150 calories per serving, not including the lemon wedges used for serving.

MALAYSIAN BBQ PORK

Char Siew, a Cantonese style barbecued pork, has become a beloved staple in Malaysia, appreciated for its sweet yet savory glaze and succulent texture. Often roasted whole in ovens or over an open flame, this dish adapleavor melts in your mouth. This wok version allows you to recreate the essence of Char Siew at home, imparting a delicious caramelized char without the need for specialized equipment.

INGREDIENTS

- 500g pork shoulder, sliced into 2-inch thick strips
- 3 tablespoons honey
- 2 tablespoons soy sauce
- 2 tablespoons oyster sauce
- 1 tablespoon Shaoxing wine
- 1 tablespoon hoisin sauce
- 1 tablespoon brown sugar
- 2 cloves garlic, finely minced
- 1 teaspoon Chinese five-spice powder
- 1 teaspoon red food coloring (optional)
- 1/2 teaspoon white pepper
- 2 tablespoons vegetable oil

DIRECTIONS

1. In a bowl, mix together honey, soy sauce, oyster sauce, Shaoxing wine, hoisin sauce, brown sugar, minced garlic, Chinese five-spice powder, red food coloring (if using), and white pepper to create the marinade.
2. Add the pork slices to the marinade, ensuring each piece is well-coated. Cover and refrigerate for a minimum of 2 hours, preferably overnight.
3. Remove pork from the refrigerator 30 minutes before cooking to allow it to come to room temperature.
4. Heat vegetable oil in a wok over high heat until just smoking.
5. Carefully place the marinated pork strips into the wok. Do not overcrowd the wok; cook in batches if necessary.
6. Sear pork for 2 minutes on each side until it starts to caramelize. Reduce heat to medium if the wok gets too hot.
7. Once all sides are nicely charred and caramelized, add the remaining marinade to the wok.
8. Continue to cook the pork, frequently turning, until the sauce reduces to a thick glaze and the pork is cooked through, about 10-12 more minutes.
9. Transfer the Char Siew to a cutting board, letting it rest for a few minutes before slicing.
10. Cut the pork into bite-sized pieces, drizzle with the reduced glaze from the wok, and serve.

DIETARY MODIFICATIONS

Vegetarian: Substitute pork with firm tofu or seitan. Press and drain tofu to remove excess moisture before marinating. Adjust cooking time as needed, since tofu or seitan will not require as long to cook as pork.

Vegan: Follow the vegetarian modifications, and replace honey with maple syrup and oyster sauce with a vegan mushroom-based sauce.

Gluten-Free: Use gluten-free soy sauce and hoisin sauce. Confirm that all other ingredients are gluten-free, including the Shaoxing wine and Chinese five-spice powder.

INGREDIENT SPOTLIGHT: SHAOXING WINE

Shaoxing wine is a Chinese rice wine used for cooking. Originating from the region of Shaoxing in the Zhejiang province of eastern China, it has been produced for over 2,000 years. This ingredient is key to adding depth and authenticity to the marinade for Char Siew. It imparts a subtle sweetness and a complexity that enhances the flavors of the sauces and spices used, creating a rounder, more balanced taste profile that is quintessential in many Chinese dishes.

CHEF'S TIPS

- Always slice meat against the grain to ensure tender bites.
- Reserve some of the marinade to baste the pork halfway through cooking for additional glaze and flavor.
- Open windows or use a kitchen fan when searing meat at high temperatures to ensure proper ventilation.
- Let the cooked Char Siew rest before slicing to allow juices to redistribute throughout the meat.
- Use a cast-iron wok if possible, as it retains heat better, applying the perfect seal for the marinade and imparting a smoky note.

POSSIBLE VARIATIONS OF THE RECIPE

- **Honey-Glazed:** Increase honey to 1/4 cup and eliminate brown sugar for a sweeter, stickier glaze.
- **Spicy Kick:** Add 1 tablespoon of chili paste or sliced fresh chili to the marinade for a spicy version.
- **Thai Twist:** Replace hoisin sauce with tamarind paste and add a tablespoon of fish sauce to the marinade for a tangy, Thai-inspired take.

HEALTH NOTE & CALORIC INFORMATION

Char Siew is a rich and flavorful dish, with the primary caloric content coming from the pork and the sugars in the marinade. A typical serving size could range roughly between 300 to 400 calories, containing good amounts of protein and moderate fat content. It is, however, high in sodium and sugar, so its consumption should be enjoyed in moderation within a balanced diet.

STIR-FRIED LETTUCE

Rooted in the efficiency of Chinese cuisine, stir-frying crisp greens like lettuce is both unconventional and refreshingly simple. Often overshadowed by bok choy or spinach in stir-fries, lettuce – particularly iceberg or romaine – takes center stage in this dish. This recipe elevates humble lettuce to a vibrant side dish, proving that with a few aromatics and high heat, even the most basic ingredients can deliver bold flavors.

INGREDIENTS

- 1 large head romaine or iceberg lettuce
- 5 cloves garlic, minced
- 2 tablespoons vegetable oil
- 1 teaspoon sesame oil
- 1 tablespoon soy sauce
- 1 teaspoon sugar
- 1/2 teaspoon salt, adjust to taste
- 1/2 teaspoon ground white pepper
- 1 tablespoon Shaoxing wine (optional)
- 1 teaspoon cornstarch mixed with 1 tablespoon water (cornstarch slurry, optional for thickening)
- 1 green onion, chopped (optional for garnish)

DIRECTIONS

1. Begin by washing the lettuce thoroughly. Separate the leaves and pat them dry to ensure there is no excess water.
2. Tear or cut the lettuce leaves into bite-sized pieces.
3. Preheat a wok or large skillet over high heat. Swirl in the vegetable oil to coat the bottom.
4. Add the minced garlic to the wok. Stir-fry briefly until aromatic but not browned – about 15-20 seconds.
5. Quickly add the lettuce pieces to the wok. Stir rapidly to prevent the garlic from burning.
6. Splash in the Shaoxing wine around the perimeter of the wok, if using, to add depth of flavor.
7. Season the lettuce with soy sauce, sugar, salt, and white pepper. Keep tossing the lettuce for 2-3 minutes until it is tender and bright green.
8. If a thicker sauce is desired, stir in the cornstarch slurry and cook for another minute until the sauce has thickened and clings to the lettuce.
9. Drizzle with sesame oil and give everything a final toss to combine.
10. Plate up the stir-fried lettuce, optionally garnishing with green onions. Serve immediately with steamed rice.

DIETARY MODIFICATIONS

Vegetarian: The given recipe is already vegetarian, so no modifications are required.
Vegan: Ensure that the soy sauce is vegan-friendly as some brands may use animal products in the fermentation process. The rest of the recipe is suitable for a vegan diet.
Lactose Intolerance: This recipe contains no dairy and is suitable for individuals with lactose intolerance.

INGREDIENT SPOTLIGHT: SESAME OIL

The spotlight ingredient for this recipe is sesame oil. With origins in East Asia, sesame oil is made from pressed sesame seeds and imparts a nutty, aromatic flavor that is unmistakable in many Asian dishes. While there are different varieties, including light and dark sesame oils, this recipe calls for lightly colored and richly flavored oil. Its intense aroma and taste are best when used as a finishing touch to a dish, as heat can diminish its character. Sesame oil is a key component in this recipe as it adds a hint of richness and depth that contrasts the crisp, fresh texture of the lettuce.

CHEF'S TIPS

- Make sure your wok is very hot before adding the oil; this practice known as 'longyau' ensures food doesn't stick and cooks quickly.
- Dry the lettuce thoroughly after washing to prevent splattering and to enhance the stir-fry's texture.
- Keep the garlic moving once you add it to the hot oil to prevent it from burning and becoming bitter.
- Use high heat throughout the cooking process to maintain the crisp texture of the lettuce.
- Add the sesame oil off the heat or at the end of cooking to maximize its aroma and flavor.

POSSIBLE VARIATIONS OF THE RECIPE

- **Spicy:** Add a teaspoon of chili flakes or a tablespoon of chili paste with the garlic for a spicy kick.
- **Protein-Packed:** Stir in strips of tofu or seitan with the garlic for added protein.
- **Mushroom Medley:** Add a cup of sliced mushrooms before you add the lettuce, and stir-fry until they're golden for an earthy flavor boost.

HEALTH NOTE & CALORIC INFORMATION

A typical serving of stir-fried lettuce with garlic is low in calories but packed with vitamins A and C. It's also low in fat, with most of it coming from the healthy oils used in the recipe. Depending on portion size, a serving could have approximately 50-100 calories. With the full recipe making about 4 servings, the sodium content can be moderated by adjusting the soy sauce and salt to taste. However, always be cautious with the sauces to manage sodium intake.

JAPANESE YAKI UDON

Yaki Udon is a Japanese stir-fried noodle dish that's incredibly versatile, allowing chefs and home cooks alike to incorporate a variety of vegetables and proteins. It is believed that Yaki Udon originated in the post-World War II period as a creative and filling meal when ingredients were scarce. Today, it's a comfort food staple, offering the satisfying chew of udon noodles paired with a savory sauce and a medley of crisp vegetables.

INGREDIENTS

- 2 packages of pre-cooked udon noodles (200g each)
- 2 tablespoons vegetable oil
- 1 medium onion, thinly sliced
- 1 bell pepper, julienne
- 1 cup shredded cabbage
- 1 medium carrot, julienned
- 2 cloves garlic, minced
- 1 tablespoon fresh ginger, grated
- 4 green onions, chopped into 1-inch pieces
- 2 tablespoons soy sauce
- 1 tablespoon oyster sauce (substitute with vegetarian stir-fry sauce for vegetable variation)
- 1 tablespoon mirin (Japanese sweet rice wine)
- 1 teaspoon sesame oil
- Salt and pepper, to taste
- 1 tablespoon sesame seeds (for garnish)
- 1 sheet of nori (seaweed), shredded (for garnish)

DIRECTIONS

1. Prep Containers: Gather all your ingredients and measure out the sauces. Have all the vegetables cut according to the list above.
2. Noodles: If the udon is refrigerated and firm, briefly rinse the noodles under hot water to separate them, then drain well.
3. Stir-Fry Vegetables: Heat vegetable oil in a large pan or wok over medium-high heat. Add the onion, bell pepper, cabbage, and carrot. Stir-fry for about 3-5 minutes until the vegetables are tender but still have a crunch. Add garlic and ginger and cook for another minute until fragrant.
4. Noodles & Sauce: Add the udon noodles to the pan with the vegetables. Pour in the soy sauce, oyster sauce, and mirin. Toss everything together and stir-fry for another 3-4 minutes until the noodles are heated through.
5. Seasoning & Serve: Drizzle with sesame oil and adjust seasoning with salt and pepper. Mix in the green onions and stir-fry for a final minute.
6. Plating: Serve the Yaki Udon hot, garnished with sesame seeds and shredded nori. Enjoy your delicious Japanese stir-fry!

DIETARY MODIFICATIONS

Vegetarian: Replace oyster sauce with a vegetarian stir-fry sauce or hoisin sauce to retain the depth of flavor without using seafood-based products.

Vegan: Follow the vegetarian suggestions and make sure to use vegan udon noodles. Also, substitute mirin with a vegan sugar syrup or agave nectar if preferred.

Gluten-Free: Use gluten-free soy sauce and make sure your udon noodles are labeled as gluten-free. Be cautious with mirin as some brands may contain gluten; opt for a gluten-free alternative if necessary.

INGREDIENT SPOTLIGHT: UDON NOODLES

Udon noodles are the soul of this dish. Originating from Japan, these thick, chewy noodles are traditionally made from wheat flour and are a staple in Japanese cuisine. They are versatile and can be served cold in salads, in hot broths, or stir-fried as in this recipe. Udon's plump and tender texture is key to Yaki Udon, providing a satisfying bite that absorbs the flavors of the sauces and complements the crunch of the vegetables.

CHEF'S TIPS

- Control the heat: Constant, high heat keeps vegetables crisp and noodles chewy without overcooking.
- Prep ahead: Having all ingredients ready before cooking ensures that the dish comes together quickly.
- Season to taste: Adjust soy sauce or salt in increments to avoid overpowering the dish.
- Use a wok: If available, cook in a wok for an authentic flavor and even heat distribution.
- Noodle separation: Loosen the noodles with your hands before adding them to prevent clumping.

POSSIBLE VARIATIONS OF THE RECIPE

- Spicy Kick: Add a spoonful of chili sauce or a sprinkle of red pepper flakes when adding the garlic and ginger for a spicy version.
- Protein-Packed: Introduce thinly sliced chicken, beef, tofu, or shrimp at the vegetable stir-fry stage for an added protein boost.
- Curry Infusion: Stir in a tablespoon of Japanese curry powder with the sauces to give your Yaki Udon a warm, spiced twist.

HEALTH NOTE & CALORIC INFORMATION

A serving of this Yaki Udon with Vegetables is relatively balanced with carbohydrates from the noodles, vitamins and fiber from the vegetables, and some protein. It's also customizable to accommodate various dietary restrictions. The exact calorie content can vary based on the specific ingredients and portion size but expect a range of approximately 350-450 calories per serving. For more detailed nutritional information, it's best to calculate based on the specific brands and quantities of ingredients used.

WOK-FRIED SHRIMP

Originating from the vibrant kitchens of Coastal China where seafood plays a pivotal role, Wok-Fried Shrimp with Snow Peas is a dish that reflects the philosophy of Chinese cuisine—harmony in color, aroma, and taste. This dish is cherished for its crisp vegetables and succulent shrimp, brought to life with the fire of the wok and the balancing act of simple, yet profound flavors.

INGREDIENTS

- 1 pound of large shrimp, peeled and deveined
- 2 cups of snow peas, trimmed
- 2 tablespoons of vegetable oil
- 3 cloves of garlic, minced
- 1 tablespoon of ginger, minced
- 1 tablespoon of Shaoxing wine (or dry sherry)
- 1 teaspoon of sesame oil
- 2 tablespoons of soy sauce
- 1 teaspoon of cornstarch
- 1 teaspoon of sugar
- 2 tablespoons of water
- Salt to taste
- White pepper to taste
- 1 teaspoon of toasted sesame seeds (for garnish)

DIRECTIONS

1. Prep the Shrimp: In a bowl, toss the shrimp with a pinch of salt and white pepper. Let them marinate for about 10 minutes.
2. Prepare the Sauce: In a small bowl, mix together soy sauce, Shaoxing wine, sesame oil, cornstarch, sugar, and water until well combined. Set aside.
3. Blanch Snow Peas: Bring a pot of water to a boil. Add the snow peas and blanch for 30 seconds. Drain and immediately plunge into an ice bath to stop the cooking process.
4. Wok Time: Heat 1 tablespoon of vegetable oil in a wok over high heat until it starts to smoke.
5. Cook the Shrimp: Add the shrimp to the wok in a single layer. Sear for about 30 seconds on each side until they are pink and slightly golden. Remove the shrimp from the wok and set aside.
6. Aromatics: Lower the heat to medium and add the remaining tablespoon of vegetable oil. Sauté the garlic and ginger until fragrant, approximately 1 minute.
7. Combine Everything: Return the shrimp to the wok along with the blanched snow peas. Stir-fry for a minute.
8. Add the Sauce: Pour in the sauce mixture and toss everything together for another minute or until the sauce thickens and coats the shrimp and snow peas.
9. Finishing Touches: Taste and adjust seasoning with salt if necessary. Sprinkle with toasted sesame seeds.
10. Serve: Serve hot with steamed rice or as a stand-alone entrée.

DIETARY MODIFICATIONS

Gluten-Free: Use tamari or a certified gluten-free soy sauce instead of traditional soy sauce. Ensure all other ingredients like Shaoxing wine are gluten-free as well.

Vegetarian: Substitute shrimp with firm tofu or tempeh, cut into bite-sized pieces. Press the tofu beforehand to remove excess moisture and allow it to crisp up in the wok.

Vegan: Follow the vegetarian modifications and also make sure the soy sauce, wine, and sugar are vegan-friendly, as some may process using animal products.

INGREDIENT SPOTLIGHT: SOY SAUCE

This ancient condiment stretches back to the Eastern Zhou dynasty in China over 2,500 years ago. Originating as a way to stretch salt, an expensive commodity at times, soy sauce is made from fermented soybeans, wheat, salt, and water. The fermentation process gives it a complex flavor profile—salty, umami, with hints of sweetness. The deep, rich color also adds visual appeal to any dish, making it an indispensable tool in both Asian and increasingly global kitchens.

CHEF'S TIPS

- Proper Heat Management: Keep the wok really hot to cook the shrimp quickly and give snow peas a crispy texture while retaining their bright green color.
- Avoid Overcooking the Shrimp: Shrimp cook very rapidly; overcooking them leads to a rubbery texture. A quick sear on each side is sufficient.
- Marinate in Stages: Marinating the shrimp with salt and pepper ahead of time allows for deeper flavor penetration.
- Freshness is Key: Use fresh, high-quality shrimp and snow peas for the best texture and taste.
- Serve Immediately: For the best eating experience, this dish should be served as soon as it's ready to enjoy the contrast between the crisp snow peas and tender shrimp.

POSSIBLE VARIATIONS OF THE RECIPE

- Spicy Kick: Add a tablespoon of chili sauce or a sprinkling of red pepper flakes to the sauce for a spicy variation.
- Nutty Crunch: Toss in a handful of cashews or peanuts with the snow peas for an added crunch and protein boost.
- Citrus Twist: Add a splash of fresh orange juice and some orange zest to the sauce for a sweet and tangy flavor.

HEALTH NOTE & CALORIC INFORMATION

This dish is typically high in protein and low in carbohydrates, making it a great option for those on a balanced diet. The shrimp provide an excellent source of lean protein and essential omega-3 fatty acids. Snow peas are low in calories and contain dietary fiber, antioxidants, and a good mix of vitamins, particularly Vitamin C. Depending on portion size, one serving of Wok-Fried Shrimp with Snow Peas is approximately 200-250 calories. Remember that condiments and serving sizes can affect the calorie content.

LEMONGRASS CHICKEN

Stemming from the fragrant streets of Vietnam, Lemongrass Chicken is a symphony of flavors that speak to the essence of Southeast Asian cuisine. This aromatic dish is deeply rooted in the diverse culinary traditions of the region, where the allure of fresh herbs and the spirit of home cooking create a vibrant food culture. Traditionally marinated to perfection and skillfully grilled or stir-fried, this dish effortlessly turns an ordinary meal into an exotic adventure.

INGREDIENTS

- 2 pounds of chicken thighs, boneless and skinless
- 4 stalks of fresh lemongrass, outer layers removed and finely minced
- 4 garlic cloves, minced
- 2 shallots, minced
- 2 bird's eye chilies (optional), finely chopped
- 1 tablespoon ginger, grated
- 3 tablespoons soy sauce
- 2 tablespoons fish sauce
- 2 tablespoons brown sugar
- 2 tablespoons lime juice
- 3 tablespoons vegetable oil
- Fresh cilantro leaves, for garnish
- Lime wedges, for serving
- Steamed rice or rice noodles, for serving

DIRECTIONS

1. Begin by preparing the chicken thighs. Cut them into bite-size pieces and set aside in a large mixing bowl.
2. In a food processor, combine the minced lemongrass, garlic, shallots, chilies (if using), and ginger to form a fragrant paste.
3. Add the soy sauce, fish sauce, brown sugar, and lime juice to the paste and blend until well incorporated.
4. Pour the marinade over the chicken pieces, ensuring each piece is adequately coated. Let the chicken marinate for at least 30 minutes, or for better flavor absorption, refrigerate for 2 hours or overnight.
5. Heat the vegetable oil in a large pan or wok over medium-high heat. Once hot, carefully add the marinated chicken pieces in batches. Stir-fry until the chicken is golden brown and cooked through, about 8-10 minutes per batch.
6. Once all the chicken has been cooked, return all pieces to the pan and stir well to heat evenly.
7. Garnish with fresh cilantro leaves and serve hot alongside lime wedges, with steamed rice or rice noodles.

DIETARY MODIFICATIONS

Vegetarian: Substitute chicken with firm tofu or seitan. Press the tofu to remove excess water before cutting it into cubes and marinating it as you would with the chicken.

Vegan: Follow the vegetarian option and replace fish sauce with vegan fish sauce or an extra tablespoon of soy sauce mixed with a pinch of seaweed flakes for that umami flavor.

Gluten-Free: Use tamari instead of soy sauce and ensure that the fish sauce is gluten-free. Many brands offer gluten-free fish sauce options.

INGREDIENT SPOTLIGHT: LEMONGRASS

Lemongrass is a tall, stalky plant with a lemony scent that is indigenous to tropical regions of Asia and Africa. It is widely used in cooking and herbal medicine. This citrus-flavored herb adds a zesty, fresh fragrance and flavor to dishes, and its subtle sharpness is indispensable in many Vietnamese and Thai recipes. Lemongrass has been used for centuries not just in cooking but also in perfumes and as a pesticide.

CHEF'S TIPS

- To extract maximum flavor, bash the lemongrass stalks with the back of a knife before mincing.
- Marinating the chicken overnight will deepen the flavors, making the dish more aromatic and tasty.
- For an authentic charred taste, consider grilling the marinated chicken instead of stir-frying.
- To avoid a bitter taste, remove the very outer layers of the lemongrass and only use the tender part of the stalk.
- If bird's eye chilies are too spicy for your preference, deseed them or use less pungent chili varieties.

POSSIBLE VARIATIONS OF THE RECIPE

- **Coconut Lemongrass Chicken:** Add a creamy twist by simmering the stir-fried chicken in coconut milk during the last 5 minutes of cooking.
- **Lemongrass Chicken Skewers:** Thread the marinated chicken pieces onto skewers and grill them for a finger-food variation that's perfect for parties.
- **Lemongrass Chicken Salads:** Toss sliced, cooked lemongrass chicken with mixed greens, herbs, and a Vietnamese-inspired dressing for a light yet flavorful meal.

HEALTH NOTE & CALORIC INFORMATION

Lemongrass Chicken is a high-protein meal that is fairly low in carbohydrates when served without rice or noodles. The chicken provides an excellent source of lean protein, while the lemongrass and other herbs contribute negligible calories but a plethora of nutrients and antioxidants. A typical serving of Lemongrass Chicken (without rice) contains approximately 310 calories, with 35g of protein, 18g of fat, and 4g of carbohydrates. The exact calorie content can vary based on the specific ingredients used and portion sizes.

DUCK BREAST

Influenced by the rich culinary traditions of China, Wok-Seared Duck Breast with Plum Sauce is a modern fusion dish that draws from the aromatic, sweet, and savory elements iconic to Chinese cuisine. The dish pays homage to Peking duck yet is designed for the home cook looking for an elegant but accessible meal to serve on special occasions.

INGREDIENTS

- 2 boneless duck breasts (with skin)
- Salt and freshly ground black pepper, to taste
- 1 tablespoon vegetable oil
- 1 shallot, finely chopped
- 1 clove garlic, minced
- 1/2 cup plum jam
- 2 tablespoons soy sauce
- 1 tablespoon rice vinegar
- 1 teaspoon five-spice powder
- 1 teaspoon grated fresh ginger
- 1/4 cup water
- 1 tablespoon chopped fresh cilantro (for garnish)

DIRECTIONS

1. Pat the duck breasts dry with paper towels. With a sharp knife, score the skin of the duck breasts in a crisscross pattern, being careful not to cut into the flesh.
2. Season the duck breasts generously with salt and freshly ground black pepper.
3. Heat a wok (or heavy skillet) over medium-high heat. Add the vegetable oil and swirl to coat the bottom.
4. Place the duck breasts skin-side down in the wok and cook until the skin is golden and crisp, about 5-7 minutes.
5. Turn the duck breasts over and cook for another 4-5 minutes for medium-rare (internal temperature of 135°F), or until desired doneness. Remove the duck from the wok and let rest on a cutting board, loosely covered with foil.
6. Pour off all but a tablespoon of fat from the wok. Add the shallot and garlic, and stir-fry for 1-2 minutes until fragrant.
7. Add the plum jam, soy sauce, rice vinegar, five-spice powder, and grated ginger to the wok. Stir to combine.
8. Pour in the water and bring the sauce to a simmer. Cook, stirring occasionally until the sauce thickens slightly, about 3 minutes.
9. Slice the rested duck breasts thinly.
10. Serve the duck slices with warm plum sauce drizzled over the top and garnish with chopped fresh cilantro.

DIETARY MODIFICATIONS

Vegetarian: Replace duck breasts with thick slices of tofu or seitan, and pan-sear as you would the duck. Use a vegetarian oyster sauce instead of soy sauce for depth of flavor.

Gluten-Free: Ensure the soy sauce is a gluten-free variety, and use gluten-free plum jam. Also, verify that the five-spice powder is gluten-free.

Low-Fat: Opt for skinless duck breasts or a leaner protein such as chicken breasts. Reduce the vegetable oil to a teaspoon just to prevent sticking and use a sugar-free plum jam.

INGREDIENT SPOTLIGHT: PLUM JAM

Plum jam is the star ingredient in the sauce accompanying the duck. With a history of fruit preservation that dates back centuries in China, plum jam embodies a balance of sweetness and a gentle tartness, making it an ideal accompaniment to rich meats like duck. It's used widely in Asian cuisine, incorporated into sauces, marinades, and even as a standalone condiment. The jam brings a fruity depth to the dish and helps create an alluring glaze that compliments the spicy notes of the five-spice powder.

CHEF'S TIPS

- Score the duck skin deeply but don't cut the meat; this allows fat to render and skin to get crispy.
- Begin cooking the duck on a cold wok or pan to slowly render the fat out for a crisper finish.
- Rest the duck breast after cooking to allow the juices to redistribute; cut into it too early, and the juices will run out.
- Never rush the sauce; allow it to simmer and thicken so the flavors can fully develop.
- Finely chop the shallots and garlic to ensure they release their flavors quickly during the brief stir-frying step.

POSSIBLE VARIATIONS OF THE RECIPE

- **Spicy Plum Sauce:** Add a teaspoon of chili flakes or a tablespoon of finely chopped chili peppers to the plum sauce to give it a spicy kick.
- **Crunchy Topping:** Add toasted sliced almonds or sesame seeds as a garnish for an extra layer of texture and nuttiness.
- **Citrus Twist:** Introduce a zest of an orange to the plum sauce for a twist of brightness, complementing the rich flavors of the duck.

HEALTH NOTE & CALORIC INFORMATION

A single serving of Wok-Seared Duck Breast with Plum Sauce (based on an 8-ounce duck breast) provides approximately 460 calories, with 28 grams of fat, 30 grams of carbohydrates, and 24 grams of protein. This dish is high in B-vitamins, phosphorus, and selenium, but also high in sodium and cholesterol. Remember that the crispy skin contributes to the higher fat content. If looking to cut fat and cholesterol, serving the duck without the skin will significantly change the nutritional values.

GARLIC TOFU STIR-FRY

Tofu, a staple in Asian cuisine for centuries, is enjoyed across the continent in countless forms. Its versatility allows it to soak up flavors, making it a favorite for stir-fries. This Asian Garlic Tofu Stir-Fry is inspired by the balance of savory, sweet, and spicy flavors prevalent in East Asian cooking, specifically drawing influence from Chinese-style stir-fries that have delighted families for generations.

INGREDIENTS

- 400g firm tofu
- 2 tablespoons soy sauce
- 1 tablespoon hoisin sauce
- 1 tablespoon rice vinegar
- 2 teaspoons sesame oil
- 2 teaspoons cornstarch
- 4 cloves garlic, minced
- 1-inch piece ginger, grated
- 2 tablespoons vegetable oil
- 1 red bell pepper, sliced
- 1 green bell pepper, sliced
- 3 green onions, chopped
- 1 teaspoon red pepper flakes (optional)
- Sesame seeds for garnish
- Cooked white or brown rice, for serving

DIRECTIONS

1. Press the tofu by wrapping it in a clean cloth and setting a heavy object on top for about 15 minutes to remove excess water.
2. Cut the pressed tofu into 1-inch cubes.
3. In a bowl, whisk together soy sauce, hoisin sauce, rice vinegar, sesame oil, and cornstarch to make the sauce. Set aside.
4. Heat vegetable oil in a large pan or wok over medium-high heat.
5. Add the tofu cubes to the pan and fry them, turning occasionally until all sides are golden brown. This should take about 5-7 minutes.
6. Remove the tofu and set it aside on a paper towel-lined plate.
7. In the same pan, add a bit more oil if needed, and stir-fry the minced garlic, ginger, and red pepper flakes for about 1 minute until fragrant.
8. Add the sliced bell peppers to the pan and stir-fry for 2-3 minutes until slightly softened.
9. Return the tofu to the pan with the peppers and pour the sauce over the mixture.
10. Toss everything to coat evenly and cook for another 2-3 minutes until the sauce thickens.
11. Top with chopped green onions and a sprinkle of sesame seeds before serving.
12. Serve hot over cooked rice.

DIETARY MODIFICATIONS

Vegetarian: This dish is already vegetarian-friendly.
Vegan: Ensure the hoisin sauce used is vegan, as some may contain honey. Check labels carefully.
Gluten-Free: Opt for gluten-free soy sauce and hoisin sauce to accommodate this dietary need.

INGREDIENT SPOTLIGHT: HOISIN SAUCE

Hoisin Sauce. This thick, fragrant sauce is a staple in Chinese cooking, often referred to as Chinese barbecue sauce. Made from a blend of soybeans, garlic, chilies, and various spices, it provides a sweet and savory element that's essential in many Asian dishes, particularly stir-fries and meat marinades. Hoisin sauce is the cornerstone of this recipe's flavor, offering depth and richness that marries well with the zesty garlic and warm ginger.

CHEF'S TIPS

- Pressing the tofu is crucial for achieving the right texture; it helps the tofu stay firm and absorb more flavor.
- Cutting the tofu in similar-sized cubes ensures even cooking.
- To prevent the tofu from sticking to the pan, ensure the pan is hot before adding oil and the oil is shimmering before adding the tofu.
- Allowing the sauce to thicken on the pan will create a tasty glaze on the tofu and vegetables.
- Serve immediately after cooking to enjoy the combination of textures, from the crispy tofu to the tender-crisp vegetables.

POSSIBLE VARIATIONS OF THE RECIPE

- **Spicy Maple Tofu:** Replace hoisin sauce with maple syrup and add extra red pepper flakes for a sweet and spicy twist.
- **Peanut Butter Tofu:** Add a tablespoon of creamy peanut butter to the sauce mixture for a nutty flavor dimension.
- **Citrus Zest Tofu:** Incorporate orange zest into the sauce for a citrusy fragrance that complements the ginger and garlic.

HEALTH NOTE & CALORIC INFORMATION

A serving of Asian Garlic Tofu Stir-Fry, not including rice, contains approximately 200-250 calories, assuming the recipe yields 4 servings. It's high in plant-based protein and provides a modest amount of healthy fats from the sesame oil and vegetable oil. The dish is also high in vitamins A and C, courtesy of the bell peppers. Keep in mind that hoisin sauce and soy sauce are high in sodium, so those watching their salt intake should consume this dish in moderation.

CHICKEN AND BEANS

Bridging the culinary traditions of China's Cantonese cuisine with modern kitchen panache, our Succulent Chicken with Aromatic Black Bean Sauce is a crave-worthy fusion of hearty protein and bold flavors. Fermented black beans, or douchi, are the cornerstone of this dish—they bring a depth of flavor that has been celebrated in Chinese cooking for centuries. While black bean sauce is a staple in many stir-fries, this recipe showcases its rich, savory profile as a starring accompaniment to tender chicken.

INGREDIENTS

- 500g skinless, boneless chicken thighs, cut into bite-sized pieces
- 2 tablespoons vegetable oil
- 1 red bell pepper, diced
- 1 green bell pepper, diced
- 1 yellow bell pepper, diced
- 3 tablespoons fermented black beans, rinsed and roughly chopped
- 2 garlic cloves, minced
- 1 tablespoon ginger, minced
- 2 scallions, sliced
- 2 tablespoons soy sauce
- 1 tablespoon oyster sauce
- 1 teaspoon sugar
- 1 tablespoon cornstarch
- 60ml chicken stock (or water)
- 1 teaspoon sesame oil
- Salt, to taste
- Pepper, to taste

DIRECTIONS

1. In a bowl, mix the chicken pieces with cornstarch and a pinch of salt and pepper. Ensure each piece is well coated.
2. Heat the vegetable oil in a wok or large frying pan over medium-high heat.
3. Add the chicken to the wok and stir-fry until golden and cooked through, about 5-7 minutes. Remove the chicken and set aside.
4. In the same wok, add a bit more oil if needed, then add the bell peppers. Stir-fry for about 2 minutes until they soften slightly.
5. Add the minced garlic and ginger to the wok and fry for another minute until fragrant.
6. Stir in the fermented black beans and cook for another minute.
7. Return the chicken to the wok and mix well with the peppers and black beans.
8. In a small bowl, combine soy sauce, oyster sauce, sugar, and chicken stock. Mix until the sugar dissolves.
9. Pour the sauce mixture into the wok and bring to a simmer. Cook for a further 2-3 minutes, allowing the sauce to thicken slightly.
10. Drizzle with sesame oil and garnish with scallions before removing from heat.
11. Serve the chicken with aromatic black bean sauce over steamed rice or your preferred grain.

DIETARY MODIFICATIONS

Vegetarian: Use firm tofu or tempeh instead of chicken. Ensure that the tofu is pressed and drained well to soak up the flavors of the sauce.
Vegan: Along with substituting chicken for tofu or tempeh, replace oyster sauce with a vegan mushroom sauce to retain the umami depth without any animal products.
Lactose Intolerance: This recipe is naturally lactose-free, so no modifications are necessary.

INGREDIENT SPOTLIGHT: DOUCHI

Fermented black beans, also known as douchi, are the spotlight ingredient of this dish. They are made by fermenting and salting black soybeans. This ancient ingredient dates back to over 2,000 years ago in China, and is critical for adding the unique, umami-rich, and slightly bitter flavor that is typical in many Chinese dishes. Their complex taste is a key to adding authenticity to our black bean sauce.

CHEF'S TIPS

- Pat the chicken dry before coating it with cornstarch to ensure it gets a nice sear.
- The fermentation of black beans means they're potent; a little goes a long way.
- Cook garlic and ginger just until fragrant to avoid burning, which can introduce bitterness.
- When stir-frying, keep things moving in the wok to cook evenly and prevent overcooking.
- Tasting as you go allows you to adjust seasoning for the perfect balance of flavors.

POSSIBLE VARIATIONS OF THE RECIPE

- **Spicy Kick:** Incorporate a diced hot pepper or a spoonful of chili paste with garlic for those who appreciate a fiery touch.
- **Nutty Crunch:** Add a handful of cashews or peanuts into the stir-fry for some crunch and additional protein.
- **Citrus Twist:** A splash of fresh orange juice can add a tangy note to the sauce, complementing the savory black beans beautifully.

HEALTH NOTE & CALORIC INFORMATION

A serving of Chicken with Aromatic Black Bean Sauce is rich with protein, while providing a moderate amount of calories. The fermented black beans add beneficial probiotics, and the array of colored bell peppers boosts the dish's vitamin C content. Depending on portion size, expect around 250-350 calories per serving, not including the steamed rice or grain of choice. It's also a low-lactose dish suitable for most diets, and with slight modifications, can meet vegetarian and vegan needs.

TOFU AND BROCCOLI

Tofu and Broccoli in Garlic Sauce is a staple in Chinese-American cuisine, offering a delectable blend of textures and flavors. It nods to traditional Sichuan cooking methods, embodying the spirit of 'yu xiang,' which means "fish-fragrant," a term describing a particular combination of salty, sweet, and spicy ingredients. Despite the name, no fish is involved in this dish, making it a favorite among vegetarians. Adapted for Western tastes, this recipe brings a harmonious balance of umami-rich tofu, crunchy broccoli, and a robust, garlicky sauce to delight the palate.

INGREDIENTS

- 14 oz block of firm tofu
- 2 cups broccoli florets
- 4 tablespoons vegetable oil
- 3 cloves garlic, minced
- 1-inch piece of ginger, minced
- 1/4 cup soy sauce
- 2 tablespoons brown sugar
- 1 tablespoon cornstarch
- 1/2 teaspoon crushed red pepper flakes
- 1/2 cup vegetable broth
- 1 tablespoon sesame oil
- 2 teaspoons rice vinegar
- Green onions, sliced for garnish
- Sesame seeds, for garnish

DIRECTIONS

1. Drain and press the tofu to remove excess moisture. Cut into 3/4-inch cubes.
2. Blanch the broccoli in boiling water for 2 minutes, then immediately plunge into ice water to stop the cooking process. Drain well.
3. In a small bowl, whisk together the soy sauce, brown sugar, cornstarch, red pepper flakes, vegetable broth, sesame oil, and rice vinegar until the cornstarch is fully dissolved. Set aside.
4. Heat 2 tablespoons of vegetable oil in a large skillet or wok over medium-high heat. Add the tofu cubes, and pan-fry until golden brown on all sides, about 8 minutes. Remove tofu and set aside.
5. In the same skillet, add the remaining 2 tablespoons of oil and sauté the minced garlic and ginger until fragrant, about 1-2 minutes, being careful not to burn them.
6. Pour in the sauce mixture and stir until it thickens slightly, about 2 minutes.
7. Return the tofu to the skillet, and add the broccoli. Toss everything together to coat with the sauce and heat through.
8. Garnish with green onions and sesame seeds.
9. Serve hot with steamed rice or noodles of your choice.

DIETARY MODIFICATIONS

For **Gluten-Free:** Replace the soy sauce with a gluten-free tamari or coconut aminos. Ensure all other ingredients are certified gluten-free.

For **Vegan:** This dish is naturally vegan. Simply ensure that your sugar is certified vegan (some sugars are processed with animal bone char).

For **Nut Allergies:** This recipe is already nut-free. Ensure that there is no cross-contamination with nuts in your ingredients, particularly if using pre-packaged items like tofu or vegetable broth.

INGREDIENT SPOTLIGHT: TOFU

Tofu, also known as bean curd, is made by coagulating soy milk and then pressing the resulting curds into blocks of varying softness. It has been a key component in East Asian and Southeast Asian cuisines for over 2,000 years. Tofu's origins can be traced back to Han China, and its versatility has allowed it to spread across various cuisines globally. In this recipe, tofu acts as a sponge, absorbing the potent garlic sauce and providing a protein-rich component that stands up to the strong flavors while offering a textural counterpoint to the crunchy broccoli.

CHEF'S TIPS

- To achieve the best texture for the tofu, press it for at least 30 minutes to extract as much water as possible. This helps it crisp up when pan-fried.
- For an authentic touch, lightly fry the garlic and ginger first in a small amount of oil and use this infused oil to cook the rest of the dish.
- Don't overcook the broccoli. It should be bright green and tender-crisp to provide a textural contrast to the tofu.
- If you like a saucier dish, double the sauce ingredients and simmer to the desired thickness before adding the tofu and broccoli.
- Use a non-stick skillet or well-seasoned wok to prevent the tofu from sticking and breaking apart during frying.

POSSIBLE VARIATIONS OF THE RECIPE

- **Spicy Orange:** Infuse the garlic sauce with fresh orange juice and zest for a citrusy kick, complementing the sweetness and heat.
- **Peanutty Tofu:** Add 2 tablespoons of natural peanut butter to the sauce for a creamy, nutty twist. Great with added bell peppers!
- **Mushroom Medley:** Alongside broccoli, integrate a variety of mushrooms, such as shiitake or oyster, to introduce a savory depth and an additional layer of umami.

HEALTH NOTE & CALORIC INFORMATION

This dish is relatively low in calories but rich in protein and vitamins thanks to the tofu and broccoli. The garlic sauce, while flavorful, is moderate in sodium especially if low-sodium soy sauce is used. A single serving, based on 4 servings per recipe, is approximately 280-320 calories, with 18 grams of protein, 20 grams of fat, and 15 grams of carbohydrates. This nutritional content can vary based on the exact ingredients used and portion sizes.

OKRA WITH SAMBAL

Okra, also known as "ladies' fingers," has been a staple in cuisines around the world, particularly in African, Middle Eastern, Greek, Turkish, Indian, Caribbean, and Southern U.S. dishes. This recipe infuses okra with the fiery spirit of Southeast Asian cuisine, featuring sambal—a piquant chili paste that is essential in Indonesian and Malaysian kitchens. The combination of sambal's heat and the sweetness of shallots creates a harmony of flavors that emboldens the okra without overshadowing its natural, earthy taste.

INGREDIENTS

- 500g fresh okra
- 4 tablespoons vegetable oil
- 8 shallots, thinly sliced
- 3 cloves garlic, minced
- 2 tablespoons sambal oelek
- 1 tablespoon soy sauce
- 1 teaspoon fish sauce (optional)
- 1 teaspoon tamarind paste
- 1 tablespoon brown sugar
- Salt to taste
- Fresh lime wedges for serving

DIRECTIONS

1. Begin by washing the okra under cold water. Pat them dry with a kitchen towel, as moisture can cause sliminess when cooking. Trim the ends and cut the okra into 2-inch pieces.
2. Heat 2 tablespoons of oil in a large skillet or wok over medium-high heat. Add the okra in a single layer, and cook for about 5 to 6 minutes, or until the okra is lightly browned and tender. Stir occasionally to ensure even cooking. Once cooked, transfer the okra to a plate and set aside.
3. In the same skillet, heat the remaining 2 tablespoons of oil over medium heat. Add the thinly sliced shallots and cook, stirring frequently, until they become soft and start to caramelize, about 5 minutes.
4. Add the minced garlic to the shallots and cook for another 1 minute, until fragrant.
5. Stir in the sambal oelek, soy sauce, fish sauce (if using), tamarind paste, and brown sugar. Mix well and cook for about 2 minutes to allow the flavors to meld.
6. Return the sauteed okra to the skillet and toss well to coat with the sambal shallot mixture. Season with salt to taste.
7. Cook everything together for an additional 3 minutes, making sure the okra is heated through and well coated with the sauce.
8. Serve hot with lime wedges on the side, allowing everyone to add a spritz of fresh lime juice to taste.

DIETARY MODIFICATIONS

Vegetarian: Omit the fish sauce or substitute with a vegetarian fish sauce alternative.
Vegan: Follow the vegetarian modifications and ensure the sambal oelek and soy sauce used are vegan-friendly (some brands may include shrimp paste or other non-vegan ingredients).
Gluten-Free: Use tamari or a gluten-free soy sauce instead of regular soy sauce to make the dish gluten-free.

INGREDIENT SPOTLIGHT: SAMBAL OELEK

Sambal oelek is a traditional Southeast Asian chili paste that is a cornerstone of Indonesian and Malaysian cuisines. Composed of ground chilies, vinegar, and salt, its history dates back to when traders and immigrants introduced new types of chilies to Southeast Asia. Sambal oelek's bright heat and tangy undertones make it versatile, ideal for marinades, condiments, and as an integral part of cooking. It brings the heat to this okra dish, balancing the sweetness of shallots and the natural mildness of okra.

CHEF'S TIPS

- Ensure that the okra is completely dry before cooking to minimize sliminess.
- Don't overcrowd the pan when browning the okra; otherwise, they may steam rather than fry.
- Adjust the quantity of sambal oelek to suit your heat preference. Start with less if you're cautious about spice levels.
- Allow the shallots to brown properly before adding garlic, to avoid the garlic from burning.
- Use fresh lime juice over bottled for a brighter flavor.

POSSIBLE VARIATIONS OF THE RECIPE

- **Shrimp Combo:** Stir in cooked shrimp in the final 2 minutes for a protein-packed dish.
- **Coconut Creaminess:** Add a splash of coconut milk with the sambal for a creamier, milder sauce.
- **Crispy Garnish:** Top with crispy fried onions for added texture and rich flavor.

HEALTH NOTE & CALORIC INFORMATION

This Okra with Sambal and Shallots dish is loaded with fiber, vitamin C, and antioxidants while being low in calories. It's a healthful side that contributes to your daily vegetable intake. An approximate calorie count for a serving is around 150-200 kcal, depending on the modifications and portion sizes used. Okra is also known for its beneficial effects on blood sugar control, making it a great choice for those managing diabetes. The sambal brings a good dose of capsaicin, which is linked to boosting metabolism and reducing inflammation.

PORK MELON STIR-FRY

Bitter melon, also known as bitter gourd, has been a staple in Asian cuisine for centuries, particularly in China, India, and Southeast Asia. It's prized not only for its unique bitter flavor, which is believed to stimulate digestion, but also for its medicinal properties. This Pork and Bitter Melon Stir-Fry is a classic Chinese dish, often enjoyed in the hotter months for its cooling effect on the body. It's a delicious harmony of flavors and textures, with the tenderness of pork contrasting the crunchy bitterness of the melon.

INGREDIENTS

- 2 medium-sized bitter melons
- 200 grams pork tenderloin, thinly sliced
- 2 tablespoons soy sauce
- 1 tablespoon oyster sauce
- 1 teaspoon cornstarch
- 1 teaspoon sugar
- 2 tablespoons vegetable oil
- 3 cloves garlic, minced
- 1 tablespoon ginger, minced
- Salt to taste
- Ground black pepper to taste
- 1 scallion, sliced for garnish
- 1 red chili, thinly sliced (optional, for heat)

DIRECTIONS

1. Prepare the bitter melon by slicing it in half lengthwise and then use a spoon to scoop out the seeds and white pith. Slice the halves into thin, half-moon shapes. Sprinkle them with salt, let them sit for about 10 minutes, then rinse under cold water and drain. This helps to reduce the bitterness.
2. Mix the pork slices with 1 tablespoon of soy sauce, cornstarch, and a bit of pepper. Let marinate for at least 15 minutes.
3. Heat 1 tablespoon of vegetable oil in a wok or large skillet over high heat. Add the pork in a single layer and stir-fry until it's just cooked through, about 2-3 minutes. Remove the pork from the wok and set aside.
4. In the same wok, add another tablespoon of vegetable oil. Sauté the garlic and ginger until aromatic, about 1 minute.
5. Add the bitter melon and stir-fry for about 2 minutes, or until it starts to soften.
6. Return the pork to the wok, add the remaining soy sauce, oyster sauce, sugar, and a splash of water. Stir well to combine.
7. Cook for another 2-3 minutes, until the sauce has thickened slightly and the bitter melon is tender but still crisp. Taste and adjust seasoning with salt and pepper, if necessary.
8. Dish out and garnish with scallions and red chili, if using. Serve immediately with steamed rice.

DIETARY MODIFICATIONS

Vegetarian: Replace the pork with firm tofu or tempeh sliced into strips. Marinate and cook similarly. For the oyster sauce, use a vegetarian mushroom oyster sauce.

Vegan: Follow the vegetarian substitutions and ensure that the soy sauce is vegan (some brands ferment with animal products). Double check the sugar to ensure it's vegan as some sugar is processed with bone char.

Low-carb: Omit the sugar in the stir-fry sauce, and serve with a side of cauliflower rice instead of traditional rice to reduce the carbohydrate content.

INGREDIENT SPOTLIGHT: BITTER MELON

The bitter melon, also known as karela or goya, is a member of the gourd family and is a key ingredient in this dish. Originating in India and introduced to China during the 14th century, it is not only part of the culinary landscape but also used in traditional medicine to treat diabetes and other ailments. The bitterness comes from compounds called cucurbitacins, which are thought to have antioxidant and anti-inflammatory properties. It's often paired with strong flavors like meat or spices to balance its bitterness.

CHEF'S TIPS

- Don't skip the step of salting and rinsing the bitter melon slices; it's crucial for reducing the bitterness.
- Ensure your wok is very hot before adding the pork to get a nice sear without overcooking.
- Cut the pork thinly and against the grain for the most tender texture.
- Constantly stir while stir-frying to cook evenly and prevent sticking.
- Add a splash of water while stir-frying if the wok becomes too dry; this creates steam for a more even cook.

POSSIBLE VARIATIONS OF THE RECIPE

- **Spicy:** Add extra red chilies or a tablespoon of spicy bean paste for a hotter dish, appealing to lovers of fiery flavors.
- **Sweet and Sour:** Incorporate pineapple chunks and a splash of rice vinegar to the stir-fry for a tangy twist on the traditional recipe.
- **Black Bean Sauce:** Replace oyster sauce with fermented black bean paste to introduce a robust, salty flavor that complements the bitter melon beautifully.

HEALTH NOTE & CALORIC INFORMATION

A serving of Pork and Bitter Melon Stir-Fry is approximately 220 calories. The dish is rich in protein from the pork and low in carbohydrates. Bitter melon contributes dietary fiber, vitamins A and C, and a range of minerals, including magnesium and potassium. Note that altering ingredients for dietary needs will affect the nutritional content.

CHAO NIAN GAO

Hailing from the Shanghai region of China, Chao Nian Gao, or stir-fried rice cakes, is a beloved dish rooted in Chinese New Year celebrations. The name Nian Gao roughly translates to "year cake" or "Chinese new year's cake," symbolizing prosperity and the promise of better days. Historically, families gather to enjoy this dish, appreciating the chewy texture of the rice cakes, often complemented by the freshness of seasonal vegetables.

INGREDIENTS

- 200g sliced rice cakes (nian gao), soaked in water if they're dried
- 2 tablespoons vegetable oil
- 2 garlic cloves, finely chopped
- 1 teaspoon ginger, freshly grated
- 1 medium carrot, julienned
- 150g Napa cabbage, chopped
- 100g shiitake mushrooms, stems removed and thinly sliced
- 2 tablespoons light soy sauce
- 1 tablespoon Shaoxing wine (Chinese cooking wine)
- 1 teaspoon sesame oil
- 1 teaspoon sugar
- Salt to taste
- Freshly ground black pepper to taste
- 2 green onions, chopped
- A handful of fresh cilantro leaves for garnish

DIRECTIONS

1. Prepare the rice cakes according to the package instructions. If they're dried, soak them in warm water until they're soft, for about an hour.
2. Heat a wok or a large frying pan over medium-high heat. Add the vegetable oil, swirling to coat the surface.
3. Add the minced garlic and grated ginger to the wok, stir-frying for about 30 seconds, just until aromatic.
4. Increase the heat to high and add the carrots, stir-frying for 2 minutes until they start to soften.
5. Toss in the Napa cabbage and shiitake mushrooms, continuing to stir-fry for another 3 minutes, or until the vegetables are tender and the mushrooms have released their moisture.
6. Drain the rice cakes and add them to the wok with the vegetables.
7. Pour the soy sauce, Shaoxing wine, sesame oil, sugar, and a pinch of salt and pepper over the rice cakes and vegetables. Stir well to combine everything, making sure the rice cakes don't stick to the pan.
8. Stir-fry for another 5-7 minutes, until the rice cakes are tender and have absorbed the flavors of the sauce.
9. Taste and adjust the seasoning if necessary. Turn off the heat.
10. Sprinkle chopped green onions and cilantro leaves over the top for garnish.
11. Serve hot as a flavorful side dish or a light main course.

DIETARY MODIFICATIONS

Vegetarian: Simply ensure the soy sauce used is vegetarian, as some brands use a small amount of fish or other animal products.

Vegan: In addition to ensuring the soy sauce is vegan, also check the rice cakes' ingredients as some may contain traces of animal products. Use vegan-friendly Shaoxing wine or replace it with a non-alcoholic rice vinegar.

Gluten-Free: Opt for gluten-free soy sauce and check the rice cakes for any gluten content. Substitute Shaoxing wine with a gluten-free alternative like dry sherry.

INGREDIENT SPOTLIGHT: NIAN GAO

The spotlight ingredient, Nian Gao or sliced rice cakes, has a gelatinous, chewy texture that is unlike other types of noodles or pasta. Originating from East Asian cuisine, they are made from glutinous rice flour. Consumed traditionally during Chinese New Year, these rice cakes symbolize growth, prosperity, and longevity, thus they are a central component of the dish, not just for their unique mouthfeel but also for the cultural significance they carry. The preparation of Nian Gao is an art in itself, central to the integrity of the dish, offering a canvas for the symphony of flavors.

CHEF'S TIPS

- For the best texture, keep the heat high and stir constantly to prevent the rice cakes from sticking.
- Slice the vegetables uniformly to ensure they cook evenly.
- Soak dried rice cakes sufficiently until they are thoroughly soft to guarantee a tender chewiness in the final dish.
- Use a seasoned wok to impart a smoky, "wok hei" flavor to the dish that's typical in Chinese cuisine.
- Serve immediately to enjoy the optimal texture and taste since the rice cakes can become soggy if left sitting.

POSSIBLE VARIATIONS OF THE RECIPE

- **Seafood Delight:** Add shrimp or sliced fish cakes in the stir-fry for a pescatarian twist, cooking seafood thoroughly before adding the rice cakes.
- **Spicy Kick:** Introduce a tablespoon of chilli sauce or sliced fresh chillies for those who crave a bit of heat.
- **Protein Boost:** For a heartier meal, incorporate strips of marinated tofu or chicken. Ensure the protein is cooked separately and added with the vegetables.

HEALTH NOTE & CALORIC INFORMATION

Stir-Fried Rice Cakes with Vegetables is a carbohydrate-rich meal, with rice cakes providing the bulk of the calories. A typical serving contains approximately 250-300 kcal, with a moderate amount of fiber from the vegetables and a low to moderate fat content depending on the amount of oil used in stir-frying. It's a source of protein through mushrooms and Napa cabbage, but adding tofu or meat can increase this. Always consider portion sizes and adjust serving size for specific dietary needs.

XO SAUCE FRIED RICE

XO sauce, the luxurious condiment originating from Hong Kong in the 1980s, gives a rich umami depth and seafood aroma to dishes. Named after the prestigious XO (extra-old) cognac for its high quality and similarly sophisticated image, this sauce is often made with dried scallops, dried shrimp, chili peppers, and various seasonings. Our XO Sauce Fried Rice is an embodiment of this opulence, marrying simple home cooking with a touch of extravagance.

INGREDIENTS

- 2 cups of cooked jasmine rice, preferably day-old
- 3 tablespoons of XO sauce
- 2 tablespoons of vegetable oil
- 2 large eggs, beaten
- 4 scallions, white and green parts separated and thinly sliced
- 1 medium carrot, diced
- 1/2 cup of frozen peas, thawed
- 2 cloves of garlic, minced
- Salt, to taste
- 2 tablespoons of soy sauce
- 1 teaspoon of sesame oil

DIRECTIONS

1. Ensure your cooked jasmine rice is cold and grains are separate. If using fresh rice, spread it out on a tray and place it in the refrigerator for a few moments to cool down and dry out a bit.
2. Heat a wok or large skillet over high heat and add 1 tablespoon of vegetable oil, swirling to coat the bottom.
3. Pour in the beaten eggs and quickly scramble until just set. Remove the eggs to a plate and set aside.
4. Add the remaining tablespoon of vegetable oil to the wok. When hot, add the white parts of the scallions, carrot, and garlic and stir-fry for about 2 minutes until just softened.
5. Increase the heat to high, add the rice and break up any clumps with a spatula. Stir-fry for about 3 minutes until the rice is heated through.
6. Add the XO sauce, stirring well to evenly coat the rice.
7. Mix in the soy sauce and sesame oil, and continue to stir-fry for an additional minute, integrating all the flavors.
8. Incorporate the scrambled eggs and thawed peas, and cook for another 2 minutes, tossing everything together.
9. Finish by adding the green parts of the scallions. Stir well and adjust the seasoning with salt if necessary.
10. Serve hot, garnished with additional scallion greens or sesame seeds if desired.

DIETARY MODIFICATIONS

Vegetarian: Substitute XO sauce with a vegetarian umami sauce blend of shiitake mushroom soy sauce, miso paste, and a pinch of smoked paprika.
Vegan: Follow the vegetarian modifications and replace eggs with firm tofu crumbled and fried until golden.
Gluten-free: Ensure that gluten-free soy sauce is used, and check that your XO sauce or its substitute does not contain any gluten ingredients.

INGREDIENT SPOTLIGHT: XO SAUCE

XO Sauce is the star ingredient in our fried rice. It was created in the 1980s in Hong Kong and quickly became popular for its complex blend of savory, sweet, and spicy flavors. Traditional XO sauce packs a punch with dried scallops—known as conpoy—and dried shrimp, which provide an intense seafood umami. These are combined with chili peppers, onions, garlic, and oil. Quality XO sauce is characterized by its chunky texture and rich brown color. Its luxurious status comes from the cost of dried scallops, making it a premium addition to any pantry.

CHEF'S TIPS

- Use day-old rice for the best texture; freshly cooked rice may turn mushy.
- Keep the wok on high heat to achieve the characteristic 'wok hei'—the slightly smoky flavor of good fried rice.
- Prepare all ingredients before you start cooking; the process is quick and doesn't leave time for chopping.
- Be bold with the XO sauce; it should be the dominant flavor, but adjust according to your taste.
- If you don't have XO sauce available, you can use any other umami-rich sauce as a base and customize with additional chili, shallots, and dried seafood.

POSSIBLE VARIATIONS OF THE RECIPE

- **Seafood Delight:** Add sautéed prawns, scallops, or squid for a more luxurious dish.
- **Chicken XO Fried Rice:** Incorporate diced chicken thighs, marinated in soy sauce and sesame oil, stir-fried before adding the rice.
- **Spicy Kick:** For those who love heat, add chopped fresh red chili or a spoonful of chili oil in the final stages of cooking.

HEALTH NOTE & CALORIC INFORMATION

This dish is a high-carbohydrate meal, with rice making up the bulk of the calories. The vegetable oil, XO sauce, and eggs provide fats, while the peas and carrot add fiber and a modest amount of vitamins. One serving of XO Sauce Fried Rice is approximately 350 to 400 calories, with variations depending on the exact ingredients and portion sizes. The dish also contains protein from the eggs and any additional seafood or meat, and the use of sesame oil adds a small amount of healthy fat. Remember that XO sauce can be high in sodium, so those with salt-sensitive diets should be mindful of portion sizes.

BEEF WITH GINGER

A staple dish in Chinese cuisine, stir-fried beef with ginger and spring onion brings together the warm spice of ginger with the freshness of spring onions, paired with tender slices of beef. It is a quick and easy dish that demonstrates the principles of wok hei, or the "breath of the wok," where the high heat cooking imparts a unique seared flavor.

INGREDIENTS

- 500g beef sirloin, thinly sliced
- 2 tablespoons soy sauce
- 1 tablespoon oyster sauce
- 1 teaspoon cornstarch
- 2 teaspoons sugar
- 1 tablespoon Chinese rice wine (Shaoxing wine)
- 3 tablespoons vegetable oil
- 2 inches fresh ginger, julienned
- 4 spring onions, cut into 2-inch lengths
- 1 garlic clove, minced
- Salt and pepper to taste
- Optional: 1 teaspoon sesame oil for finishing

DIRECTIONS

1. In a bowl, mix 1 tablespoon soy sauce, oyster sauce, cornstarch, sugar, and Chinese rice wine. Add the sliced beef to the marinade, ensuring each piece is coated. Let it marinate for at least 15 minutes.
2. Heat 2 tablespoons vegetable oil in a wok or a large skillet over high heat. Once the oil is hot, add the beef in a single layer. Sear the beef until it is browned, then stir to cook all sides evenly. This should take about 2-3 minutes. Remove the beef and set aside.
3. In the same wok, add the remaining 1 tablespoon of oil. Add the ginger and garlic. Stir-fry for about 30 seconds until fragrant.
4. Add the spring onions and the remaining 1 tablespoon of soy sauce. Stir-fry the mixture for about 1 minute.
5. Return the beef to the wok, stirring to mix all the ingredients well. Stir-fry for another 2 minutes or until the spring onions are tender but still crisp.
6. Season with salt, pepper, and optional sesame oil. Serve immediately with steamed rice.

DIETARY MODIFICATIONS

Vegetarian: Substitute beef with firm tofu, sliced and pressed to remove excess moisture. Use a vegetarian oyster sauce.
Vegan: Follow the vegetarian suggestions and ensure soy sauce is vegan. Substitute honey with agave syrup if sweetening is necessary.
Gluten-Free: Use gluten-free tamari or coconut aminos instead of soy sauce. Ensure the oyster sauce is gluten-free or use a gluten-free alternative.

INGREDIENT SPOTLIGHT: GINGER

Ginger is a rhizome that has been used in cooking and medicine for thousands of years, particularly in Asian and Indian cultures. Its pungent and spicy flavor is essential in many dishes, and it's also known for its anti-inflammatory and digestive properties. In this recipe, ginger adds warmth and zest, balancing the rich flavors of the beef and the savory sauces. The fresh, sharp bite of ginger is a key contrast to the sweetness of the spring onions, making it indispensable in this dish.

CHEF'S TIPS
- Slice the beef against the grain for tenderness.
- Ensure the wok is preheated to a high temperature before adding ingredients for proper wok hei.
- Do not overcrowd the wok; cook in batches if necessary to maintain high heat.
- Cut the spring onions at a diagonal angle for aesthetic and to expose more surface area for cooking.
- Adding a small splash of water can help to deglaze the wok if ingredients start to stick.

POSSIBLE VARIATIONS OF THE RECIPE
- **Spicy Version:** Add sliced chili peppers or a teaspoon of chili flakes when stir-frying the ginger.
- **Pepper Beef:** Incorporate bell peppers of different colors, cut into bite-sized pieces, for added sweetness and crunch.
- **Orange Ginger Beef:** Introduce a zesty twist by adding orange zest and a tablespoon of orange juice to the marinade.

HEALTH NOTE & CALORIC INFORMATION
This dish is high in protein and contains a moderate amount of fat, mainly from the vegetable oil used for frying. It also provides ingredients with potential health benefits like ginger, which aids in digestion. A typical serving contains approximately 300-400 calories, assuming the dish serves four and is served with a modest portion of steamed rice. Please note this is an estimate and actual calories may vary.

OJINGEO BOKKEUM

Ojingeo Bokkeum is a beloved spicy squid dish from the coastal regions of Korea, known for its robust flavor and quick preparation, making it an ideal dish for a fast-paced lifestyle. Traditionally eaten with a bowl of steaming rice, it showcases Korea's affinity for seafood and its mastery of balancing spice, sweetness, and savory flavors in a single dish.

INGREDIENTS

- 400 grams of fresh squid, cleaned and sliced into rings
- 2 tablespoons of gochujang (Korean red chili paste)
- 1 tablespoon of soy sauce
- 1 tablespoon of oyster sauce
- 1 tablespoon of gochugaru (Korean red chili flakes)
- 1 tablespoon of sesame oil
- 1 tablespoon of vegetable oil
- 3 cloves of garlic, minced
- 1 teaspoon of grated ginger
- 1 medium onion, sliced
- 1 carrot, julienned
- 2 green onions, chopped
- 1 tablespoon of honey or sugar
- 1 teaspoon of toasted sesame seeds (for garnish)
- Salt to taste

DIRECTIONS

1. Prepare the squid by rinsing under cold water and slicing it into bite-sized rings, and tentacles into manageable pieces.
2. In a mixing bowl, combine gochujang, soy sauce, oyster sauce, gochugaru, honey or sugar, minced garlic, and grated ginger to make the sauce.
3. Heat sesame oil and vegetable oil in a large skillet or wok over medium-high heat. Add the sliced onion and carrots, sautéing until they begin to soften, about 3 minutes.
4. Add the squid to the skillet and stir-fry for about 2 minutes until it starts to turn opaque. Be careful not to overcook the squid as it can become rubbery.
5. Pour the sauce over the squid and vegetables, stirring well to ensure everything is coated evenly with the sauce. Stir-fry for another 2-3 minutes.
6. Incorporate the green onions into the stir-fry and cook for an additional minute.
7. Remove from heat and taste, adjusting for salt if necessary.
8. Garnish with toasted sesame seeds and serve hot with steamed rice.

DIETARY MODIFICATIONS

Vegetarian: Use mushrooms such as oyster or king oyster mushrooms as a substitute for squid. Adjust the cooking time appropriately as mushrooms will cook faster than squid.

Vegan: Follow the vegetarian substitutes and replace oyster sauce with a vegan stir-fry sauce or hoisin sauce. Ensure that the gochujang is vegan-friendly as some brands may use fish sauce.

Gluten-Free: Use a gluten-free soy sauce and ensure that the gochujang and oyster sauce are gluten-free. Many brands offer gluten-free options for these ingredients.

INGREDIENT SPOTLIGHT: GOCHUJANG

Gochujang is a quintessential Korean condiment with a history stretching back to the 18th century. It's a fermented paste made from chili powder, glutinous rice, fermented soybeans, and salt, known for its deep red color and a unique balance of sweet, spicy, and savory flavors. It's the heart of many Korean dishes, and in this recipe, it brings both heat and a touch of sweetness that is crucial for the authenticity of the flavor profile.

CHEF'S TIPS

- Dry the squid thoroughly after cleaning to prevent sogginess and spatter during stir-frying.
- Preheat the skillet or wok before adding the oil to ensure a quick sear on the ingredients, locking in flavors.
- Slice the squid into uniform pieces for even cooking.
- Do not overcook the squid—quick high-heat cooking is key to a tender result.
- For added complexity, consider a splash of rice wine or mirin in the sauce.

POSSIBLE VARIATIONS OF THE RECIPE

- **Seafood Medley:** Add different types of seafood such as shrimp, scallops, or mussels along with the squid to turn it into a mixed seafood stir-fry.
- **Extra Spice:** For those who love heat, increase the amount of gochugaru or add slices of fresh hot peppers towards the end of cooking.
- **Sweet and Crunchy:** Introduce a sweet element like pineapple or bell peppers for a sweet crunch, providing a contrast to the spicy sauce.

HEALTH NOTE & CALORIC INFORMATION

This dish is relatively low in calories, with the main contributor to its nutritional value being the squid, which is rich in protein. Depending on the portion size, a serving can range between 200-300 calories. The vegetables add fiber and a variety of vitamins. Be mindful of the sodium content due to the sauces; using low-sodium soy sauce may reduce sodium intake. Gochujang contains some sugar, contributing to the carbs count in the dish.

SAMBAL KANGKONG

Sambal Kangkong is a beloved Southeast Asian dish known for its fiery blend of flavors. In Malaysia, Indonesia, and Singapore, Kangkong (water spinach) is a common vegetable, often found growing in water or damp soil. When stir-fried with sambal—a spicy chili paste—and other aromatics, this humble green transforms into a mouthwatering dish that's full of zest. It's a common fixture in home cooking as well as hawker centers, where it's loved for its simplicity and bold taste.

INGREDIENTS

- 500g Kangkong (water spinach), cut into 2-inch lengths
- 2 tablespoons cooking oil
- 3 cloves garlic, minced
- 1 small onion, sliced
- 1 red chili, sliced
- 2 tablespoons sambal oelek (chili paste)
- 1 tablespoon belacan (shrimp paste)
- 1 teaspoon sugar
- 2 tablespoons tamarind juice (mix tamarind pulp with water and strain)
- Salt to taste

DIRECTIONS

1. Rinse the Kangkong thoroughly in cold water to remove any dirt or grit. Drain and set aside.
2. In a mortar and pestle or a food processor, blend the belacan with the sambal oelek, garlic, onion, red chili, and sugar to make a fragrant paste.
3. Heat the cooking oil in a wok or large frying pan over medium-high heat.
4. Add the sambal belacan paste into the wok and stir-fry for 2-3 minutes until aromatic, being careful not to burn the mixture.
5. Increase the heat to high, and add the Kangkong to the wok. Stir quickly to combine with the sambal mixture.
6. Pour in the tamarind juice and continue to stir-fry for another 2-3 minutes until the Kangkong is wilted but still vibrant green.
7. Season with salt to taste—you might not need much as belacan is quite salty.
8. Remove from heat and serve immediately with steamed rice.

DIETARY MODIFICATIONS

Vegetarian: Replace belacan with a vegetarian shrimp paste substitute, which can be made by combining miso paste with a touch of soy sauce and sugar.

Vegan: Alongside the vegetarian substitute for belacan, ensure that the sambal oelek used does not contain shrimp or fish sauce, which can be present in some varieties.

Gluten-Free: Confirm that the sambal oelek and belacan (or its substitutes) are gluten-free, since some brands may contain gluten as an additive.

INGREDIENT SPOTLIGHT: BELACAN

The spotlight ingredient in this recipe is belacan, a fermented shrimp paste that's a cornerstone of Malaysian and Indonesian cuisine. Made by fermenting tiny shrimp mixed with salt, belacan is then sun-dried and cut into blocks. This condiment packs a pungent aroma and a powerful boost of umami that's indispensable in many Southeast Asian dishes. Although the smell can be strong to the uninitiated, the flavor it imparts is rich and deeply savory, providing a distinctive character to Sambal Kangkong.

CHEF'S TIPS

- Remove any tough, woody stems from the Kangkong before cooking.
- Ensure that the wok is properly heated before adding the oil and sambal mixture, as this will help to bring out the flavors.
- When stir-frying, keep the ingredients moving to avoid burning, especially the garlic, which can turn bitter if overcooked.
- Preparing the sambal paste ahead of time can allow the flavors to meld and deepen.
- If you prefer less heat, deseed the chili or adjust the amount of sambal oelek to suit your spice tolerance.

POSSIBLE VARIATIONS OF THE RECIPE

- **Seafood Lover's Twist:** Stir in a handful of prawns or squid in the last few minutes of cooking for an added seafood dimension.
- **Protein Boost:** Add cubes of firm tofu or tempeh to the stir-fry for some added protein and texture.
- **Mild and Kid-Friendly:** Reduce the chili paste and add a splash of coconut milk towards the end of cooking for a creamier, milder version that's great for those with a low spice threshold.

HEALTH NOTE & CALORIC INFORMATION

Kangkong is rich in vitamins A and C and is also a good source of iron. The dish is relatively low in calories, with the majority coming from the oil and shrimp paste. For those watching their salt intake, belacan is high in sodium, so it's advisable to add less salt during cooking or seek low-sodium alternatives. The exact calorie content will vary based on the specific ingredients used, but a single serving (without rice) typically contains approximately 80-120 calories, with 4-6 grams of fat, 2-3 grams of protein, and a carbohydrate count largely dependent on the amount of sugar and tamarind juice used.

THAI CASHEW CHICKEN

Infused with the colorful culinary traditions of Thailand, Thai Cashew Chicken is a stir-fry dish that embraces the harmony of sweet, savory, and spicy flavors typical to Thai cuisine. A popular dish in Thai restaurants worldwide, its roots lie in the Chinese influence on Thai cooking, which is masterfully represented by the use of cashews—a nut that was brought to Thailand by Chinese merchants. This dish is a fusion that celebrates the blend of cultures, featuring the aromatic blend of Thai herbs and spices with the rich, buttery crunch of cashews.

INGREDIENTS

- 1 pound (450g) chicken breast, cut into bite-sized pieces
- 1/3 cup roasted cashews
- 3 tablespoons vegetable oil
- 5-6 dried red chilies, cut into halves and seeds removed
- 1 bell pepper, sliced
- 1 onion, sliced
- 2 cloves garlic, minced
- 1 teaspoon minced ginger
- 2 green onions, chopped
- 1 tablespoon soy sauce
- 1 tablespoon oyster sauce
- 1 tablespoon fish sauce
- 2 teaspoons sugar
- 1/2 teaspoon ground white pepper

DIRECTIONS

1. Heat the vegetable oil in a wok or large frying pan over medium-high heat until the oil is hot but not smoking.
2. Add the dried red chilies to the oil and stir-fry for about 30 seconds, or until they darken slightly.
3. Add the minced garlic and ginger, and stir-fry for another 30 seconds until aromatic.
4. Introduce the chicken pieces to the wok and stir-fry for 4-5 minutes, or until they are mostly cooked through.
5. Toss in the sliced onion and bell pepper, continuing to stir-fry for 2-3 minutes until the vegetables soften.
6. Sprinkle in the sugar, soy sauce, oyster sauce, fish sauce, and ground white pepper, mixing well to coat the chicken and vegetables in the sauce.
7. Finally, add the roasted cashews and green onions, stir well, and cook for an additional minute.
8. Once the chicken is fully cooked and the vegetables are tender-crisp, remove the wok from the heat.
9. Serve your Thai Cashew Chicken hot, ideally over steamed jasmine rice.

DIETARY MODIFICATIONS

Vegetarian: Substitute the chicken with extra-firm tofu that has been pressed and cut into cubes. Pan-fry the tofu until golden brown and use it in place of the chicken. Use vegetarian oyster sauce or mushroom sauce instead of the regular oyster sauce.

Vegan: Follow the vegetarian modifications and replace fish sauce with a vegan fish sauce alternative or simply add additional soy sauce to taste.

Gluten-Free: Ensure that the soy sauce is gluten-free, or use tamari instead. Also, check that your oyster sauce is gluten-free, or use a gluten-free hoisin sauce as a substitute.

INGREDIENT SPOTLIGHT: CASHEW NUT

The cashew nut, a product initially native to Brazil, was brought to Southeast Asia by the Portuguese in the 16th century. It quickly became a staple in many Asian cuisines. The cashew's creamy texture and mild nutty flavor provide a delightful contrast to the zesty elements of Thai dishes. Roasting enhances their natural sweetness, making them an essential component in this recipe for their flavor and the appealing crunch they bring.

CHEF'S TIPS

- Slice the chicken evenly to ensure consistent cooking. Thin slices cook faster and absorb the sauce better, enhancing the flavor.
- Dry-roast the cashews in a pan before using them in the dish to release their natural oils and intensify the flavor.
- Use a wok for authentic stir-frying, which allows for quick cooking at high temperatures, making ingredients crispy and not soggy.
- Ensure all ingredients are prepped and ready to go before you start cooking since stir-frying is done at high heat and moves quickly.
- Adjust the number of dried chilies to suit your heat preference. The seeds are the hottest part, so remove them if you prefer a milder dish.

POSSIBLE VARIATIONS OF THE RECIPE

- **Pineapple Cashew Chicken:** Add chunks of fresh pineapple with the bell peppers to introduce a sweet, tangy flavor that complements the cashews.
- **Thai Basil Cashew Chicken:** Stir in a handful of fresh Thai basil leaves at the end of cooking for an aromatic twist.
- **Cashew Shrimp:** Substitute chicken with equal amounts of shrimp and adjust the cooking time accordingly, frying until the shrimp are pink and just cooked through.

HEALTH NOTE & CALORIC INFORMATION

Thai Cashew Chicken is a protein-rich dish with the added benefits of vitamins and fiber from the vegetables. Cashews bring in healthy fats and a boost of minerals. However, the sauces could contribute to high sodium levels, so it is advisable to consume in moderation. A single serving without rice typically contains around 300-400 calories, depending on the preparation.

LAO STIR FRY

Lao cuisine is one of the culinary treasures of Southeast Asia, known for its fresh ingredients, bold flavors, and herbs. This recipe is a take on the traditional Lao stir fry, with a focus on the harmonious blend of savory, sweet, and spicy flavors that characterize Lao food. The stir fry often includes a variety of fresh vegetables and herbs, typically seasoned with fish sauce and padaek (Lao fermented fish sauce) for depth. Chicken is frequently used, although variations with beef or pork are also popular.

INGREDIENTS

- 500g chicken breast, thinly sliced
- 1 tbsp vegetable oil
- 2 cloves garlic, finely minced
- 3 small shallots, sliced
- 2 red chilies, sliced (adjust to taste)
- 1 bell pepper, julienned
- 1 carrot, julienned
- 100g green beans, trimmed and halved
- 1 small handful of Thai basil leaves
- 1 tbsp oyster sauce
- 1 tbsp fish sauce
- 1 tbsp soy sauce
- 1 tsp sugar
- 1 tbsp Lao fermented fish sauce (padaek), optional
- 1 tbsp toasted rice powder (khao khua), for garnish
- Fresh lime wedges, for serving

DIRECTIONS

1. Marinate the chicken with soy sauce, fish sauce, and sugar for at least 20 minutes.
2. Heat oil in a large wok or frying pan over high heat. Add garlic and shallots, stir-fry until fragrant.
3. Add the chicken and stir-fry until it starts to brown.
4. Toss in the red chilies, bell pepper, carrot, and green beans. Stir-fry for about 3-5 minutes or until the vegetables are tender but still crisp.
5. Stir in the oyster sauce, and Lao fermented fish sauce if using, and cook for another minute.
6. Turn off the heat, and mix in the fresh Thai basil leaves until they just begin to wilt.
7. Serve the stir fry hot, garnished with toasted rice powder and lime wedges on the side.

DIETARY MODIFICATIONS

Vegetarian: Substitute chicken with tofu or a mix of mushrooms. Use soy sauce in place of fish sauce and mushroom oyster sauce for the oyster sauce.

Vegan: Follow the vegetarian modifications and ensure that the soy sauce and sugar used are vegan-friendly. Skip the toasted rice powder garnish unless you're sure it's vegan.

Gluten-Free: Use gluten-free soy sauce and a gluten-free oyster sauce substitute. Ensure all other sauces are gluten-free as well.

INGREDIENT SPOTLIGHT: THAI BASIL

Thai basil is a variety of basil native to Southeast Asia. Its flavor is a distinctive combination of basil sweetness with notes of anise and licorice. Unlike the sweet basil used in Italian cooking, Thai basil holds up well under high cooking temperatures, which makes it perfect for stir-fries. It's not just a flavoring – Thai basil is said to support digestion and has anti-inflammatory properties. Its robust flavor is the backbone of this dish, bringing the quintessential Lao aroma to the stir fry.

CHEF'S TIPS

- Prepare all ingredients before you start cooking. Stir-frying is a quick process and requires immediate addition of ingredients in sequence.
- Marinate the chicken to ensure it is flavorful and tender after cooking.
- Maintain high heat throughout cooking to achieve a good sear on the chicken and crisp-tender vegetables.
- Add the Thai basil last to prevent it from burning and to retain its vibrant flavor and color.
- Use a wok if possible for even heat distribution and authentic taste; otherwise, a large frying pan will suffice.

POSSIBLE VARIATIONS OF THE RECIPE

- **Lao Beef Stir Fry:** Substitute chicken with thinly sliced beef and add a touch of dark soy sauce for a deeper flavor.
- **Seafood Delight:** Replace chicken with a mix of seafood such as shrimp and squid for a pescatarian version.
- **Spicy Eggplant Stir Fry:** Add sliced eggplant and increase the chilies for a vegetarian option with more heat and texture.

HEALTH NOTE & CALORIC INFORMATION

A serving of Lao Stir Fry typically contains a balance of lean protein from the chicken, fiber, and vitamins from the varied vegetables, and healthy fats from the vegetable oil. The use of fresh herbs and moderate amounts of sauces keeps the dish relatively low in calories, with an estimated calorie count of approximately 250-300 calories per serving. It is also a good source of vitamin C and iron. The addition of fermented sauces contributes to the sodium content, which diners with dietary restrictions may need to monitor.

GARLIC CHIVE AND EGG

Garlic chives, known as 'jiu cai' in Mandarin, hold a cherished spot in various Asian cuisines, especially in Chinese cooking. They are celebrated for their robust flavor, which is more intense than that of common chives. This Garlic Chive and Egg Stir-Fry is a homage to the simple yet delicious home-cooked meals found throughout China. Quick to prepare, it showcases the perfect harmony between the fragrant garlic chives and the soft, fluffy texture of scrambled eggs.

INGREDIENTS

- 4 large eggs
- 2 cups garlic chives, chopped into 1-inch pieces
- 2 tablespoons vegetable oil
- 2 cloves garlic, minced
- 1 teaspoon soy sauce
- 1/2 teaspoon sesame oil
- Salt, to taste
- White pepper, to taste

DIRECTIONS

1. In a bowl, crack the eggs and beat them until the yolks and whites are fully combined. Season with a pinch of salt and white pepper.
2. Heat a wok or large frying pan over medium-high heat. Add 1 tablespoon of vegetable oil and swirl to coat the bottom.
3. Pour in the eggs and gently stir with a wooden spoon or spatula, pushing the cooked egg towards the center and letting the uncooked egg flow to the edges. Cook to the desired level of doneness, then remove the eggs to a separate plate.
4. In the same wok, add the remaining tablespoon of oil and sauté the minced garlic until fragrant, about 30 seconds.
5. Add the chopped garlic chives and stir-fry for about 2 minutes or until the chives are tender but still bright green.
6. Return the scrambled eggs to the wok and add the soy sauce and sesame oil. Gently fold the eggs into the chives to combine.
7. Taste and adjust for seasoning, then immediately remove from heat to avoid overcooking.
8. Serve the garlic chive and egg stir-fry hot with steamed rice or as a side dish with other main courses.

DIETARY MODIFICATIONS

Vegetarian: This recipe is already suitable for vegetarians.
Vegan: Replace the eggs with a mixture of tofu scramble made from crumbled firm tofu, turmeric for color, nutritional yeast for a cheesy flavor, and a pinch of black salt for an eggy flavor.
Gluten-Free: Ensure that the soy sauce used is a gluten-free tamari soy sauce to accommodate gluten intolerance without altering the dish's taste profile significantly.

INGREDIENT SPOTLIGHT: GARLIC CHIVES

Garlic chives, also known as Chinese chives, are a unique herb with flat, green leaves and a subtle garlic flavor. They are more robust than common chives, which makes them ideal for cooking. Originating in the mountainous regions of the Chinese province of Shanxi, garlic chives have been cultivated for over 4,000 years. In traditional Chinese medicine, they are reputed to have mild stimulant, diuretic, and antiseptic properties. Their pungent taste and versatility in the kitchen make them an essential ingredient in stir-fries, dumplings, and pancakes.

CHEF'S TIPS
- For fluffy eggs, beat them thoroughly before cooking to incorporate air.
- Don't overcook the garlic to avoid bitterness; it should be just aromatic.
- High heat is key for a good stir-fry but constantly stir to prevent burning.
- Adding the eggs back into the wok at the end keeps them tender.
- Cook garlic chives just until wilted to preserve color and nutrients.

POSSIBLE VARIATIONS OF THE RECIPE
- **Shrimp Addition:** Stir in peeled and deveined shrimp before adding the chives for a protein boost and a hint of seafood flavor.
- **Spicy Kick:** Add a teaspoon of chili flakes or a tablespoon of chili sauce to the stir-fry for heat lovers.
- **Meat Lovers:** Include slices of cooked pork or chicken as an extra savory element to this versatile dish.

HEALTH NOTE & CALORIC INFORMATION
This dish is relatively low in calories, with a single serving containing about 150-200 calories, largely due to the use of eggs and vegetables. Garlic chives are a good source of vitamins A and C, while the eggs provide high-quality protein and fats. It is also low in carbohydrates, making it a suitable dish for low-carb diets. The actual calorie count may vary depending on the specific ingredients used and any additional ingredients in the variations.

WOK-FRIED SPICY EGGPLANT

Hailing from Sichuan province in southwestern China, this fiery and fragrant eggplant dish captures the essence of Szechuan cuisine, renowned for its bold flavors—especially the piquancy and pungency resulting from the liberal use of garlic, chili peppers, and Sichuan peppercorns. Traditionally served as a part of a shared meal, wok-fried spicy eggplant hits all the right notes: It's sweet, sour, and delightfully numbing.

INGREDIENTS

- 2 medium-sized Chinese eggplants (about 500g in total)
- 2 tablespoons soy sauce
- 1 tablespoon Chinese black vinegar
- 1 tablespoon Shaoxing wine
- 2 teaspoons sugar
- 1 teaspoon cornstarch
- 1/2 teaspoon ground Sichuan peppercorns
- 4 tablespoons vegetable oil
- 4 cloves garlic, minced
- 2 teaspoons grated ginger
- 2 green onions, sliced into 1-inch pieces
- 1-2 red chili peppers, thinly sliced (adjust to taste)
- 1 teaspoon sesame oil
- Salt to taste
- Fresh cilantro for garnish (optional)

DIRECTIONS

1. Begin by slicing the eggplants into batons approximately 3 inches long and 1/2 inch thick. Soak the eggplant pieces in water for about 15 minutes to remove any bitterness. Drain and pat dry with paper towels.
2. In a small bowl, whisk together the soy sauce, Chinese black vinegar, Shaoxing wine, sugar, cornstarch, and ground Sichuan peppercorns. This will be your sauce mixture; set it aside.
3. Heat 2 tablespoons of vegetable oil in a wok over high heat. Once smoking, add half the eggplant pieces. Stir-fry until they are soft and the edges are slightly browned, about 3 to 4 minutes. Remove the eggplant from the wok and set aside. Repeat with the remaining eggplant and oil.
4. Lower the flame to medium-high and add the garlic, ginger, green onions, and red chili peppers to the wok. Stir-fry for about a minute until aromatic.
5. Add the cooked eggplant back into the wok, give the sauce mixture a quick stir, and then pour it over the eggplants. Toss everything quickly to combine and coat the eggplants evenly.
6. Cook for an additional 1 to 2 minutes until the sauce has thickened slightly and is clinging to the eggplants.
7. Turn off the heat, drizzle sesame oil over the top, and toss to combine. Taste and adjust with salt if necessary.
8. Transfer to a serving dish, garnish with fresh cilantro if desired, and serve hot as a side dish or with steamed rice for a complete meal.

DIETARY MODIFICATIONS

Gluten-Free: Replace soy sauce with tamari or a gluten-free soy sauce alternative and ensure that the Shaoxing wine and Chinese black vinegar are gluten-free as well.

Vegan: The recipe is already vegan; just double-check your wine and sugar for non-vegan processing methods if you adhere strictly to vegan standards.

Low FODMAP: Omit garlic and onion and use garlic-infused oil and the green parts of spring onions to retain some of the flavors. Replace the black vinegar with a low FODMAP-friendly vinegar like red wine vinegar.

INGREDIENT SPOTLIGHT: SICHUAN PEPPERCORNS

Sichuan peppercorns are not actually peppercorns but the dried husks of the prickly ash tree's berries. They are famed for their unique aroma and the slight numbing sensation that they create on the palate, a characteristic integral to Sichuan cuisine's "málà" (numbing and spicy) flavor profile. Over time, these "peppercorns" have become indispensable in Chinese cooking, contributing a distinct tang that can't quite be replicated by any other spice.

CHEF'S TIPS

- Eggplants absorb oil like sponges, so make sure your wok is very hot before adding the oil and the eggplants; this helps to sear them quickly and prevents too much oil absorption.
- Keep the skin on the eggplants for added texture, color, and nutrients.
- To enhance the umami flavor, a small pinch of MSG can be added to the sauce mixture if desired.
- The numbing sensation from the Sichuan peppercorns is an acquired taste; start with less and add more as you become accustomed to the sensation.
- Letting the dish sit for a few minutes before serving allows the flavors to meld together better.

POSSIBLE VARIATIONS OF THE RECIPE

- **Aubergine & Minced Pork:** Brown some minced pork before adding the garlic and ginger for a heartier main dish.
- **Kung Pao Eggplant:** Add peanuts and diced bell peppers for a vegetarian twist on the classic Kung Pao Chicken.
- **Sweet & Sour Eggplant:** Modify the sauce with pineapple juice and ketchup for a sweet and sour note that contrasts the spice.

HEALTH NOTE & CALORIC INFORMATION

This spicy eggplant dish is a nutrient-dense, low-calorie option that is rich in fiber, vitamins, and minerals. It's particularly high in vitamin B1, potassium, and magnesium. The calorie content of one serving (the recipe makes about 4 servings) can be estimated to be approximately 200 to 250 calories depending on the amount of oil absorbed during cooking.

TOFU WITH VEGETABLES

Drawing inspiration from the health-conscious and flavor-packed traditions of Asian cuisines, stir-frying as a cooking method has ancestral roots that can be traced back to the Han Dynasty. This dish combines firm tofu — a staple in vegetarian diets — with a vibrant array of vegetables, melding the philosophies of balance and variety inherent in many Asian cultures.

INGREDIENTS

- 14 oz (400 g) firm tofu
- 2 tablespoons vegetable oil
- 1 bell pepper, cut into strips
- 2 medium carrots, julienned
- 1 zucchini, sliced
- 1 cup broccoli florets
- 1 cup snap peas, trimmed
- 2 cloves garlic, minced
- 1 inch piece ginger, minced
- 2 tablespoons soy sauce
- 1 tablespoon rice vinegar
- 1 tablespoon sesame oil
- 1 teaspoon cornstarch
- 1 teaspoon sugar
- 1/2 teaspoon crushed red pepper flakes (optional)
- Salt to taste
- Fresh cilantro leaves, for garnish
- Toasted sesame seeds, for garnish

DIRECTIONS

1. Press the tofu between paper towels to remove excess moisture, then cut it into 1-inch cubes.
2. Heat 1 tablespoon of vegetable oil in a large non-stick skillet or wok over medium-high heat.
3. Add tofu cubes to the skillet and fry until they are golden brown on all sides, about 7-8 minutes. Remove the tofu and set it aside.
4. In the same skillet, add the remaining tablespoon of vegetable oil, followed by the bell pepper, carrots, broccoli, and snap peas. Stir-fry for 3-4 minutes until the vegetables are just tender but still crisp.
5. Add the minced garlic and ginger, and continue to stir-fry for another 30 seconds until fragrant.
6. In a small bowl, whisk together the soy sauce, rice vinegar, sesame oil, cornstarch, sugar, and red pepper flakes if using. This will be your sauce.
7. Add the zucchini to the skillet with the other vegetables and return the tofu to the pan. Stir everything for another minute.
8. Pour the sauce into the skillet and toss all ingredients together until the sauce thickens and evenly coats the tofu and vegetables, about 1-2 minutes.
9. Taste and add salt if needed. Stir again and turn off the heat.
10. Serve hot, garnished with cilantro leaves and toasted sesame seeds.

DIETARY MODIFICATIONS

For **Gluten-Free:** Substitute soy sauce with tamari or a gluten-free soy sauce alternative to ensure that the dish is gluten-free.

For **Vegan:** This dish is already vegan-friendly, so no modifications are needed. Just ensure that all sauces used are also certified vegan.

For **Nut Allergies:** Simply omit the sesame oil and replace it with a nut-free oil such as sunflower or additional vegetable oil to cater to those with nut allergies.

INGREDIENT SPOTLIGHT: TOFU

Tofu, also known as bean curd, is the spotlight ingredient in this recipe. Its origins date back over 2,000 years to ancient China. Made by coagulating soy milk and pressing the resulting curds into solid blocks, tofu is celebrated for its versatility and ability to absorb flavors. It is a key component of many vegetarian and vegan diets due to its high protein content and is essential in this stir-fry as it provides a satisfying texture and protein base.

CHEF'S TIPS

- Press the tofu well to remove excess water; this ensures it will crisp up nicely.
- Preheat your pan or wok before adding oil to prevent sticking and achieve a good sear on the tofu.
- Cut your veggies uniformly to ensure even cooking.
- Adding garlic and ginger midway through cooking prevents them from burning and releases maximum flavor.
- Stir the sauce before adding it to the pan to redistribute the cornstarch, which may have settled.

POSSIBLE VARIATIONS OF THE RECIPE

- **Spicy Kick:** If you enjoy heat, add a finely chopped chili or a spoonful of chili paste to the stir-fry for a spicy variant.
- **Peanut Tofu:** For a nutty version, add a tablespoon of peanut butter to the sauce. Serve with chopped peanuts on top.
- **Tropical Flair:** Introduce pineapple chunks and a dash of lime juice for a sweet and tangy twist. Cashews also make a crunchy addition.

HEALTH NOTE & CALORIC INFORMATION

A serving of Stir-Fried Tofu with Mixed Vegetables is high in protein, thanks to the tofu, and rich in vitamins and fiber from the variety of vegetables used. It's a low-calorie option that's ideal for those looking to maintain a balanced diet. The use of minimal oil and the absence of heavy sauces also make it a heart-healthy and diabetes-friendly meal. Depending on portion size, a serving may range from 200 to 400 calories.

SWEET AND SOUR PORK RIBS

Sweet and Sour Pork Ribs marry the bright, tangy taste of traditional sweet and sour sauce with succulent pork ribs, a dish that has its roots in Chinese cuisine. Its lineage can be traced back to a range of regional styles, including Cantonese and Sichuan cooking. An all-time favorite at family dinners and festive occasions, this dish has travelled globally, adapting to local tastes and ingredients, yet always retaining its delightful contrast of flavors.

INGREDIENTS

- 1 kg pork spare ribs, cut into 2-3 inch pieces
- Salt and pepper to taste
- 1 teaspoon five-spice powder
- 4 tablespoons cornflour
- Vegetable oil for deep frying
- 2 garlic cloves, minced
- 1-inch piece of ginger, minced
- 1 bell pepper, cut into bite-sized pieces
- 1 onion, cut into wedges
- 3 tablespoons tomato ketchup
- 2 tablespoons rice vinegar
- 2 tablespoons brown sugar
- 1 tablespoon soy sauce
- 1 tablespoon oyster sauce
- ½ cup pineapple juice
- ½ cup water
- Chopped spring onions and sesame seeds, for garnish

DIRECTIONS

1. Season the pork ribs with salt, pepper, and five-spice powder.
2. Dust the ribs lightly with cornflour until they are coated evenly.
3. Heat a generous amount of vegetable oil in a deep pan or wok over medium-high heat.
4. Once the oil is hot, carefully add the ribs in batches. Fry until golden brown and crispy, about 5-7 minutes per batch. Remove and drain on paper towels.
5. Drain the excess oil from the pan, leaving about 2 tablespoons behind.
6. Over medium heat, sauté garlic and ginger until fragrant, about 1 minute.
7. Add the bell pepper and onion. Stir-fry for 2 minutes or until slightly softened.
8. In a bowl, mix tomato ketchup, rice vinegar, brown sugar, soy sauce, oyster sauce, pineapple juice, and water. Stir until well combined.
9. Pour this sauce over the sautéed vegetables and bring to a simmer.
10. Return the fried ribs to the pan and toss to coat evenly with the sauce.
11. Simmer for an additional 10-12 minutes, or until the sauce has thickened and the ribs are glazed.
12. Garnish with chopped spring onions and sesame seeds before serving.

DIETARY MODIFICATIONS

Vegetarian: Swap pork ribs for portobello mushrooms cut into thick slices or strips. Use mushroom sauce instead of oyster sauce.

Vegan: In addition to the vegetarian modifications, replace honey with maple syrup and ensure that the ketchup and soy sauce used are vegan-friendly.

Gluten-Free: Ensure soy sauce is gluten-free (such as tamari), and use a gluten-free flour like rice flour for dusting the ribs.

INGREDIENT SPOTLIGHT: FIVE-SPICE POWDER

Five-spice powder is a hallmark of Chinese cuisine, consisting of star anise, cloves, Chinese cinnamon, Sichuan peppercorns, and fennel seeds. This blend embodies the five flavor elements of sweet, sour, bitter, pungent, and salty—offering a perfect snapshot of Asian culinary philosophy. Integral to this recipe, five-spice powder imparts a deeply aromatic and complex flavor that accentuates the pork's richness and balances the sweet and sour sauce.

CHEF'S TIPS

- Pat the ribs dry before seasoning and dusting with flour to ensure they get a nice crust when fried.
- Use a thermometer to keep the oil temperature consistent while frying.
- For a healthier option, ribs can be oven-baked until crispy before being coated in sauce.
- Adjust the sweetness and tanginess of the sauce to your taste by altering the amounts of sugar and vinegar.
- Let the ribs simmer in the sauce for the recommended time to allow flavors to penetrate and to achieve a sticky glaze.

POSSIBLE VARIATIONS OF THE RECIPE

- **Pineapple Twist:** Add chunks of pineapple for an extra tangy sweetness and a tropical touch.
- **Spicy Kick:** Introduce a teaspoon of chili flakes or a spoon of chili sauce to the sweet and sour mix for a fiery variation.
- **Orange Zest:** Incorporate the zest and juice of an orange for a citrusy flavor that compliments the traditional sweet and sour profile.

HEALTH NOTE & CALORIC INFORMATION

A serving of sweet and sour pork ribs is high in protein and offers a range of vitamins and minerals from the vegetables and sauce ingredients. However, it is also high in calories and fats due to deep-frying and the sugar content in the sauce. A serving typically contains approximately 450-550 calories, depending on the size and exact ingredients used. To make this dish healthier, consider using leaner cuts of pork, reducing the sugar, or frying in a less calorie-dense method such as air-frying.

NOODLES WITH VEGETABLES

Stir-fried longevity noodles, known as "Chang Shou Mian" in China, symbolize a wish for a long and healthy life. Traditionally served at birthdays and Lunar New Year, this dish features long, uncut noodles that represent longevity. Each slippery strand is a reminder to cherish the time we have and to live it to its fullest. With a medley of colorful vegetables, this recipe is a healthful twist on an ancient tradition, bringing good fortune with every bite.

INGREDIENTS

- 200 grams of Yi Mein (Chinese egg noodles)
- 1 medium carrot, julienned
- 1 red bell pepper, sliced thinly
- 1 cup of snow peas, trimmed
- 2 green onions, chopped
- 3 cloves of garlic, minced
- 1 tablespoon of ginger, minced
- 2 tablespoons of soy sauce
- 1 tablespoon of oyster sauce (optional)
- 1 teaspoon of sesame oil
- 1 tablespoon of vegetable oil
- Salt and pepper to taste
- Sesame seeds for garnishing

DIRECTIONS

1. Start by preparing the noodles according to the package instructions until they are just al dente. Drain and set aside.
2. Heat the vegetable oil in a large wok or skillet over medium-high heat. Swirl to coat the surface.
3. Add the minced garlic and ginger to the wok. Stir-fry for about 30 seconds until fragrant, being cautious not to burn them.
4. Toss in the julienned carrots and sliced red bell peppers. Stir-fry for 2-3 minutes until the vegetables are slightly softened but still crisp.
5. Add the snow peas to the wok and continue to stir-fry for an additional minute.
6. Incorporate the cooked noodles into the wok with the vegetables. Gently toss everything together.
7. Pour the soy sauce, oyster sauce (if using), and sesame oil over the noodles. Stir-fry the mixture for a few more minutes, making sure the sauces evenly coat the noodles and vegetables.
8. Season your dish with salt and pepper to taste. Transfer to a serving plate.
9. Garnish with chopped green onions and a sprinkle of sesame seeds before serving.

DIETARY MODIFICATIONS

Vegetarian: Omit the oyster sauce or use a vegetarian mushroom-based "oyster" sauce. This modification maintains the umami flavor while adhering to vegetarian standards.

Vegan: Follow the vegetarian substitution and also ensure that the noodles are egg-free. There is a variety of wheat-based Chinese noodles available that can be used instead.

Gluten-Free: Use gluten-free tamari sauce instead of soy sauce and ensure the noodles are gluten-free. A variety of rice or mung bean-based noodles can be suitable alternatives to Yi Mein.

INGREDIENT SPOTLIGHT: YI MEIN

Yi Mein, also known as e-fu noodles or longevity noodles, are a key ingredient in this dish. Made from wheat flour, these noodles are known for their spongy texture and their ability to absorb flavors. Originating from the Cantonese cuisine, Yi Mein are traditionally served at celebrations, symbolizing a wish for longevity, hence the name. What makes Yi Mein unique is the process of frying and then drying, which gives them a distinctive texture that's quite different from that of regular noodles. Their symbolic meaning and delicious flavor make them indispensable for this recipe.

CHEF'S TIPS
- Make sure to not overcook the noodles, as they will continue to cook with the vegetables and should remain al dente.
- Pre-heat the wok or pan well before adding the oil and ingredients for a true stir-fry experience.
- Use a high smoke-point oil such as peanut or canola oil to avoid burning, especially if cooking at high heat.
- Keep the ingredients moving in the wok to achieve an even cook and to prevent burning.
- Prep all your ingredients before cooking, as the dish comes together very quickly once you start stir-frying.

POSSIBLE VARIATIONS OF THE RECIPE
- **Protein Boost:** Stir in strips of tofu, chicken, or shrimp for added protein. Make sure to cook the protein thoroughly before adding the vegetables.
- **Spicy Kick:** Add a drizzle of chili oil or a sprinkle of red pepper flakes to the dish to give it some heat.
- **Nutty Crunch:** Incorporate a handful of toasted cashews or peanuts for a delightful crunch and additional layer of flavor.

HEALTH NOTE & CALORIC INFORMATION
This Stir-Fried Longevity Noodles with Vegetables dish is a balanced meal with a variety of nutrients from the vegetables. It's high in vitamins such as Vitamin A from the carrots and Vitamin C from the red bell peppers. The noodles provide a source of carbohydrates for energy. Using vegetable oil and limiting the use of sauces can help in controlling the total fat and sodium content. A typical serving size of this dish can range from 350 to 450 calories, depending on the portions and specific ingredients used. It's also a dish rich in dietary fiber.

CHICKEN CHOW HO FUN

Originating from the Guangdong province in China, Chow Ho Fun is a popular Cantonese dish cherished for its tender rice noodles (Ho Fun), vibrant stir-fry, and rich, savory sauces. The dish is a testament to the Cantonese love for wok hei (the breath of the wok), which is the essence of stir-fry cooking. This quick and easy stir-fry meal is often found sizzling away in dimly lit street stalls and bustling eateries, feeding the souls of those looking for a comforting and hearty repast.

INGREDIENTS

- 400g (14oz) fresh wide Ho Fun (rice noodles)
- 200g (7oz) chicken breast, thinly sliced
- 1 cup of bean sprouts
- 1 medium-sized onion, sliced
- 2 spring onions, chopped
- 3 cloves of garlic, minced
- 3 tablespoons of vegetable oil
- 2 tablespoons of soy sauce
- 1 tablespoon of oyster sauce
- 1 teaspoon of sesame oil
- 1/2 teaspoon of sugar
- 1/4 teaspoon of white pepper
- Salt to taste

DIRECTIONS

Preparation:

1. Begin by slicing the chicken breast into thin strips. Marinate with 1 tablespoon of soy sauce, a pinch of salt, and white pepper. Set aside for 15 minutes.
2. Peel and slice the onion. Rinse the bean sprouts and spring onions, then chop the spring onions.
3. If the rice noodles are refrigerated, blanch them in boiling water for about 1 minute to soften, then drain and set aside.

Cooking:

1. Heat 1 tablespoon of vegetable oil in a wok or large frying pan over high heat.
2. Once the oil is hot, stir-fry the marinated chicken slices until they are fully cooked (about 3-4 minutes). Remove the chicken and set aside.
3. Add another 1 tablespoon of oil to the wok. Sauté the minced garlic and sliced onion until fragrant.
4. Add the rice noodles, making sure to gently separate any clumps with a spatula. Stir-fry for a minute or two until the noodles warm up.
5. Mix in the cooked chicken, bean sprouts, remaining soy sauce, oyster sauce, sesame oil, and sugar. Stir-fry for 2-3 minutes until everything is well combined and the noodles have taken on the color of the sauces.
6. Sprinkle the chopped spring onions on top and give one final quick stir.
7. Taste and adjust with salt if necessary.

Serving:

1. Dish out your Chicken Chow Ho Fun onto plates and serve immediately to enjoy the wok hei.

DIETARY MODIFICATIONS

Vegetarian: Substitute chicken with firm tofu cut into thin slices and marinate in the same way. Replace oyster sauce with a vegetarian mushroom-flavored sauce to maintain umami flavors.

Gluten-Free: Use gluten-free soy sauce and ensure that the oyster sauce is also gluten-free. Rice noodles are naturally gluten-free, making them suitable for this dietary need.

Low-Sodium: Reduce both the soy sauce and oyster sauce by half. To compensate for the reduced sauces, enhance flavors with additional garlic, pepper, and a splash of rice wine vinegar.

INGREDIENT SPOTLIGHT: HO FUN

One of the most treasured staples in Southeast Asian cuisine, Ho Fun is crafted from rice flour and water. These noodles vary in width but are best known for being broad and flat. They have a chewy texture that absorbs flavors effectively, making them perfect for stir-fries. Ho Fun is also prominent in Vietnamese pho, showcasing its versatility across different culinary traditions.

CHEF'S TIPS

- Always use a wok or a pan with high sides to allow room for tossing and turning the noodles.
- The key to perfect Chow Ho Fun is high heat. Wok hei can only be achieved through quick cooking on a very hot surface.
- Slice the chicken thinly to ensure quick and even cooking without drying it out.
- It is important not to over-soak or over-soften the rice noodles prior to stir-frying, as they cook quickly and can become mushy if overdone.
- Do not over-stir the noodles in the wok to avoid breaking them. Gently fold them over for even cooking.

POSSIBLE VARIATIONS OF THE RECIPE

- **Seafood Chow Ho Fun:** Replace the chicken with a mix of seafood like shrimp, scallops, and squid for a pescatarian twist on this classic.
- **Beef Chow Ho Fun:** Substitute chicken with thinly sliced beef and add a touch of Chinese black bean sauce for a different layer of flavor.
- **Spicy Chow Ho Fun:** Introduce a tablespoon of chili sauce or sliced fresh chili peppers while stir-frying to add some heat for those who like a spicy kick.

HEALTH NOTE & CALORIC INFORMATION

A single serving of Chicken Chow Ho Fun is roughly 500-600 calories, depending on portion size. It is a carb-heavy dish due to the rice noodles, with moderate protein from the chicken. There is a low to moderate fat content, mostly from the cooking oil, and minimal fiber from the bean sprouts and onions. It's recommended to balance this dish with a side of vegetables for a more nutritionally rounded meal.

CHESTNUTS AND CHICKEN

This dish is a nod to the blend of textures and flavors found in Cantonese cuisine, where stir-fries are a staple. The water chestnut is valued for its ability to stay crisp amid the heat of the wok, providing a refreshing crunch against the tender chicken. Historically in southern China, water chestnuts have been cultivated and cherished for their nourishing qualities and are often incorporated into both savory and sweet dishes.

INGREDIENTS

- 1 lb (450g) chicken breast, thinly sliced
- 1 cup water chestnuts, sliced
- 2 bell peppers (red and yellow), julienned
- 4 green onions, sliced diagonally
- 3 cloves garlic, minced
- 1-inch piece of ginger, minced
- 3 tablespoons soy sauce
- 2 tablespoons oyster sauce
- 1 tablespoon Shaoxing wine (or dry sherry)
- 1 teaspoon sesame oil
- 1 teaspoon sugar
- 2 tablespoons vegetable oil
- 1 teaspoon cornstarch (mixed with 1 tablespoon water)
- Salt and pepper to taste

DIRECTIONS

1. Begin by marinating the chicken. In a bowl, combine the chicken slices with 1 tablespoon of soy sauce, sesame oil, and a dash of salt and pepper. Let it sit for 15 minutes.
2. Heat your wok over high heat until it's almost smoking. Add the vegetable oil and swirl to coat the bottom.
3. Add the chicken in a single layer and let it sear for a minute before stir-frying until it's no longer pink. Once cooked through, remove the chicken and set it aside.
4. In the same wok, add a bit more oil if needed. Toss in the minced garlic and ginger. Stir-fry briefly until aromatic.
5. Add the bell peppers and stir-fry for about two minutes, maintaining their crispness.
6. Toss in the water chestnuts and continue to stir-fry for another minute.
7. Return the chicken to the wok and stir to combine.
8. Quickly mix in the remaining soy sauce, oyster sauce, Shaoxing wine, and sugar. Ensure everything is evenly coated and simmer for a minute.
9. Add the cornstarch slurry to thicken the sauce slightly, stirring well.
10. Finally, throw in the green onions, give the mixture a few final stirs and remove from heat.
11. Serve hot with steamed rice or noodles.

DIETARY MODIFICATIONS

Vegetarian: Substitute chicken with firm tofu or seitan. Add at the same step as you would the chicken, ensuring to cook it until it's heated through and slightly browned.

Vegan: Follow the vegetarian instructions but also substitute oyster sauce with a vegan mushroom sauce, which will mimic the umami taste.

Gluten-Free: Use tamari or gluten-free soy sauce and ensure that the oyster sauce and Shaoxing wine are gluten-free. Many brands offer a gluten-free version of these sauces.

INGREDIENT SPOTLIGHT: WATER CHESTNUTS

Despite their name, water chestnuts are not nuts but aquatic tuber vegetables that grow in marshes, underwater in the mud. With a crisp, white flesh, they can be eaten raw or cooked and have been a part of Chinese cuisine for over 3000 years. Their ability to stay crunchy even when cooked makes them a unique ingredient, especially valued in stir-fries. Water chestnuts also offer a subtly sweet flavor, which balances savory dishes wonderfully and adds an enticing contrast in texture.

CHEF'S TIPS

- Ensure that your wok is thoroughly heated before adding your ingredients to achieve the signature sear and smoky wok hei' flavor.
- Cutting the chicken thinly allows for quick and even cooking, essential in a fast-paced stir-fry.
- If the wok gets too dry when cooking the vegetables, add a small splash of water instead of more oil to prevent things from burning.
- Keep ingredients moving in the wok to cook them evenly and to prevent them from sticking.
- Make sure the cornstarch slurry is well-mixed before adding it to the wok. This prevents clumping and ensures a smooth sauce.

POSSIBLE VARIATIONS OF THE RECIPE

- **Thai Twist:** Add a splash of fish sauce and a handful of Thai basil leaves with the green onions for a Thai-inspired flavor profile.

- **Nut Crumble:** Garnish with crushed peanuts or cashews for extra crunch and nuttiness.

- **Spicy Kick:** Introduce a teaspoon or two of chili paste or fresh sliced chilies when adding the garlic and ginger if you enjoy heat.

HEALTH NOTE & CALORIC INFORMATION

A serving of Wok-Fried Water Chestnuts and Chicken is low in carbohydrates and high in protein, making it a healthy option for those looking to maintain a balanced diet. The inclusion of fresh vegetables contributes to your daily intake of vitamins and fiber. A typical serving contains approximately 220-260 calories, depending on the amounts of oil and sauce used. Please be mindful of sodium content due to the soy and oyster sauces, and adjust according to dietary needs.

BEEF WITH MUSHROOMS

Stir-frying is a technique that originated in China and has spread throughout many Asian cuisines. The method involves cooking food quickly in a small amount of very hot oil while stirring continuously, ideally in a wok. This Asian Beef Stir-Fry with Mushrooms is a testament to the versatile and fast-paced cooking style that brings out the vibrant flavors and textures of the ingredients. With influences from various Asian culinary traditions, this dish is both hearty and aromatic, with succulent pieces of beef, earthy mushrooms, and a rich, savory sauce.

INGREDIENTS

- 500g beef sirloin, thinly sliced
- 300g mixed mushrooms (e.g., shiitake, oyster, button), sliced
- 2 tbsp vegetable oil
- 1 large onion, sliced
- 3 cloves garlic, minced
- 1-inch piece of ginger, finely grated
- 1 red bell pepper, sliced
- 1 green bell pepper, sliced
- 3 green onions, chopped
- 2 tbsp soy sauce
- 1 tbsp oyster sauce
- 1 tbsp hoisin sauce
- 1 tsp sesame oil
- 1 tsp cornstarch
- Salt and pepper, to taste
- Sesame seeds, for garnish
- Fresh cilantro leaves, for garnish

DIRECTIONS

1. Place the beef slices in a mixing bowl. Season with salt and pepper, and sprinkle cornstarch over them, tossing to coat evenly. Set aside.
2. In a small bowl, combine soy sauce, oyster sauce, hoisin sauce, and sesame oil. Stir well to create the stir-fry sauce. Set aside.
3. Heat a wok or large skillet over high heat and add 1 tablespoon of vegetable oil. Swirl to coat the surface.
4. Add the beef in a single layer and stir-fry until browned and just cooked through, about 1-2 minutes per side. Remove the beef from the wok and set aside on a plate.
5. In the same wok, add the remaining tablespoon of vegetable oil if needed. Add the onions and stir-fry for about 2 minutes until they start to soften.
6. Add the garlic and ginger; stir-fry for 30 seconds until fragrant.
7. Add the mixed mushrooms, and continue to stir-fry for another 3-4 minutes until the mushrooms are tender.
8. Add the bell peppers and green onions to the wok, and stir-fry for an additional 2 minutes.
9. Return the beef to the wok and pour the sauce over the top. Stir-fry everything together for another 2 minutes, ensuring the sauce coats all ingredients and heats through.
10. Taste and adjust the seasoning if necessary.
11. Garnish with sesame seeds and fresh cilantro leaves before serving.
12. Serve hot with steamed rice or noodles as desired.

DIETARY MODIFICATIONS

Vegetarian: Substitute beef with firm tofu or tempeh. Ensure the tofu or tempeh is drained and pressed to remove excess moisture, then slice and stir-fry as with the beef.

Vegan: Follow the vegetarian modifications and also replace oyster sauce with vegan stir-fry sauce or mushroom-based sauce to mimic the umami flavor.

Gluten-Free: Use tamari or a certified gluten-free soy sauce and gluten-free hoisin sauce. Ensure all other ingredients, including oyster sauce, are gluten-free varieties.

INGREDIENT SPOTLIGHT: OYSTER SAUCE

Oyster sauce is a thick, brown sauce that is a staple in Chinese cooking, known for its savory, slightly sweet, and rich umami flavor. Originating in southern China during the late 19th century, oyster sauce was supposedly created by accident by a man named Lee Kum Sheung, the founder of the Lee Kum Kee company, when he overcooked oysters. Today, it is made by caramelizing oyster juices, salt, and sugar, sometimes mixed with cornstarch and coloration. This sauce is a key ingredient in many Asian dishes and provides depth and complexity to the stir-fry, marrying well with the beef and mushrooms.

CHEF'S TIPS

- Freeze the beef for 20-30 minutes before slicing. Partially frozen meat is easier to cut into thin, even slices.
- Preheat the wok until it's almost smoking to get a good sear on the meat and vegetables, which adds a distinctive flavor known as 'wok hei.'
- Do not overcrowd the wok. Cook the beef in batches if necessary to maintain high heat and avoid stewing the meat.
- Constantly move the ingredients around in the wok for even cooking and to prevent burning.
- Cut all ingredients into similar-sized pieces to ensure even cooking times.

POSSIBLE VARIATIONS OF THE RECIPE

- **Spicy Kick:** Add sliced chili peppers or a tablespoon of chili garlic sauce to the stir-fry sauce for a spicy version of the dish.
- **Szechuan Style:** Incorporate Szechuan peppercorns and a bit of Chinese black vinegar in the sauce for a numbing and tangy twist.
- **Extra Veggies:** For a more robust vegetable presence, add broccoli, snap peas, or baby corn alongside the original vegetables, and stir-fry until tender but still crisp.

HEALTH NOTE & CALORIC INFORMATION

Each serving of Asian Beef Stir-Fry with Mushrooms is high in protein and full of various vitamins and minerals from the vegetables. The beef provides iron and zinc, while the mushrooms offer selenium and B vitamins. However, the sauces contain sodium, so those watching salt intake should use low-sodium options. Traditional preparation without any rice or noodles contains approximately 350 calories per serving, with 22g of protein, 15g of fat, and 20g of carbohydrates.

BABY BOK CHOY

Baby bok choy, a tender and mild Chinese cabbage, has graced tables in Asian cuisine for centuries. The practice of sautéing it with flavorful aromatics like ginger and garlic not only dates back to ancient cooking styles but also reflects the emphasis on freshness and the medicinal properties of foods in traditional Chinese culture. This easy yet elegant dish is known for its delicate texture and is often served as a side to balance more robust, spicy entrees.

INGREDIENTS

- 500 grams (about 1 pound) baby bok choy, cleaned and halved lengthwise
- 2 tablespoons extra virgin olive oil
- 4 cloves garlic, minced
- 2 inches fresh ginger root, peeled and julienned
- 2 tablespoons low-sodium soy sauce
- 1 tablespoon oyster sauce (optional for added umami flavor)
- 1 teaspoon sesame oil
- Salt, to taste
- Freshly ground black pepper, to taste
- 1 teaspoon toasted sesame seeds (for garnish)
- 2 green onions, thinly sliced (for garnish)

DIRECTIONS

1. Begin by preparing the baby bok choy. Rinse the bok choy under cold water, making sure to remove any dirt trapped in the leaves. Cut the stalks in half lengthwise, so they can cook evenly.
2. Mince the garlic cloves and julienne the ginger root to obtain thin, matchstick pieces.
3. Heat the olive oil in a large skillet or wok over medium heat. Once the oil is shimmering, add the minced garlic and julienned ginger. Sauté for about 1 minute, or until they are fragrant but not browned.
4. Increase the heat to medium-high and add the baby bok choy to the skillet. Toss gently to coat with the oil, garlic, and ginger.
5. Stir in the soy sauce, and if using, the oyster sauce. Cook for 2-3 minutes, or until the leaves start to wilt and the stalks are tender but still retain some crispness.
6. Drizzle with sesame oil and season with salt and black pepper to taste. Give everything a final gentle toss.
7. Transfer to a serving platter, sprinkle with toasted sesame seeds, and garnish with sliced green onions.
8. Serve immediately as a side dish to your favorite Asian main course, or enjoy as a nutritious and flavorful light meal on its own.

DIETARY MODIFICATIONS

For a **vegetarian version,** omit the oyster sauce or use a vegetarian oyster sauce substitute made from mushrooms to retain the umami depth.

To make this recipe **vegan,** ensure to use a vegan oyster sauce alternative and double-check that the soy sauce brand used does not contain any animal products.

For those with **gluten sensitivity,** opt for tamari or a certified gluten-free soy sauce to avoid any gluten content often found in traditional soy sauces.

INGREDIENT SPOTLIGHT: BABY BOK CHOY

Baby bok choy, also known as Pak choi or Shanghai green, is a member of the cruciferous vegetables family. It originates from China, where it has been cultivated for over 5,000 years. The vegetable is rich in vitamins A, C, and K, as well as calcium, magnesium, and iron. Its mild flavor makes it extremely versatile in the kitchen, and its delicate texture allows it to cook quickly, making it a perfect candidate for stir-fries, steaming, and sautéing.

CHEF'S TIPS

- Pat the bok choy dry after washing to ensure better sautéing and to prevent splattering once it hits the oil.
- When sautéing, keep the aromatics moving to prevent them from burning, which would impart a bitter taste to the dish.
- Avoid overcrowding the pan when adding the bok choy to ensure each piece makes contact with the heat directly, thus encouraging a good sear.
- Sesame oil has a low smoke point; hence, it is used near the end of cooking to preserve its flavor and nutrients.
- Let the dish rest for a minute before serving to allow the flavors to meld together better.

POSSIBLE VARIATIONS OF THE RECIPE

- Spice it up by adding a tablespoon of chili flakes or a sliced chili pepper along with garlic and ginger for a spicy kick.
- Try adding a protein like tofu, shrimp, or sliced chicken breast to turn this side dish into a wholesome main course.
- Give it a Thai twist by substituting soy sauce with fish sauce and adding a dash of lime juice and chopped cilantro before serving.

HEALTH NOTE & CALORIC INFORMATION

This dish is low in calories but high in vitamins and minerals. A serving of Garlic-Ginger Baby Bok Choy typically contains approximately 50 calories. It's a suitable side dish for those seeking a nutrient-rich, low-fat option. Baby bok choy is also a good source of dietary fiber. Always remember to adjust portions and seasoning to align with individual dietary goals.

NAKJI BOKKEUM

Nakji Bokkeum is a fiery dish that represents Korea's love for spice and seafood. Originating from the coastal cities, this dish leverages the country's abundant seafood and reflects the bold flavors favored in Korean cuisine. Customarily served with a bowl of rice to balance the heat, Nakji Bokkeum has become a popular dish both within Korea and at Korean eateries worldwide.

INGREDIENTS

- 2 medium-sized octopuses, cleaned and cut into bite-sized pieces
- 2 tablespoons vegetable oil
- 1 tablespoon sesame oil
- 4 cloves garlic, minced
- 1 teaspoon ginger, grated
- 1 medium onion, sliced
- 2 carrots, julienned
- 1 bell pepper, sliced
- 4 green onions, cut into 1-inch pieces
- 2 tablespoons soy sauce
- 2 tablespoons gochujang (Korean red pepper paste)
- 1 tablespoon sugar
- 1 tablespoon Korean red pepper flakes (gochugaru)
- 1 teaspoon black pepper
- 1 tablespoon toasted sesame seeds (for garnish)
- Steamed rice, for serving

DIRECTIONS

1. Prepare the octopus by cleaning it thoroughly and cutting it into bite-sized pieces. Make sure to remove the beak and any internal organs.
2. In a large skillet or wok, heat vegetable oil and sesame oil over medium-high heat.
3. Add minced garlic and grated ginger to the skillet and sauté for about 30 seconds or until fragrant.
4. Incorporate the sliced onion, julienned carrots, and bell pepper. Stir-fry them for about 2 to 3 minutes until they start to soften.
5. Add the octopus to the skillet and cook for about 2 minutes, or until it begins to firm up.
6. While the octopus is cooking, mix soy sauce, gochujang, sugar, gochugaru, and black pepper in a small bowl to make the sauce.
7. Pour the sauce over the octopus and vegetables in the skillet. Mix everything thoroughly to ensure the sauce coats all the ingredients evenly.
8. Allow the dish to cook for another 4 to 5 minutes, stirring occasionally, until the octopus is fully cooked and tender.
9. Toss in the green onions and cook for an additional minute.
10. Remove from heat and garnish the dish with toasted sesame seeds.
11. Serve hot with steamed rice to help temper the dish's spiciness.

DIETARY MODIFICATIONS

Vegetarian: Substitute octopus with firm tofu or king oyster mushrooms sliced into bite-sized pieces. Adjust the cooking time as these will require less time to cook than octopus.

Vegan: Along with the vegetarian substitutes, ensure that the gochujang used is vegan as some brands contain fish sauce. Use a vegan sugar.

Gluten-Free: Use tamari or a certified gluten-free soy sauce instead of regular soy sauce and double-check that the gochujang is gluten-free.

INGREDIENT SPOTLIGHT: GOCHUJANG

Gochujang is a savory, sweet, and spicy fermented condiment made from red chili, glutinous rice, fermented soybeans, and salt. This staple of Korean kitchens dates back to the 18th century. Not only is it crucial for adding depth and heat in Nakji Bokkeum, but it also offers umami and a hint of sweetness that balances fiery dishes. Gochujang's versatility extends beyond stir-fries; it's also used in marinating meats, as a base for stews, and as a condiment.

CHEF'S TIPS

- Use a high heat and quick stir-frying method to ensure the octopus cooks evenly and remains tender.
- Slice the vegetables uniformly for even cooking.
- It is important to have all the ingredients prepped and ready to go before you start cooking, as the stir-frying process is fast-paced.
- If the heat is too intense, adjust the amount of gochugaru to suit your spice tolerance.
- Garnishing with sesame seeds and chopped green onions at the end of cooking adds texture and a fresh flavor contrast.

POSSIBLE VARIATIONS OF THE RECIPE

- **Seafood Medley:** Add other seafood such as shrimp, scallops, or squid to the mix to create a diverse range of textures and flavors.
- **Mild Nakji Bokkeum:** For those who prefer less spice, decrease the amount of gochujang and gochugaru, and add a touch of honey for a sweeter profile.
- **Stir-Fried Octopus with Noodles:** Add cooked Korean sweet potato noodles (japchae noodles) to the stir-fry for a heartier meal that soaks up the spicy sauce.

HEALTH NOTE & CALORIC INFORMATION

Spicy Stir-Fried Octopus is rich in protein and contains a variety of vitamins and minerals from the mix of seafood and vegetables. The dish is relatively low in carbohydrates unless served with rice. However, it can be high in sodium due to the soy sauce and gochujang; low-sodium alternatives can be used to adjust this. Depending on portion sizes and specific ingredients used, a serving without rice is roughly estimated to contain around 250 to 300 calories.

HONEY WALNUT SHRIMP

Honey Walnut Shrimp is a beloved dish known for its creamy and sweet flavor profile, commonly found in Chinese-American cuisine. This dish likely evolved from Shanghai-style sweet creamy dishes, adapted with local ingredients and tastes to appeal to American palates. It balances succulent shrimp with the crunch of candied walnuts, all enveloped in a luscious honey-mayonnaise sauce. This wok version creates a fast, high-heat method that mimics the quick cooking style of traditional Chinese wok stir-frying.

INGREDIENTS

- 1 pound large shrimp, peeled and deveined
- 1 cup water
- 2/3 cup white sugar
- 1 cup walnut halves
- 4 egg whites
- 2/3 cup cornstarch
- Vegetable oil for frying
- 1/4 cup mayonnaise
- 2 tablespoons honey
- 1 tablespoon condensed milk
- 1 tablespoon lemon juice
- 1/2 cup scallions, chopped (for garnish)

DIRECTIONS

1. Begin by candying the walnuts. In a small pot, bring 1 cup of water to a boil. Add the sugar and stir until completely dissolved. Add the walnut halves and simmer for 2 minutes. Drain and place on a baking sheet to dry.
2. In a medium bowl, whisk the egg whites until frothy. Add the cornstarch and continue to whisk until the mixture forms a smooth batter.
3. Toss the shrimp in the batter until they are well coated.
4. Heat vegetable oil in a wok over high heat; the oil should reach 350°F (175°C). Carefully add the shrimp and fry until golden brown, approximately 2 minutes each side. Do not overcrowd the wok; fry in batches if necessary. Remove the shrimp and drain on paper towels.
5. In a large bowl, mix together mayonnaise, honey, condensed milk, and lemon juice to make the sauce.
6. Toss the fried shrimp in the sauce until evenly coated.
7. Serve the shrimp on a platter, sprinkle with candied walnuts and chopped scallions for garnish.

DIETARY MODIFICATIONS

Gluten-Free: Replace cornstarch with arrowroot powder or a gluten-free flour blend to cater to those with gluten intolerance or celiac disease.

Low-Sugar: Use a sugar substitute such as stevia or erythritol to candy the walnuts and lower the overall sugar content of the dish without sacrificing sweetness.

Dairy-Free: Substitute the condensed milk with coconut condensed milk or omit it entirely and add a bit more honey for those with lactose intolerance or a dairy-free diet.

INGREDIENT SPOTLIGHT: WALNUT

The walnut is more than just a crunchy addition; it's a nutritional powerhouse packed with omega-3 fatty acids, antioxidants, and vitamins. Originating from ancient Persia, walnuts have been a cherished ingredient across many cultures for millennia, symbolizing intelligence due to their brain-like appearance. Walnuts not only add a textural contrast in this recipe but also a subtle bitterness that perfectly complements the sweet and creamy sauce.

CHEF'S TIPS

- Ensure the oil is at the correct temperature before frying; too low and the shrimp will absorb oil and become soggy, too high and the outside will burn before the inside is cooked.
- Dry the candied walnuts thoroughly for a crispier texture.
- When mixing the shrimp with the sauce, use a gentle folding motion to avoid breaking the crispy batter.
- Frying in small batches ensures even cooking and prevents the shrimp from sticking together.
- Make the sauce ahead of time and chill it in the refrigerator to allow the flavors to meld together.

POSSIBLE VARIATIONS OF THE RECIPE

- **Spicy Kick:** Add a teaspoon of Sriracha or hot chili sauce to the honey-mayo sauce for a sweet and spicy twist on the classic.
- **Tropical Twist:** Incorporate a tablespoon of pineapple juice and some fresh pineapple chunks into the dish for a pop of tropical flavor.
- **Nut-Free Option:** For those with nut allergies, replace walnuts with toasted sesame seeds to maintain the crunchy texture without the nuts.

HEALTH NOTE & CALORIC INFORMATION

A typical serving of Honey Walnut Shrimp contains high protein and low fiber content. The dish is calorie-dense, mainly due to the frying process and the rich sauce. A serving can contain approximately 500-600 calories, with a significant amount of sugar and fat due to the candied walnuts and creamy sauce. Consumption should be considered in the context of a balanced diet, possibly as an occasional indulgence rather than a daily meal.

BRUSSEL SPROUTS AND SHALLOTS

In the bustling streets of Southeast Asia, a sizzling wok is a telltale sign of mouthwatering street food. One unconventional yet delightful dish is wok-charred Brussel sprouts, borrowing from the tradition of stir-frying vegetables for a quick, flavorful bite. This dish takes these humble sprouts and, with a hint of char and the crunch of shallots, turns them into a warmly-received side dish that could steal the show.

INGREDIENTS

- 500g Brussel sprouts, trimmed and halved
- 3 shallots, thinly sliced
- 4 tablespoons vegetable oil
- 1 tablespoon soy sauce
- 1 tablespoon oyster sauce
- 2 teaspoons fish sauce
- 1 teaspoon brown sugar
- 3 cloves garlic, minced
- 1 red chili, deseeded and finely sliced (optional)
- Salt to taste
- Fresh ground black pepper to taste
- A handful of fresh cilantro leaves for garnish
- Lime wedges for serving

DIRECTIONS

1. Heat 2 tablespoons of vegetable oil in a large wok or heavy skillet over high heat until it just starts to smoke.
2. Add the Brussel sprouts, cut side down, and let them sear without moving them for about 2 minutes, or until they start to char.
3. Toss the sprouts and cook for an additional 3-4 minutes until they're tender-crisp and charred to your liking. Transfer them to a bowl.
4. Reduce the heat to medium and add the remaining 2 tablespoons of oil to the wok.
5. Add the sliced shallots to the wok. Stir often and cook until they are crispy and golden brown, about 3-5 minutes. Watch them closely to prevent burning. Once done, transfer them to a paper towel-lined plate to drain.
6. Quickly wipe out the wok with paper towels and return it to medium heat.
7. Add the minced garlic (and red chili if using) to the wok, and stir-fry for about 30 seconds until you can smell the aroma.
8. Add the soy sauce, oyster sauce, fish sauce, and brown sugar to the wok. Stir until the sugar dissolves.
9. Return the Brussel sprouts to the wok and toss to coat evenly in the sauce. Cook for another 1-2 minutes to heat through.
10. Season with salt and pepper to taste.
11. To serve, transfer the Brussel sprouts to a serving dish, top with the crispy shallots, garnish with fresh cilantro leaves, and serve with lime wedges on the side.

DIETARY MODIFICATIONS

Vegetarian: Substitute oyster sauce with a vegetarian oyster sauce made from mushrooms and use a vegetarian fish sauce or increase the soy sauce slightly to compensate.

Vegan: Follow the vegetarian modifications and also use a vegan fish sauce alternative. For the garnish, swap out fish sauce in dressings or dips with soy sauce mixed with a bit of seaweed flakes to mimic the umami flavor.

Gluten-Free: Make sure to use a gluten-free soy sauce and check that the vegetarian/vegan oyster and fish sauce alternatives are also gluten-free.

INGREDIENT SPOTLIGHT: SHALLOT

The shallot is a type of onion but offers a sweeter, more subtle flavor than its robust relatives. Historic references trace its origins back to Asia, possibly in or around Palestine. Globally recognized for their contribution to gastronomy, shallots become exceptionally sweet when cooked, and frying them until crisp transforms the texture and intensifies their flavor. In this recipe, crispy shallots not only provide a contrasting crunch but also a depth of sweetness that complements the charred Brussel sprouts perfectly.

CHEF'S TIPS

- Make sure the Brussel sprouts are completely dry before searing to ensure a good char without steaming.
- Do not overcrowd the wok; if necessary, char the Brussel sprouts in batches to maintain high heat and achieve a nice char.
- Adjust the heat as needed to prevent the garlic and shallots from burning. They should develop color slowly for the best flavor.
- For an extra kick, adding a splash of rice wine vinegar to the sauce will balance the richness with a touch of acidity.
- Use a high smoke point oil for frying the shallots and sprouts to avoid any bitter, burnt flavors.

POSSIBLE VARIATIONS OF THE RECIPE

- **Spicy Kick:** Add extra red chilis or a spoon of chili flakes while stir-frying for those who prefer their greens with a bit of heat.
- **Nutty Tryst:** Toss in a handful of crushed peanuts or cashews with the Brussel sprouts for added texture and richness.
- **Sweet and Tangy:** A splash of balsamic vinegar added with the sauces can provide a sweet, tart glaze that complements the char on the Brussel sprouts beautifully.

HEALTH NOTE & CALORIC INFORMATION

This dish is rich in vitamins C and K, coming from the Brussel sprouts, and offers a good source of dietary fiber. Shallots add a modest amount of iron and antioxidants. One serving of wok-charred Brussel sprouts with crispy shallots contains approximately 200 calories. The majority of these calories come from the vegetable oil used for frying. It's also relatively low in carbohydrates, with about 15 grams per serving.

BLACK PEPPER CRAB

Singapore Black Pepper Crab is one of the signature dishes of Singapore's vibrant food scene. This indulgent, savory, and spicy dish has found its way to the hearts (and stomachs) of both locals and tourists alike. The black pepper crab first gained popularity in the 1950s, where the use of fresh crabs paired with a robust pepper sauce showcased the country's penchant for bold flavors. Its fame continues to be celebrated in seafood restaurants and hawker centers across the island state.

INGREDIENTS

- 2 large live mud crabs (about 1-1.5 kg each)
- 1 cup of unsalted butter
- 4 tablespoons of coarsely crushed black peppercorns
- 5 cloves of garlic, minced
- 1-2 red chilies, finely chopped (optional for extra heat)
- 3 tablespoons of oyster sauce
- 2 tablespoons of dark soy sauce
- 2 tablespoons of light soy sauce
- 1 tablespoon of sugar
- 1/2 cup of chicken stock or water
- 6 stalks of spring onions, cut into 2-inch lengths
- Vegetable oil, for frying

DIRECTIONS

1. Humanely euthanize the crabs before cooking. Clean the crabs by scrubbing with a brush and rinsing under cold water. Pat dry.
2. Twist off the claws and legs, crack them gently with a nutcracker, and set aside.
3. Cut the body into quarters and crack the shells slightly.
4. Heat a large wok over high heat and add enough vegetable oil to deep fry the crabs. In batches, deep fry the crab pieces until they are half cooked, about 2-3 minutes each batch. Drain on paper towels.
5. Drain off all but 3 tablespoons of oil from the wok. Over medium heat, add the butter and allow it to melt.
6. Sauté the garlic, chilies, and black peppercorns until fragrant.
7. Add the oyster sauce, dark and light soy sauce, and sugar. Stir well to combine into a paste.
8. Pour in chicken stock or water and bring the mixture to a simmer.
9. Add the pre-fried crab pieces to the wok and toss to coat in the sauce.
10. Cover the wok and let simmer for another 5-8 minutes, or until the crabs are fully cooked and coated with the sauce.
11. Lastly, toss in the spring onions and cook for another minute.
12. Serve the black pepper crab hot with extra napkins on the side – it's a deliciously messy affair!

DIETARY MODIFICATIONS

Gluten-Free: Replace both dark and light soy sauce with tamari or gluten-free soy sauce. Ensure all other sauces and stocks are certified gluten-free.

Vegetarian: Substitute fresh crabs with king oyster mushrooms cut into large pieces. Follow the same recipe but reduce cooking time after adding mushrooms to the sauce.

Less Spicy: For those who prefer milder flavors, reduce the amount of black peppercorns to 1 or 2 tablespoons and omit the red chilies.

INGREDIENT SPOTLIGHT: BLACK PEPPERCORNS

Black peppercorns are the dried berries of the Piper nigrum vine, native to Southern India but now grown in other tropical regions. They have been a prized spice since ancient times, traded globally and used not just in food but also as currency. Black peppercorns give our Black Pepper Crab its signature piquant kick. The heat from freshly crushed black peppercorns is more robust and complex than pre-ground pepper, which makes it an essential ingredient in this dish. They not only provide heat but also add depth and an earthy flavor which balances the richness of the crab and butter.

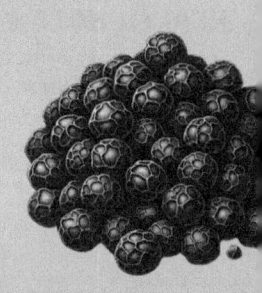

CHEF'S TIPS

- Ensure your wok is heated to the right temperature before adding your crabs - too cool, and the crabs will absorb oil; too hot, and the shell can burn.
- Fry the crabs in batches to keep the oil temperature consistent.
- Freshly crush your black peppercorns just before cooking to maximize the flavor and heat.
- Do not skimp on the butter; it is integral to the rich, velvety texture of the sauce.
- When tossing the crab in the sauce, do so gently to avoid breaking the delicate meat.

POSSIBLE VARIATIONS OF THE RECIPE

- **Creamy Pepper Crab:** Introduce heavy cream toward the end of cooking to create a more indulgent, creamy sauce.
- **Stir-Fry Pepper Crab:** Skip the deep-frying, and stir fry the crab directly in the pepper sauce for a lighter version.
- **Black Pepper Crab with Basil:** Add Thai basil leaves at the same time as spring onions for a fragrant twist.

HEALTH NOTE & CALORIC INFORMATION

This dish is high in protein and contains beneficial omega-3 fatty acids from the crab. However, it is also high in cholesterol and should be enjoyed in moderation by those monitoring their intake. A single serving of black pepper crab can range from 500 to 800 calories depending on the size of the crab and the amount of butter and oil used in preparation.

JAPCHAE

Japchae, a traditional Korean dish dating back to the 17th century, was first created for a royal banquet at the Joseon Dynasty court. Originally made without noodles, japchae has evolved into a beloved stir-fry dish featuring sweet potato noodles, a medley of vegetables, and often meat. This recipe offers a vegetable-focused version, maintaining the harmony of colors and textures prominent in Korean cuisine.

INGREDIENTS

- 200g sweet potato glass noodles
- 1 medium carrot, julienned
- 1 red bell pepper, thinly sliced
- 1 yellow bell pepper, thinly sliced
- 1 small zucchini, julienned
- 1 cup spinach leaves, roughly chopped
- 5 shiitake mushrooms, thinly sliced
- 2 green onions, chopped
- 3 tablespoons soy sauce
- 2 tablespoons brown sugar
- 2 tablespoons sesame oil
- 1 tablespoon vegetable oil
- 4 cloves garlic, minced
- 1 teaspoon freshly ground black pepper
- 1 tablespoon toasted sesame seeds
- Salt to taste

DIRECTIONS

1. Prepare the noodles by soaking them in hot water for about 10 minutes or until they are soft. Drain and set aside.
2. While the noodles are soaking, prepare a sauce by whisking together the soy sauce, brown sugar, and 1 tablespoon of sesame oil in a small bowl until the sugar has dissolved. Set the sauce aside.
3. Heat the vegetable oil in a large skillet or wok over medium-high heat. Once hot, add the garlic and sauté until fragrant, about 30 seconds.
4. Add the carrots and cook for 2 minutes, then add the red and yellow bell peppers, stirring occasionally for another 2 minutes.
5. Introduce the zucchini and mushrooms to the skillet, and continue cooking for another 2 minutes. Sprinkle with a pinch of salt.
6. Toss in the spinach leaves and cook until they begin to wilt, about 1 minute.
7. Add the drained noodles and the sauce to the vegetables. Stir thoroughly to ensure all the ingredients are coated with the sauce. Cook for an additional 5 minutes, stirring constantly to prevent the noodles from sticking.
8. Remove from heat, then stir in the green onions, the remaining tablespoon of sesame oil, and ground black pepper.
9. Garnish with toasted sesame seeds and serve warm.

DIETARY MODIFICATIONS

Gluten-Free: Substitute soy sauce with tamari, which is a type of soy sauce that's usually gluten-free. Ensure all other ingredients are certified gluten-free.
Low-Sodium: Use low-sodium soy sauce and reduce the quantity to 2 tablespoons. Adjust the seasonings with additional spices like ginger to compensate for the reduced salt from the soy sauce.
Vegan: The recipe is already vegan-friendly. However, if you're using alternates for ingredients in the sauce, verify that they do not contain any animal derivatives.

INGREDIENT SPOTLIGHT: DANGMYEON

Sweet potato glass noodles, also known as dangmyeon, are at the heart of any japchae recipe. Made from sweet potato starch, they boast a unique chewy texture and are naturally gluten-free. They absorb flavors superbly, harmonizing with the various components of the dish. Originating in Korea, these noodles have gained international popularity for their versatility in both hot and cold dishes.

CHEF'S TIPS

- When soaking the glass noodles, ensure the water is just hot enough to soften them without making them mushy
- Julienne the vegetables uniformly to promote even cooking and an aesthetically appealing dish.
- Constant stirring during the final cooking stage is essential to prevent the noodles from sticking together and to encourage an even distribution of flavors.
- Adding the sauce incrementally can help you manage how well the noodles and vegetables are coated and prevent the dish from becoming too salty or sweet.
- Let the noodles sit for a few minutes after cooking; this will allow the flavors to meld together beautifully.

POSSIBLE VARIATIONS OF THE RECIPE

- **Spicy Japchae:** Add 1-2 tablespoons of gochujang (Korean red chili paste) or red pepper flakes to the sauce for a fiery kick.
- **Protein-Packed Japchae:** Include thin slices of tofu or tempeh with the vegetables for added protein. If not adhering to a vegan or vegetarian diet, you could use beef, chicken, or shrimp.
- **Nutty Japchae:** Sprinkle crushed peanuts or cashews on top before serving for an extra crunch and a nutty flavor.

HEALTH NOTE & CALORIC INFORMATION

A serving of this stir-fried glass noodles with vibrant vegetables is a low-calorie, high-fiber meal rich in vitamins and minerals from the array of vegetables used. Sweet potato noodles provide complex carbohydrates for sustained energy. Typically, a serving contains around 300-400 calories, but this can vary based on portion sizes and specific ingredients used.

FIVE-SPICE WOK CHICKEN

Originating from the diverse culinary landscape of China, stir-frying is a quick-cook method ideal for tossing together delicious meals in a flash. Chinese five-spice powder, a blend embodying the five flavor elements of Chinese cooking—sweet, sour, bitter, savory, and salty—elevates a simple stir-fry to an aromatic dish that's both savory and nuanced. This dish is a fusion of traditional Chinese flavors with the convenience of modern cooking, perfect for a weeknight dinner.

INGREDIENTS

- 500g boneless, skinless chicken breasts or thighs, thinly sliced
- 2 tablespoons soy sauce
- 1 tablespoon oyster sauce
- 1 teaspoon Chinese five-spice powder
- 2 tablespoons vegetable oil
- 1 red bell pepper, thinly sliced
- 1 yellow bell pepper, thinly sliced
- 1 medium onion, thinly sliced
- 2 cloves garlic, minced
- 1 tablespoon ginger, minced
- 1 small carrot, julienned
- 1 teaspoon sesame oil
- Salt to taste
- Freshly ground black pepper to taste
- Green onions, chopped (for garnish)
- Sesame seeds (for garnish)

DIRECTIONS

1. In a mixing bowl, combine the sliced chicken with one tablespoon soy sauce, oyster sauce, and Chinese five-spice powder. Toss until the chicken is well coated. Let it marinate for at least 15 minutes.
2. Heat a large wok or skillet over high heat. Add one tablespoon of vegetable oil and swirl to coat the surface.
3. Add the marinated chicken to the wok. Stir-fry for about 3-5 minutes or until the chicken is cooked through and slightly browned. Remove the chicken from the wok and set aside.
4. Reduce the heat to medium-high and add the remaining vegetable oil to the wok. Add the onions and stir-fry for a minute until they start to soften.
5. Add the garlic, ginger, and carrots to the wok and stir-fry for another minute.
6. Toss in the red and yellow bell peppers, and continue to stir-fry for 2-3 minutes or until all the vegetables are tender-crisp.
7. Return the chicken to the wok, add the remaining soy sauce, and stir well to combine. Cook for another minute, ensuring the chicken is well heated.
8. Drizzle with sesame oil, and season with salt and pepper to taste.
9. Serve hot, garnished with green onions and sesame seeds.

DIETARY MODIFICATIONS

Gluten-Free: Use tamari or a gluten-free soy sauce instead of regular soy sauce, and ensure that the oyster sauce is also labeled gluten-free.

Vegetarian: Substitute the chicken with tofu or tempeh. Press and drain the tofu or tempeh before cutting into cubes, then marinate and cook as per the recipe.

Low-Carb: Exclude the carrot and serve the stir-fry over cauliflower rice instead of regular rice to reduce the carbohydrate content in the meal.

INGREDIENT SPOTLIGHT: FIVE-SPICE POWDER

Chinese five-spice powder is a significant component of Chinese cuisine, crafted from a blend of star anise, cloves, Chinese cinnamon, Sichuan peppercorns, and fennel seeds. It dates back to the ancient philosophy of balancing yin and yang in food, with each spice representing one of the five flavor elements. This powder imparts a uniquely warm and aromatic flavor that is instantly recognizable, adding complexity to simple dishes.

CHEF'S TIPS

- Slice the chicken thinly to ensure even and quick cooking.
- Preheat the wok or skillet before adding ingredients to achieve a char and prevent sticking.
- Keep the ingredients moving in the wok to avoid burning and to cook evenly.
- Cut all the vegetables uniformly to ensure they cook at the same rate.
- Use sesame oil at the end of cooking for flavor; heating it too much can diminish its taste.

POSSIBLE VARIATIONS OF THE RECIPE

- **Spicy Kick:** Add sliced chili peppers or a spoonful of chili sauce with the vegetables for an extra fiery dish.
- **Nut Crunch:** Toss in cashews or peanuts towards the end of cooking for a satisfying crunch and nutty flavor.
- **Citrus Zest:** Add a splash of orange juice or a teaspoon of orange zest with the vegetables for a fresh, citrusy note.

HEALTH NOTE & CALORIC INFORMATION

This stir-fry is a high-protein, low-calorie dish with a mix of vitamins and minerals from the vegetables. The five-spice powder adds no significant calories but contributes to the overall aromatic flavor profile. A single serving without rice is approximately 300 calories, with variations depending on the exact sizes and cuts of vegetables and chicken used.

STIR-FRIED POTATO STRIPS

In Sichuan province, the heart of bold and spicy Chinese cuisine, one can find a variety of dishes that defy the expectation of Chinese food being centered around rice and noodles. The Sichuan-Style Stir-Fried Potato Strips, known in Mandarin as "Qingjiao Tudousi," is a vibrant example. The dish boasts the hallmark numbing spice of Sichuan peppercorns paired with the unexpected crisp texture of julienned potatoes. This side dish showcases how Sichuan cooks use a seamlessly simple vegetable to deliver a burst of flavor and a unique contrast in textures.

INGREDIENTS

- 2 medium-sized potatoes (about 300g), julienned
- 1 green bell pepper, julienned
- 2 tablespoons vegetable oil
- 1 teaspoon Sichuan peppercorns
- 2 cloves garlic, minced
- 1 teaspoon ginger, minced
- 2 dried red chili peppers, chopped (optional)
- 1 tablespoon soy sauce
- 1/2 teaspoon sugar
- Salt, to taste
- 2 green onions, chopped

DIRECTIONS

1. Begin by washing the potatoes, peeling them, and cutting them into fine julienne strips. Soak the potato strips in cold water for 5 minutes to remove excess starch and prevent browning.
2. Meanwhile, julienne the green bell pepper and set aside.
3. In a small bowl, mix the soy sauce, sugar, and salt to create a seasoning sauce and set it aside.
4. Drain the potato strips completely and pat them dry with a kitchen towel or paper towels.
5. Heat a wok or a large frying pan over high heat and add vegetable oil. Once the oil is hot, add the Sichuan peppercorns and stir for about 30 seconds until fragrant. Be careful not to burn them.
6. Add the minced garlic, ginger, and dried red chili peppers (if using) to the wok and stir-fry for another 30 seconds.
7. Quickly add the drained potato strips to the wok. Keep the heat high and stir-fry the potatoes for about 2-3 minutes. They should become slightly tender but still retain a crispness.
8. Toss in the julienned green bell pepper and stir-fry for another minute.
9. Pour the prepared seasoning sauce over the stir-fried vegetables and toss everything quickly to coat evenly.
10. Cook for another minute, then add the chopped green onions, give it a final stir and remove from the heat.
11. Serve immediately for the best texture, accompanying it with rice or your choice of protein.

DIETARY MODIFICATIONS

Gluten-Free: Replace the traditional soy sauce with a gluten-free tamari to accommodate a gluten-free diet without altering the essence of the dish.

Vegan: The recipe is naturally vegan. Ensure that your soy sauce and sugar do not contain any animal products to be certain.

Low-Sodium: For those monitoring their sodium intake, use a reduced-sodium soy sauce or substitute with coconut aminos, which are naturally lower in sodium than traditional soy sauces.

INGREDIENT SPOTLIGHT: HUA JIAO

Sichuan peppercorns, also known as "hua jiao," are not actually peppercorns but the dried husks of the prickly ash shrub. Originating from the Sichuan region, these 'peppercorns' are famous for their distinctive numbing sensation and lemony aroma. They are indispensable in Sichuan cuisine, contributing a tingling complexity to dishes. In Sichuan-Style Stir-Fried Potato Strips, Sichuan peppercorns' unique numbing effect balances the potatoes' crisp texture and earthiness, making them key to this recipe's signature flair.

CHEF'S TIPS

- Ensure your wok or pan is thoroughly heated before adding any ingredients; a hot wok is crucial for a good stir-fry.
- Dry the potato strips well to avoid splattering oil and to achieve the desired crispness when stir-frying.
- Adjust the amount of Sichuan peppercorns to your tolerance level for heat and numbing sensation.
- Do not overcook the vegetables; stir-fried dishes should have a blend of softness and crunch.
- If the Sichuan peppercorns are too potent for your taste, try infusing the oil with them and then discarding the solids before proceeding with the recipe.

POSSIBLE VARIATIONS OF THE RECIPE

- **Hot and Sour:** Add a splash of black vinegar and a pinch of chili flakes for an additional depth of tanginess and heat.
- **Meaty Twist:** Include thinly sliced pork or beef for a protein-packed version; ensure to stir-fry the meat until just cooked before adding the potatoes.
- **Carrot Inclusion:** Add julienned carrots along with the potatoes for an extra pop of color and a hint of sweetness.

HEALTH NOTE & CALORIC INFORMATION

This dish is low in calories, with one serving containing approximately 150-200 calories. The potatoes provide a source of carbohydrates and fiber, while the bell peppers add vitamin C and other micronutrients. The use of Sichuan peppercorns adds no significant nutritional value but is low in calories. It's also a naturally vegan and gluten-free (if gluten-free soy sauce is used) dish, making it suitable for a wide range of dietary preferences.

KOREAN COOKBOOK

YOUR ESSENTIAL GUIDE TO THE ART OF KOREAN HOME COOKING IN 50 TRADITIONAL RECIPES

DANGMYEON

EMMA YANG

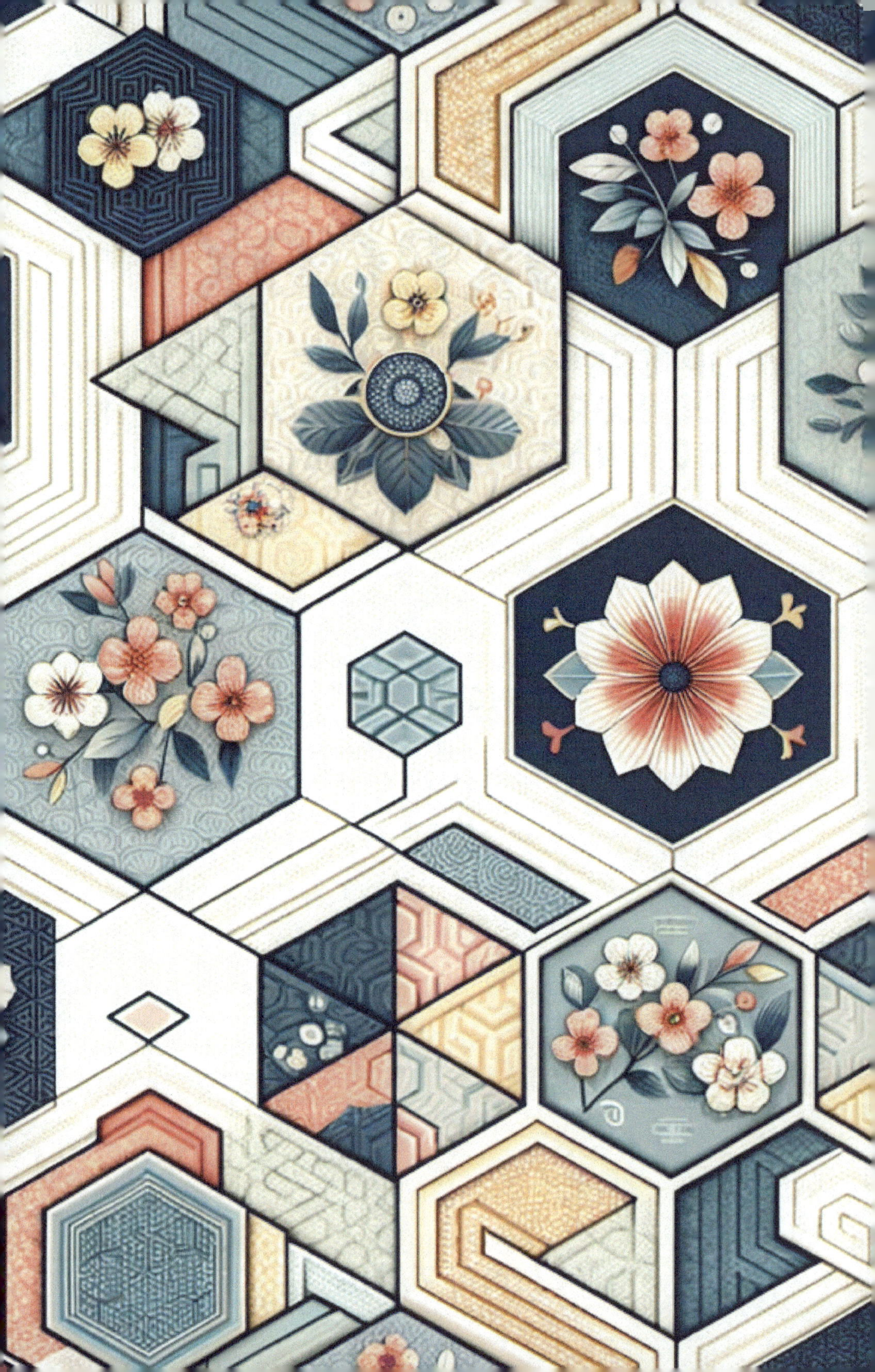

© Copyright 2024 by Emma Yang - All rights reserved.

Without the prior written permission of the Publisher, no part of this publication may be stored in a retrieval system, replicated, or transferred in any form or medium, digital, scanning, recording, printing, mechanical, or otherwise, except as permitted under 1976 United States Copyright Act, section 107 or 108. Permission concerns should be directed to the publisher's permission department.
Legal Notice

This book is copyright-protected. It is only to be used for personal purposes. Without the author's or publisher's permission, you cannot paraphrase, quote, copy, distribute, sell, or change any part of the information in this book.
Disclaimer Notice

This book is written and published independently. Please keep in mind that the material in this publication is solely for educational and entertaining purposes. All efforts have provided authentic, up-to-date, trustworthy, and comprehensive information. There are no express or implied assurances. The purpose of this book's material is to assist readers in having a better understanding of the subject matter. The activities, information, and exercises are provided solely for self-help information. This book is not intended to replace expert psychologists, legal, financial, or other guidance. If you require counseling, please get in touch with a qualified professional.

By reading this text, the reader accepts that the author will not be held liable for any damages, indirectly or directly, experienced due to the use of the information included herein, particularly, but not limited to, omissions, errors, or inaccuracies. You are accountable for your decisions, actions, and consequences as a reader.

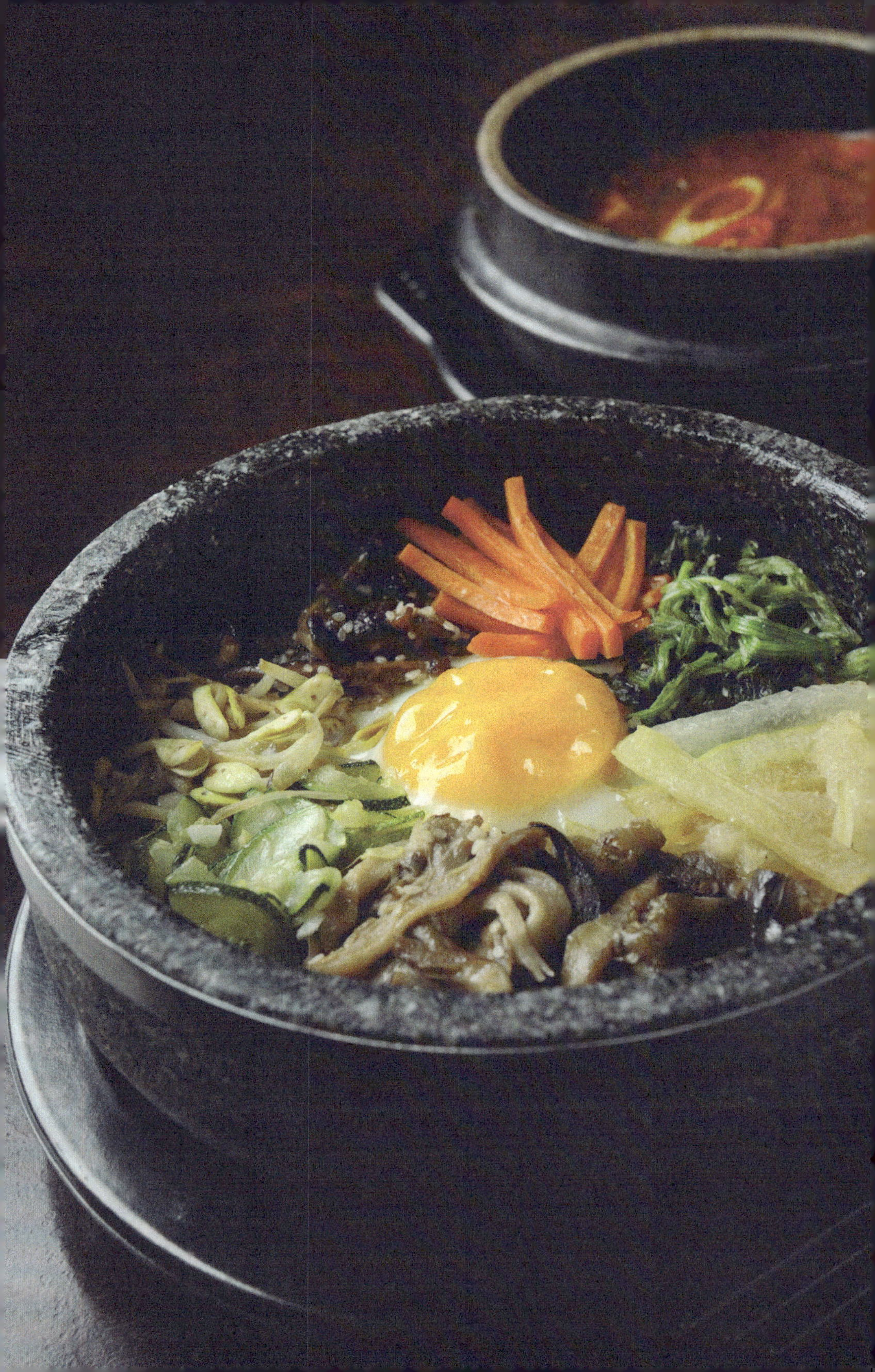

PREFACE

Welcome to the soulful symphony of Korean cuisine—a gastronomic odyssey that traverses the lush hillsides and bustling cities of Korea to bring a feast of flavors to your table. In this cookbook, we extend an invitation to immerse yourself in the diverse and delicious world of Korean cooking, a cultural journey steeped in a rich tapestry of history and contemporary creativity.

Korean food, or "hansik," is a harmonic ensemble of the five fundamental flavors—sour, bitter, sweet, spicy, and salty—that define the balance and depth of each mouthwatering dish. From the iconic, punchy zest of kimchi to the intricate layers of flavor found in a bubbling jeongol, this collection is a tribute to the varied and fascinating gastronomic landscape of Korea.

As we guide you through this flavorful quest, you will encounter both the quintessence of traditional dishes and the exciting fusion fare that bridges Korean culinary delights with global tastes. Every recipe penned here is not merely a set of instructions; it is a canvas upon which you will paint the vivid colors of Korea's culinary culture.

Beneath each title in this treasury lies a story—a tale of royal banquets, family gatherings, and resilient innovation. These pages are lined with the wisdom of generations and the evolving tastes of the Korean palate, inviting you to not just recreate these indulgent eats but also to savor the history and essence that infuse every bite.

You'll celebrate the classics like tender bulgogi, stone-pot bibimbap, and the hearty warmth of doenjang jjigae, while navigating through lesser-known, yet equally captivating, provincial specialties. This journey will also carry you to trendy cafes in Seoul, where you'll find imaginative concoctions such as kimchi tacos and bulgogi pizza—proving that the spirit of Korean cuisine is ever-adaptive and globally inclusive.

Equipped with detailed tips and chefs' secrets, we aspire to empower you with the knowledge that makes Korean cooking a craft—a ritualistic dance where preparation, presentation, and consumption form a circle of shared joy and nourishment.

As we venture into the melding of the traditional with the avant-garde, we also recognize the global desire for health-conscious choices. Thus, our recipes embrace both the heartiness of Korean dining and the principles of well-being embedded in much of the nation's dietary heritage, where meals are a balanced mosaic of nature's bounty.

This cookbook unfolds not just as a compilation of recipes, but as an openhearted celebration of Korean life, culture, and the unifying power of food. Aspiring chefs and culinary adventurers alike are welcomed to explore the nuanced aromas and textures that characterize hansik.

So, let us embark together on this culinary voyage, where centuries-old practices meet the dynamism of modern foodscapes, and where every plate is a reminder of Korea's enduring love affair with food. Welcome, and 잘 먹겠습니다 (jal meokgetseumnida)—bon appétit, Korean style!

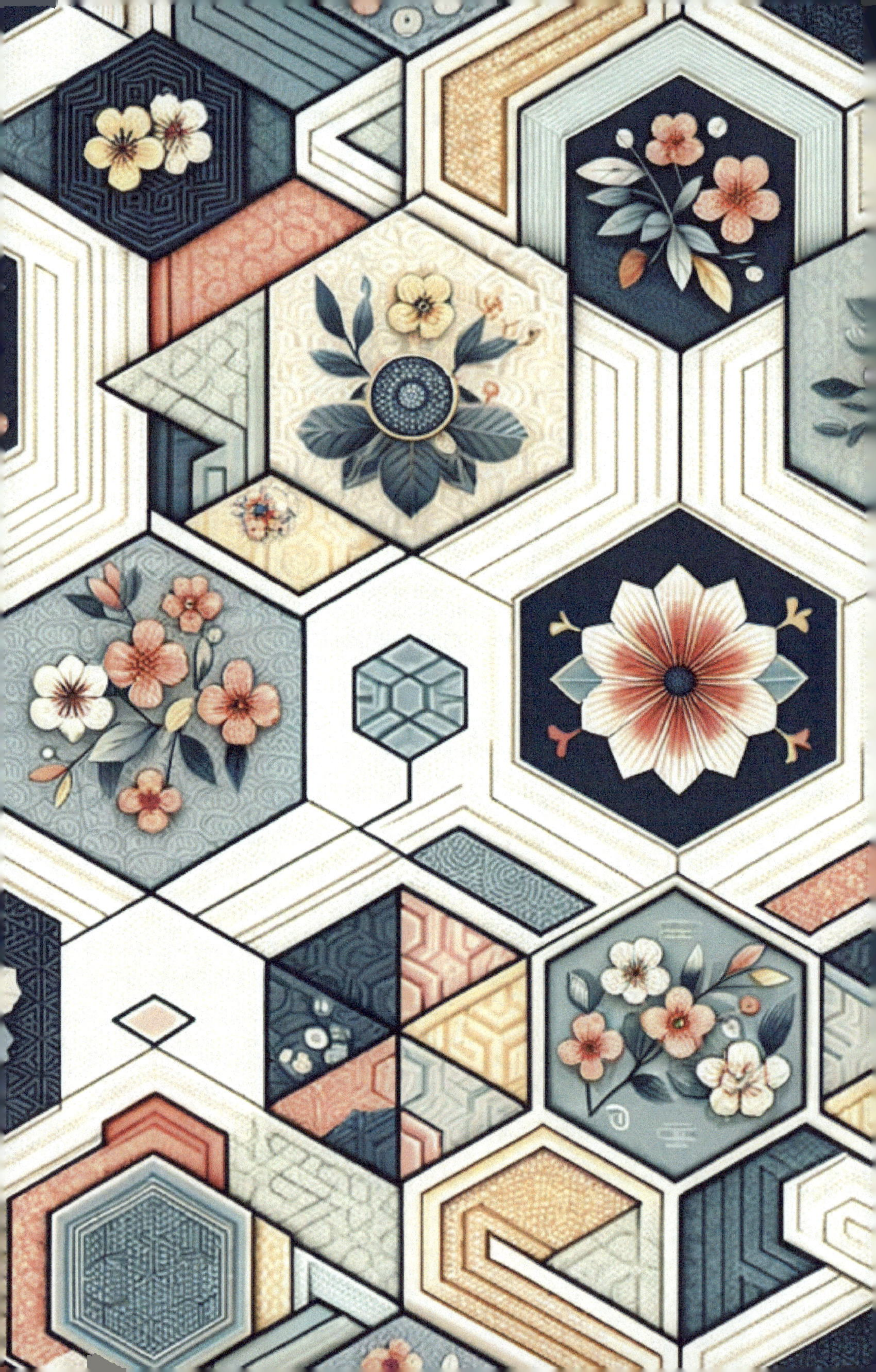

AUTHENTIC KOREAN RECIPES

NAPA CABBAGE KIMCHI

Kimchi is a quintessential Korean dish, with a history stretching back over a thousand years. Initially a way to preserve vegetables through the harsh winters, it has evolved into a culinary staple, beloved for its complex flavors and myriad health benefits. Each Korean household boasts its own unique recipe passed down through generations, adjusting spice levels and ingredients to personal taste.

INGREDIENTS

- 2 heads of Napa cabbage, quartered and cut into 2-inch pieces
- 1/2 cup of sea salt
- 12 cups of cold water
- 2 tablespoons of glutinous rice flour
- 2 tablespoons of brown sugar
- 1/2 cup of fish sauce
- 1/4 cup of salted shrimp paste (saeujeot)
- 1 1/2 cups of gochugaru (Korean red pepper flakes)
- 1 small Asian pear, peeled and grated
- 8 cloves of garlic, minced
- 2-inch piece of ginger, minced
- 4 green onions, chopped into 1-inch pieces
- 1 medium daikon radish, peeled and thinly sliced
- 1 small carrot, julienned

DIRECTIONS

1. Place the chopped cabbage in a large mixing bowl. Dissolve sea salt in the water and pour it over the cabbage. Ensure the cabbage is fully submerged by placing a plate on top with a weight. Let the cabbage soak for at least 6 hours, or ideally overnight.
2. After the soaking period, rinse the cabbage thoroughly under cold water. Drain and set aside.
3. Prepare the porridge by mixing glutinous rice flour and 1 cup of water in a small pot. Cook over medium heat, stirring continuously until it thickens into a porridge. Add the brown sugar and cook for another minute. Remove from the heat and cool to room temperature.
4. In a large mixing bowl, combine the fish sauce, salted shrimp paste, gochugaru, grated Asian pear, minced garlic, and ginger with the cooled porridge. Mix well to form a paste.
5. Add the radish, carrot, and green onions to the spice paste and toss until the vegetables are completely coated.
6. Wearing gloves to protect your hands from the spices, thoroughly massage the paste into the cabbage.
7. Pack the cabbage into a clean, airtight container or a traditional Korean fermentation jar called onggi. Press down firmly to remove any air pockets and submerge the cabbage in its own liquid.
8. Seal the container and leave it at room temperature for 1-5 days, depending on how fermented you desire your kimchi. Check it daily, pressing down to keep the cabbage submerged.
9. Once the kimchi has fermented to your preference, store it in the refrigerator. The flavor will continue to develop as it ages.

DIETARY MODIFICATIONS

Vegetarian: Substitute fish sauce and salted shrimp paste with soy sauce and kelp powder to maintain the umami flavor profile.

Vegan: Follow the vegetarian modifications, and ensure that the sugar used is organic or certified vegan.

Gluten-Free: Replace the glutinous rice flour with a gluten-free alternative, such as arrowroot powder, and use gluten-free tamari instead of soy sauce.

INGREDIENT SPOTLIGHT: GOCHUGARU

Gochugaru, or Korean red pepper flakes, is the heart of kimchi. It's made from sun-dried red chili peppers that are de-seeded and ground to a coarse texture. Gochugaru has a distinctive flavor - simultaneously sweet, smoky, and spicy, with just the right amount of heat. Without gochugaru, kimchi would not have its signature vibrant red color or its deep, complex flavor profile. This ingredient not only gives kimchi its kick but is also rich in vitamins and antioxidants.

CHEF'S TIPS

- Salt is crucial for the safety and flavor of kimchi; ensure it is distributed evenly.
- Maintain cleanliness throughout the process to avoid contamination and spoilage.
- Tasting the kimchi throughout fermentation will help you understand how the flavors develop over time.
- Use a glass or food-grade plastic container for fermentation to prevent unwanted chemical reactions.
- If the kimchi is too spicy, reduce the amount of gochugaru according to your taste.

POSSIBLE VARIATIONS OF THE RECIPE

- **White Kimchi:** For a milder version, omit the gochugaru. This results in a non-spicy kimchi known as baek-kimchi.
- **Cucumber Kimchi:** Substitute the Napa cabbage with cucumbers for a refreshing alternative, known as oi-kimchi.
- **Radish Kimchi:** Known as kkakdugi, use Korean radish (mu) instead of Napa cabbage for a crunchy variety of kimchi.

HEALTH NOTE & CALORIC INFORMATION

Kimchi is low in calories but high in fiber, vitamins A, B, and C, and the lactobacilli bacteria beneficial for gut health. The exact calorie count can vary, but a 100-gram serving typically contains about 15-30 calories, with 1-2 grams of protein and 2-3 grams of fiber. It's also rich in antioxidants and can contribute to a healthy digestive system.

TRADITIONAL BIBIMBAP

Bibimbap, which translates to "mixed rice," is a beloved Korean dish with as many variations as there are cooks who prepare it. Traditionally served in a hot stone bowl, it's a delectable mélange of rice, vegetables, a protein like beef, and a raw or fried egg, all brought together with the sweet and spicy flavor of gochujang sauce. The dish is both a staple of Korean home cooking and a canvas for creativity, most notable for its vibrant presentation and satisfying blend of textures and temperatures.

INGREDIENTS

For the rice:
- 2 cups short-grain rice
- 2 1/2 cups water
- 1 cup spinach, blanched and squeezed dry
- 1 cup bean sprouts, blanched
- 1 medium zucchini, julienned and sautéed
- 1 medium carrot, julienned and sautéed
- 1 cup shiitake mushrooms, sliced and sautéed
- 1 cup cucumber, julienned (served raw)

For the protein:
- 1/2 pound beef sirloin, thinly sliced
- 2 tablespoons soy sauce
- 1 tablespoon sesame oil
- 1 tablespoon sugar
- 1 clove garlic, minced
- 1/2 teaspoon ground black pepper

Additional ingredients:
- 4 eggs
- Salt to taste
- Vegetable oil for sautéing
- Gochujang (Korean red chili paste)
- Roasted sesame seeds
- 1 teaspoon sugar (optional for dressing)
- 1 clove garlic, minced (optional for dressing)
- 2 teaspoons sesame oil (optional for dressing)

DIRECTIONS

1. Begin by rinsing the rice under cold water until the water runs clear. Drain and cook the rice according to package instructions or use a rice cooker, then set aside and keep warm.
2. Prepare the vegetables separately, sautéing or blanching each one and seasoning lightly with salt.
3. For the beef, combine the marinade ingredients in a bowl. Add the thinly sliced beef and ensure each piece is well-coated. Set aside to marinate for at least 30 minutes.
4. In a pan over medium-high heat, sauté the marinated beef slices until fully cooked, about 2-3 minutes per side. Keep warm.
5. For the bibimbap sauce, mix gochujang with 1 teaspoon sugar, 1 clove of minced garlic, and 2 teaspoons sesame oil in a bowl. Adjust the seasoning according to your taste.
6. In a separate pan, fry the eggs sunny side up.
7. Assemble the bowl by placing a serving of rice at the bottom. Arrange the prepared vegetables and beef in sections over the rice. Place a fried egg on top of each serving.
8. Sprinkle with roasted sesame seeds and drizzle with the bibimbap sauce.
9. Serve immediately, inviting diners to mix everything thoroughly before eating.

DIETARY MODIFICATIONS

Vegetarian: Omit the beef and use tofu or a mix of mushrooms as a protein. Marinate the tofu or mushrooms in the same mixture the beef would use for a savory umami flavor.

Vegan: Follow the vegetarian modifications and replace the egg with a vegan egg substitute or additional vegetables, such as sautéed kale or avocado slices.

Gluten-Free: Ensure that the soy sauce used for beef marinade and bibimbap sauce is gluten-free, or substitute it with tamari or coconut aminos.

INGREDIENT SPOTLIGHT: GOCHUJANG

This Korean red chili paste is a fermented condiment made with red chili powder, glutinous rice, fermented soybeans, and salt. Gochujang has a complex flavor profile—it's sweet, spicy, and umami-rich, making it an indispensable ingredient in many Korean dishes. Its history traces back to the 18th century, and it is a staple in Korean cuisine, used in a variety of dishes from marinades to stews to dipping sauces. In bibimbap, gochujang is the key element that ties the individual ingredients together with a signature Korean zest.

CHEF'S TIPS

- Use a cast-iron skillet or a stone bowl (dolsot) if available, to get crispy rice at the bottom of your bowl.
- Be sure to cut vegetables into a similar size to ensure even cooking and a harmonious visual presentation.
- Season each element separately to maintain their distinctive flavors, but don't overdo it as the gochujang sauce will also add seasoning.
- When frying the eggs, make sure the whites are set but the yolks remain runny, as they will add creaminess when mixed.
- Allow the rice and toppings to gather heat if you are using a stone bowl, to add an extra layer of texture with crispy rice.

POSSIBLE VARIATIONS OF THE RECIPE

- **Seafood Bibimbap:** Substitute beef with seafood such as sautéed shrimp or squid for a pescatarian version.
- **Low-Carb Bibimbap:** Replace the rice with cauliflower rice for a low-carb alternative without sacrificing flavor.
- **Spicy Pork Bibimbap:** Marinate thinly sliced pork with gochujang-based marinade for a spicier version and pan-fry it as you would with the beef.

HEALTH NOTE & CALORIC INFORMATION

One serving of Bibimbap typically contains a balance of carbohydrates, protein, and vegetables, providing a well-rounded meal. The dish is relatively high in calories due to the rice and protein portion, averaging around 600-700 calories per serving. The high vegetable content ensures a good intake of fiber and vitamins, while the beef and egg provide a substantial amount of protein. Adjusting the amount of rice or substituting it with a lower carbohydrate alternative can significantly alter the calorie content.

BULGOGI

Bulgogi, which means "fire meat," is a classic Korean dish with a history spanning more than a thousand years. References to bulgogi date back to the Goguryeo era (37 BCE – 668 CE) when it was originally known as maekjeok and involved grilling skewered beef. Over time, the dish evolved into what's known today as bulgogi, which became popular in the 20th century. It's a beloved dish cherished for its sweet and savory flavors, tender marinated beef, and versatility in Korean cuisine.

INGREDIENTS

- 600 grams of thinly sliced ribeye steak
- 1/2 medium pear, grated
- 4 cloves garlic, minced
- 1/2 medium onion, grated
- 2 green onions, thinly sliced
- 2 tablespoons soy sauce
- 1 tablespoon brown sugar
- 1 tablespoon honey
- 1 tablespoon sesame oil
- 1 tablespoon mirin (Korean cooking rice wine)
- 1 teaspoon freshly ground black pepper
- 1 tablespoon toasted sesame seeds
- 1 tablespoon vegetable oil (for cooking)
- Lettuce leaves (for serving, optional)

DIRECTIONS

1. Begin by preparing the marinade. Combine grated pear, minced garlic, grated onion, soy sauce, brown sugar, honey, sesame oil, mirin, and black pepper in a large mixing bowl. Whisk these ingredients together until well mixed and the sugar has dissolved.
2. Place the thinly sliced ribeye into the bowl with the marinade. Add the sliced green onions and half of the toasted sesame seeds. Gently massage the marinade into the beef, ensuring each piece is well coated. Cover and marinate in the refrigerator for at least 1 hour, or overnight for deeper flavor.
3. When ready to cook, heat a tablespoon of vegetable oil in a large skillet or grill pan over medium-high heat. Ensure the pan is hot before adding the beef slices to avoid steaming the meat.
4. Working in batches to avoid overcrowding, lay the beef slices flat in the pan and cook for about 1-2 minutes on each side or until nicely seared and caramelized. If using a grill pan, you can achieve desirable grill marks.
5. Once cooked, transfer the bulgogi to a serving plate. Sprinkle the remaining toasted sesame seeds on top for garnish.
6. Serve the bulgogi hot with a side of steamed rice, lettuce leaves for wrapping, or your choice of Korean side dishes (banchan).

DIETARY MODIFICATIONS

Gluten-Free: Substitute soy sauce with tamari, ensuring it's labeled gluten-free.
Vegetarian: Use thickly sliced king oyster mushrooms in place of beef and adjust cooking time accordingly as mushrooms will cook faster.
Low-Sugar: Omit the brown sugar and honey from the marinade and replace with a sugar substitute that is appropriate for cooking, such as stevia or erythritol.

INGREDIENT SPOTLIGHT: MIRIN

Mirin is a sweet Japanese cooking wine made from glutinous rice, rice koji (a fermentation starter), and distilled liquor. It's an essential component in many Japanese dishes and adds a touch of sweetness and luster to glazes and sauces. Mirin has been a staple in Japanese cooking for centuries, and while it serves a similar purpose to sake, it has a lower alcohol content and a higher sugar content, which lends a characteristic flavor that's pivotal to the authentic taste of dishes like bulgogi.

CHEF'S TIPS

- Freeze the ribeye for about 30 minutes before slicing; this will make it easier to cut thin, even slices.
- Use a pear in the marinade, as it contains enzymes that help tenderize the beef while also adding sweetness.
- Let the beef marinate for as long as possible, preferably overnight, to allow the flavors to fully penetrate the meat.
- Cook the meat in a very hot pan in batches to ensure each piece caramelizes properly, creating a more complex flavor profile.
- Allow the cooked bulgogi to rest for a few minutes before serving; this helps retain its juices, keeping it moist and flavorful.

POSSIBLE VARIATIONS OF THE RECIPE

- **Spicy Bulgogi:** Add 1-2 tablespoons of gochujang (Korean chili paste) to the marinade for a kick of heat and a deeper red color.
- **Chicken Bulgogi:** Substitute the beef with thinly sliced chicken thigh or breast for a lighter version of the classic dish.
- **Bulgogi Bowls:** Serve over a bowl of steamed rice with pickled vegetables and a fried egg on top for a bulgogi bibimbap experience.

HEALTH NOTE & CALORIC INFORMATION

Bulgogi is a protein-rich dish that also contains essential vitamins and minerals from its various ingredients, especially if served with vegetables. The traditional recipe, however, can be high in sugars due to the ingredients in the marinade. A typical serving size (about 150 grams) of bulgogi without accompaniments is approximately 300 calories, with 23 grams of protein, 12 grams of fat, and 14 grams of carbohydrates.

JAPCHAE

Japchae is a classic Korean dish that has been around since the 17th century. Originally a royal dish, it has become a beloved staple at Korean feasts and celebrations. The name "Japchae" translates to mixed vegetables, but the dish is renowned for its sweet potato starch noodles (dangmyeon) stir-fried with a medley of colorful vegetables and sometimes beef, all tossed in a savory-sweet sauce.

INGREDIENTS

- 200g sweet potato starch noodles (dangmyeon)
- 150g spinach, washed and trimmed
- 1 medium carrot, julienned
- 1 medium onion, thinly sliced
- 1 red bell pepper, julienned
- 100g shiitake mushrooms, sliced
- 200g beef (sirloin or ribeye), thinly sliced (optional)
- 3 cloves garlic, minced
- 2 green onions, chopped
- 4 tablespoons soy sauce
- 2 tablespoons sesame oil
- 2 tablespoons sugar
- 1 tablespoon vegetable oil
- 1 tablespoon toasted sesame seeds
- Salt to taste
- Ground black pepper to taste

DIRECTIONS

1. Cook the sweet potato noodles in boiling water for about 6 minutes or until they are cooked through but still chewy. Drain and rinse under cold water to stop cooking; set aside.
2. Blanch spinach in boiling water for 30 seconds, then rinse under cold water, squeeze out excess water and season with a little salt. Set aside in a large mixing bowl.
3. Heat a tablespoon of vegetable oil in a pan over medium heat. Add the onions, carrots, and red bell pepper, sautéing until they're slightly softened but still have a bite to them. Transfer them to the bowl with the spinach.
4. In the same pan, add a little more oil if necessary, and sauté the shiitake mushrooms until they are cooked down and aromatic. Add them to the vegetable bowl.
5. If using beef, season it with a pinch of salt and pepper. Then cook it in the same pan until just browned and cooked through. Add to the vegetables.
6. In a small bowl, combine soy sauce, sesame oil, and sugar, stirring until the sugar dissolves. This is your seasoning sauce.
7. Add cooked noodles to the vegetable and beef mixture. Pour the seasoning sauce over and toss everything together until well combined. Adjust seasoning with salt if needed.
8. Garnish with green onions and toasted sesame seeds. Serve warm or at room temperature.

DIETARY MODIFICATIONS

Vegetarian: Omit the beef and add more mushrooms or tofu for a protein substitute. Ensure that the tofu is pressed and sliced into thin strips, then pan-fried until golden before adding to the dish.

Vegan: Follow the vegetarian modifications and also make sure to use a sugar substitute that aligns with vegan dietary restrictions, such as coconut sugar or agave syrup.

Gluten-free: Opt for tamari or a certified gluten-free soy sauce to ensure the dish is gluten-free without compromising the essential savory flavor of the sauce.

INGREDIENT SPOTLIGHT: SWEET POTATO

The spotlight ingredient is the sweet potato starch noodles, known as dangmyeon in Korean. These unique noodles date back to the Joseon Dynasty and are made from the starch of sweet potatoes, providing a chewy texture that is a hallmark of japchae. Unlike other noodles, dangmyeon are gluten-free and nearly transparent after being cooked. They absorb flavors from the accompanying sauce and ingredients, making them the foundation of the dish.

CHEF'S TIPS

- Soak the sweet potato noodles in warm water for about 20 minutes before cooking. This reduces the cooking time and ensures a perfect chewy texture.
- Cut the noodles with scissors after cooking for easier mixing and eating.
- Stir-fry the vegetables separately to preserve their individual flavors and textures.
- While tossing the japchae, use your hands (with gloves if desired) to mix, as it allows for the ingredients to integrate better.
- Let the japchae sit for 10 minutes after mixing to allow the flavors to meld together more cohesively.

POSSIBLE VARIATIONS OF THE RECIPE

- Spicy Japchae: Add gochujang (Korean red pepper paste) to the seasoning sauce for a spicy kick that complements the sweet and savory notes of the dish.
- Seafood Japchae: Replace the beef with a selection of seafood such as shrimp and squid for a pescatarian version, cooking them just until done to avoid chewiness.
- Wild Mushroom Japchae: Use an assortment of wild mushrooms such as oyster, enoki, and morels for an earthy, robust flavor profile that's perfect for mushroom lovers.

HEALTH NOTE & CALORIC INFORMATION

A typical serving of japchae is rich in carbohydrates due to the noodles and has a moderate amount of protein, especially if beef is included. The dish is also high in vitamins and minerals from the assortment of vegetables. Sesame oil provides healthy fats, but the dish should be consumed in moderation due to its sugar and sodium content. A serving of japchae without beef approximately contains 320 calories, whereas with beef, it is about 460 calories.

TTEOKBOKKI

Tteokbokki, a popular Korean street food, is a fiery, sweet-savory snack made with cylinder-shaped rice cakes, fish cakes, and a hearty gochujang-based sauce. This dish is beloved for its unique chewy texture and the warming, bold flavors that have become synonymous with Korean comfort food. Often sold from pojangmacha (street vendors), tteokbokki has become an emblem of lively Korean markets and bustling city life.

INGREDIENTS

- 2 cups of Korean rice cakes (tteok for tteokbokki)
- 4 cups of water
- 2 tbsp of gochujang (Korean red pepper paste)
- 1 tbsp of gochugaru (Korean red pepper flakes)
- 3 tbsp of soy sauce
- 1 tbsp of sugar
- 1 tbsp of honey
- 2 tsp of minced garlic
- 1 medium-sized onion, sliced
- 2 green onions, chopped
- 4 oz fish cakes, sliced (optional)
- 1 boiled egg (optional)
- 1 tsp of sesame seeds (for garnish)
- 1 tsp of sesame oil

DIRECTIONS

1. If using refrigerated rice cakes, soak them in warm water for about 10–15 minutes to soften. Drain and set aside.
2. In a large pan, bring the water to a boil. Add gochujang, gochugaru, soy sauce, sugar, honey, and minced garlic to the boiling water and whisk until the ingredients are well combined.
3. Lower the heat to a medium simmer and add the submerged rice cakes to the sauce, stirring gently, making sure they don't stick to each other.
4. Add the sliced onion and optional fish cakes. Continue cooking for 8–10 minutes, frequently stirring until the sauce thickens and the rice cakes are soft and chewy.
5. Stir in the sesame oil, then garnish with sesame seeds and chopped green onions on top.
6. Optional: Add a boiled egg to the dish in the last 2 minutes of cooking for an authentic touch.
7. Serve hot directly from the pan.

DIETARY MODIFICATIONS

Vegetarian: Skip the fish cakes and boiled egg. You can add a variety of vegetables like mushrooms, spinach, or carrots to maintain the volume and add nutritional value.

Vegan: Follow the vegetarian substitutes and replace honey with maple syrup or another plant-based sweetener.

Gluten-Free: Ensure the gochujang and soy sauce are labeled as gluten-free, as some brands may contain wheat.

INGREDIENT SPOTLIGHT: GOCHUJANG

Gochujang is a vibrant, crimson-red fermented paste made from chili powder, glutinous rice, fermented soybeans, and salt. It's a staple in Korean cooking, imparting a complex flavor profile that's spicy, savory, sweet, and umami. Dating back to the 18th century, gochujang is not just a condiment but a crucial ingredient that brings depth to dishes like tteokbokki, adding both heat and a unique, slightly sweet undertone that makes the dish distinctly Korean.

CHEF'S TIPS

- The right consistency of the sauce is key; it should be thick enough to evenly coat the rice cakes but not too sticky.
- Use a non-stick pan to prevent the rice cakes from sticking and to make stirring easier.
- Adjust the level of spice to your preference by varying the amount of gochujang and gochugaru.
- For a more authentic experience, try making your rice cakes from scratch if you have access to the ingredients and time.
- The freshness of the rice cakes matters; fresh or frozen rice cakes have the best texture, whereas dried ones require longer soaking times.

POSSIBLE VARIATIONS OF THE RECIPE

- **Cheese Tteokbokki:** Just before serving, top the tteokbokki with shredded mozzarella cheese, cover and let it melt for a decadent twist.
- **Seafood Tteokbokki:** Add shrimp, mussels, or squid to the dish for a hearty, ocean-inspired variation.
- **Curry Tteokbokki:** Incorporate curry powder and a bit of coconut milk into the sauce for a fusion dish with Indian influences.

HEALTH NOTE & CALORIC INFORMATION

A typical serving of tteokbokki is high in carbohydrates due to the rice cakes; however, it can also be a source of protein when including fish cakes or boiled eggs. The dish is relatively low in fat but can be high in sodium from the soy sauce and gochujang. A single serving without cheese or seafood typically contains approximately 300-400 calories, though this can vary based on portion size and specific ingredients used.

KOREAN BBQ (GALBI)

Galbi, also known as Kalbi, is a classic Korean dish known for its savory, sweet, and slightly smoky flavors. These grilled short ribs are a staple at Korean barbecues and are often enjoyed at gatherings and celebrations. The marinade, which typically includes soy sauce, sugar, and sesame oil, tenderizes the ribs and imparts a rich depth of flavor that's both distinctive and alluring. The roots of Galbi date back to the Goguryeo era (37 BC–668 AD), where it began as a skewered meat dish. Over time, it evolved with the introduction of soy sauce in the Joseon Dynasty, becoming the beloved dish we know today.

INGREDIENTS

- 3 lbs beef short ribs, Korean style (thinly sliced)
- 1 Asian pear or 1/2 cup of pear juice
- 6 cloves garlic, minced
- 1/2 cup soy sauce
- 1/2 cup brown sugar
- 2 tbsp sesame oil
- 1/4 cup water
- 1/4 cup rice wine (or mirin)
- 1 tbsp freshly grated ginger
- 2 green onions, finely chopped
- 1 tsp black pepper
- 1 tbsp toasted sesame seeds (for garnish)
- Sliced green onions (for garnish)

DIRECTIONS

1. Begin by rinsing the short ribs under cold water to remove any bone fragments. Pat dry with paper towels and set aside.
2. Peel the Asian pear and grate it until you have about 1/2 cup of pear puree. If using pear juice, measure it out.
3. In a large mixing bowl, combine garlic, soy sauce, brown sugar, sesame oil, water, rice wine, grated ginger, and chopped green onions. Mix thoroughly until the sugar has dissolved.
4. Add the pear puree or pear juice to the marinade and blend well.
5. Place the short ribs in a large dish or plastic bag. Pour the marinade over the ribs, ensuring each piece is generously coated.
6. Seal the dish with plastic wrap or close the bag, removing as much air as possible. Marinate in the refrigerator for at least 4 hours, preferably overnight.
7. Preheat the grill to medium-high heat. Ensure the grill is cleaned and oiled to prevent sticking.
8. Remove the short ribs from the marinade and shake off the excess. Grill the ribs, turning occasionally, until they are nicely caramelized and cooked through, about 3-4 minutes per side.
9. Once done, transfer the Galbi to a platter. Sprinkle with toasted sesame seeds and garnish with additional sliced green onions.
10. Serve hot with steamed rice, kimchi, and other Korean side dishes for an authentic experience.

DIETARY MODIFICATIONS

Vegetarian: Replace beef short ribs with thick slices of king oyster mushrooms. Marinate and grill similarly, ensuring not to overcook as mushrooms cook faster than meat.

Vegan: Follow the vegetarian alternative but also replace honey or traditional sugar (which may not be vegan) in the marinade with agave syrup or another vegan-friendly sweetener.

Lactose Intolerance: This recipe is naturally lactose-free, so no modifications are needed. Enjoy the Galbi as stated in the recipe above.

INGREDIENT SPOTLIGHT: ASIAN PEAR

Asian pear, also known as nashi pear, is a fruit cherished for its juicy, crisp texture and delicate sweetness. Originating in East Asia, it's often found in dishes across Korean, Japanese, and Chinese cuisines, prized for its ability to tenderize meat. In Galbi marinade, the fruit's natural enzymes aid in breaking down the proteins in beef, making the ribs exceptionally tender. This is a critical ingredient providing a subtle fruity undertone that complements and balances the savory elements of the dish.

CHEF'S TIPS

- When choosing short ribs, look for evenly marbled pieces as fat contributes to tenderness and flavor.
- Be sure to score the meat lightly, creating thin cuts across the surface to help the marinade penetrate and tenderize the meat more effectively.
- Allow the ribs to come to room temperature before grilling to ensure even cooking.
- To achieve the signature char without overcooking, make sure the grill is very hot before adding the meat.
- To prevent flare-ups and excessive charring, keep a spray bottle with water nearby to douse any flames that may rise from dripping fat.

POSSIBLE VARIATIONS OF THE RECIPE

- **Spicy Galbi:** Add 1 to 2 tablespoons of gochujang (Korean chili paste) to the marinade for a sweet and fiery kick.
- **Citrus Galbi:** Substitute half of the pear juice with fresh orange juice to add a bright citrus note to the marinade.
- **Soy-free Galbi:** For those avoiding soy, replace soy sauce with coconut aminos and adjust the sweetness as needed, as coconut aminos are slightly sweeter than regular soy sauce.

HEALTH NOTE & CALORIC INFORMATION

Korean BBQ Galbi is rich in protein due to the beef but also carries a high-fat content, particularly saturated fat. The marinade adds sugars and sodium to the dish. A typical serving may contain approximately 500-600 calories, with variations depending on the serving size and exact ingredients used. It's a nourishing dish best enjoyed in moderation and balanced with vegetables and grains.

Keep the essence of tradition in each bite while exploring the adaptability of Korean Galbi, a testament to the enduring allure of Korean barbecue. Enjoy!

KIMCHI JJIGAE

Kimchi Jjigae is a staple Korean dish made with fermented kimchi, pork, and tofu. The dish has a rich history in Korean cuisine, largely consumed in the cold winter months for its warming properties. Its origin dates back to the period when fresh vegetables were scarce, and so people turned to fermented foods for nutrition. Kimchi, being a well-preserved source of vitamins, became the star of this comforting stew. Over time, the recipe has evolved, with variations incorporating different proteins and vegetables.

INGREDIENTS

- 1 tablespoon vegetable oil
- 200 grams pork belly, thinly sliced
- 2 cups well-fermented kimchi, chopped
- 1 tablespoon kimchi juice
- 1 onion, sliced
- 2 cloves of garlic, minced
- 1 tablespoon gochugaru (Korean red chili pepper flakes)
- 1 tablespoon soy sauce
- 1 teaspoon sugar
- 2 cups chicken stock
- 1 block of tofu, cut into cubes
- 2 scallions, chopped
- 1 teaspoon sesame oil
- Cooked rice, for serving

DIRECTIONS

1. Preheat a heavy bottomed pot over medium heat and add the vegetable oil.
2. Once hot, add the pork belly slices and cook until lightly browned, about 5 minutes.
3. Add the chopped kimchi and fry with the pork belly for another 2 minutes.
4. Stir in the kimchi juice, onion, and minced garlic, cooking until the onion becomes translucent, about 3 minutes.
5. Sprinkle the gochugaru over the mixture, stirring constantly so it does not burn.
6. Add the soy sauce and sugar, mixing well to combine.
7. Pour in the chicken stock and bring the stew to a boil before reducing to a simmer. Let it cook for 15 minutes to meld the flavors.
8. Gently place the tofu cubes into the stew, letting them cook for another 5 minutes without stirring, so they keep their shape.
9. Finish the stew with a sprinkle of chopped scallions and a drizzle of sesame oil.
10. Serve hot with a side of cooked rice.

DIETARY MODIFICATIONS

Vegetarian: Substitute pork with mushrooms for umami flavor and use vegetable stock instead of chicken stock. Mushrooms offer a meaty texture and when browned, add an element similar to cooked pork.

Vegan: Follow the vegetarian substitutions and replace the traditional kimchi (which often has fish sauce) with a vegan kimchi alternative. Omit the ingredient if vegan kimchi is unavailable.

Gluten-Free: Ensure that the soy sauce is gluten-free and that the gochugaru and kimchi do not contain any gluten-containing additives. Many brands offer gluten-free soy sauce.

INGREDIENT SPOTLIGHT: GOCHUGARU

Gochugaru, or Korean red chili pepper flakes, is an essential ingredient in Korean cooking. It is made by drying and then crushing Korean red chili peppers. Gochugaru's unique flavor is slightly smoky, sweet, and with varying levels of heat. It's a fundamental component of kimchi, giving the dish its iconic red hue and spicy kick. Beyond kimchi, it's also used in a multitude of Korean dishes, from marinades to stews, and it is indispensable in adjusting a dish's spice level while adding a deep, complex flavor profile. It has been a part of Korean cuisine for centuries and continues to be a crucial spice in Korean kitchens worldwide.

CHEF'S TIPS

- The quality of kimchi significantly impacts the flavor, use well-fermented kimchi for a deeper taste.
- If preferred, remove excess fat from the pork belly for a lighter broth.
- Do not over-stir the tofu while it's in the stew to maintain its texture.
- Adjust the level of gochugaru to increase or decrease the heat to personal preference.
- Make the stew a day ahead for enhanced flavors as it sits and the ingredients meld together.

POSSIBLE VARIATIONS OF THE RECIPE

- **Seafood:** Add shrimp or mussels to the stew in the last 5 minutes of cooking for a pescatarian version that offers a fresh briny flavor profile.
- **Spicy Pork:** Increase the heat by adding extra gochugaru and sliced Korean green chili peppers to the pork as it browns, creating a bolder and spicier dish.
- **Soybean Sprout Jjigae:** For a crunchier texture and added nutrition, mix in a handful of soybean sprouts with the onion, and omit the pork for a lighter vegetarian option.

HEALTH NOTE & CALORIC INFORMATION

Kimchi Jjigae is generally moderate in calories with a balance of protein from the pork and tofu, probiotics from the kimchi, and essential nutrients from the added vegetables. The sesame oil adds healthy fats, while the gochugaru provides antioxidants. Depending on serving size and accompaniments, a single portion of Kimchi Jjigae can range from approximately 300-400 calories. It's important to note that the sodium content can be high due to soy sauce and kimchi, so it's advisable to consume this stew in moderation and be mindful if one is on a sodium-restricted diet. can be quite high in salt.

SAMGYEOPSAL

Samgyeopsal, which translates to "three-layer meat", is a beloved Korean dish that features thick, fatty slices of pork belly meat. It's a fixture in Korean barbecues and is typically cooked at the table on a grill and enjoyed communally. This method of dining not only brings a convivial atmosphere but also allows diners to cook the meat to their personal taste. As a staple in Korean cuisine, it's known not just for the taste, but also the shared experience it fosters.

INGREDIENTS

- 600 grams of pork belly slices
- 2 cloves of garlic, thinly sliced
- Salt and pepper to taste
- 1 green chili, thinly sliced (optional)
- 1 onion, sliced
- Lettuce leaves, for wrapping
- Kimchi, for serving
- Ssamjang (Korean dipping sauce), for serving
- Perilla leaves (optional)

DIRECTIONS

1. Preheat the grill (or a non-stick frying pan) to medium-high heat. Ensure that it's hot before you begin cooking the meat.
2. Once the grill is ready, place the pork belly slices onto the grill. Season them with salt and pepper.
3. Cook for about 2 to 3 minutes, then flip them over, and increase the heat to high.
4. Wait until the meat is cooked to your desired doneness—it should have a golden-brown crust.
5. While the meat is cooking, grill the sliced garlic and onions on the side of the grill until they're slightly charred and soft.
6. Once the pork is cooked, remove it from the grill and place it on a plate.
7. To enjoy, take a leaf of lettuce, place a slice of the cooked pork, grilled garlic, onion, a piece of green chili, a small scoop of kimchi, and a dab of ssamjang. Wrap it up and eat it in one bite for a burst of flavors.

DIETARY MODIFICATIONS

Vegetarian: Replace pork belly with thick slices of king oyster mushrooms. Marinate the mushrooms in a mixture of soy sauce, sesame oil, and a pinch of sugar to mimic the savory aspect of the meat.

Vegan: Follow the vegetarian replacement and ensure to use vegan kimchi (traditionally kimchi includes fish sauce) and vegan ssamjang or a soy-garlic sauce as substitutes for traditional dipping sauces.

Low-fat: Swap the pork belly for leaner cuts of pork or chicken breast. Remember to adjust cooking times, as leaner meats cook faster and can become tough if overcooked.

INGREDIENT SPOTLIGHT: PORK BELLY

Pork belly is a rich, flavorful cut of meat that has been celebrated in many cultures across the globe, from Korean samgyeopsal to Italian pancetta. Its alternating layers of meat and fat make it ideal for grilling, as the fat renders out and keeps the meat tender while providing a crispy exterior. The high-fat content delivers a luxurious mouthfeel and depth of flavor that's key to this recipe, creating a satisfying and indulgent experience.

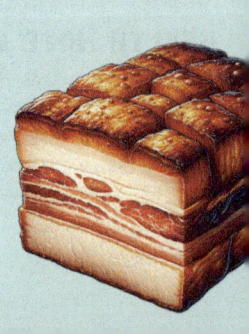

CHEF'S TIPS

- Let the pork belly come to room temperature before grilling; this ensures even cooking.
- Do not overcrowd the grill; this could cause the meat to steam instead of sear.
- If cooking indoors, ensure your space is well-ventilated as cooking pork belly can generate a significant amount of smoke.
- Always let the meat rest for a few minutes after cooking to allow the juices to redistribute.
- Make slits on the pork belly skin before grilling to prevent curling and ensure even cooking.

POSSIBLE VARIATIONS OF THE RECIPE

- Spicy Samgyeopsal: Marinate the pork belly slices in a mixture of gochujang (Korean chili paste), garlic, ginger, and soy sauce for an hour before grilling for an added kick.
- Herb-Infused Samgyeopsal: Prior to cooking, rub the pork belly with a mixture of crushed garlic, rosemary, and thyme to infuse it with herbal flavors.
- Sweet and Savory Samgyeopsal: Create a glaze with soy sauce, brown sugar, and rice wine, apply it to the pork in the last few minutes of grilling for a caramelized exterior.

HEALTH NOTE & CALORIC INFORMATION

Traditional samgyeopsal is high in calories due to the fat in pork belly, contributing to its rich flavor. A typical serving can range from 250 to 300 calories. It also contains a significant amount of protein and, depending on the side dishes, can provide a good amount of fiber (from the lettuce and garlic). Diets focusing on low-fat or low-calorie intake should consider portion sizes and meat choices carefully.

HAEMUL PAJEON

Haemul Pajeon is a popular Korean dish known for its savory and hearty quality. Pajeon, which translates to "green onion pancake," comes from the words "pa" meaning green onion and "jeon" describing a dish made by pan-frying ingredients in batter. The "haemul" part means seafood, which is a testament to Korea's long coastline and rich seafood tradition. This dish is especially enjoyed during the rainy season, believed to complement the sound of rain with its sizzling as it cooks.

INGREDIENTS

- 1 cup all-purpose flour
- 1/4 cup rice flour
- 1 1/2 cups cold water
- 1 egg
- 1/2 teaspoon salt
- 8-10 large green onions, cut into 2-inch lengths
- 1 cup mixed seafood (shrimp, squid, and scallops), chopped
- 2 fresh red chilies, sliced (optional)
- Vegetable oil for frying
- 1 tablespoon soy sauce (for dipping)
- 1 teaspoon vinegar (for dipping)
- ½ teaspoon sugar (for dipping)
- 1 clove garlic, minced (for dipping)

DIRECTIONS

1. Start by making the dipping sauce. In a small bowl, combine soy sauce, vinegar, sugar, and minced garlic. Stir until the sugar has dissolved and set aside.
2. In a large mixing bowl, sift together the all-purpose flour and rice flour. Add salt to the mixture.
3. Pour in the cold water and crack in the egg. Whisk the mixture until it forms a smooth batter, similar in consistency to thin pancake batter, making sure there are no lumps.
4. Heat a large non-stick skillet over medium heat, and add enough vegetable oil to coat the bottom.
5. Lay half of the green onions flat in the skillet, letting them sizzle for a minute. This helps to bring out their flavor.
6. Pour half of the batter over the green onions, ensuring the onions are covered.
7. Scatter half of the chopped seafood and optional red chilies evenly over the top of the batter.
8. Cook for about 4-5 minutes until the edges begin to turn golden brown, and small bubbles form on the surface.
9. Carefully flip the pancake with a large spatula, ensuring it stays intact, and continue cooking for another 3-4 minutes until the other side is crisp and golden brown.
10. Transfer the cooked pancake to a cutting board and repeat the process with the remaining ingredients for the second pancake.
11. Once both pancakes are cooked, slice them into wedges and serve immediately with the dipping sauce.

DIETARY MODIFICATIONS

Gluten-Free: Substitute the all-purpose flour with a gluten-free flour blend, and ensure that the soy sauce used for the dipping sauce is a gluten-free variety as well, such as tamari.

Vegetarian: Omit the seafood and instead insert a variety of mushrooms such as oyster or shiitake, and additional vegetables like zucchini or bell peppers to maintain the hearty consistency.

Vegan: Follow the vegetarian modifications and also substitute the egg in the batter with 1 tablespoon of ground flaxseed mixed with 3 tablespoons of water, allowing it to sit for a few minutes to thicken.

INGREDIENT SPOTLIGHT: RICE FLOUR

Rice flour is the spotlight ingredient in Haemul Pajeon. It is made from finely milled rice and introduces a hint of lightness and crispness to the batter that all-purpose flour alone cannot achieve. In Korean cuisine, it's often used to create a desirable texture in dishes like jeon (pancakes). It has a long history in Asian cooking, not just as a thickener but also for its ability to create a light, crunchy crust when fried.

CHEF'S TIPS

- For an extra crispy pancake, use ice-cold water when making the batter. This prevents the gluten in the flour from developing which can make the pancake chewy.
- Do not overcrowd the skillet with too many green onions or seafood, as it may prevent the pancake from crisping properly.
- Press down gently on the pancake with a spatula after flipping it, as this helps to create a crisper exterior.
- If you have leftover batter, you can store it in an airtight container in the refrigerator for up to a day.
- Ensure your oil is hot before adding the batter to achieve the coveted crispy edges, but avoid smoking-hot oil which can overcook the outside before the inside is done.

POSSIBLE VARIATIONS OF THE RECIPE

- **Kimchi Pajeon:** Swap out the seafood for 1 cup of chopped kimchi for a tangy, spicy version of the pancake.
- **Pa Jeon:** Focus on the scallions by omitting the seafood and adding more green onions for an authentic pa jeon, perfect for those who prefer a simpler taste.
- **Cheese Pajeon:** Sprinkle a handful of shredded mozzarella or cheddar cheese over the pancake before flipping it, creating a gooey, cheesy twist to the traditional recipe.

HEALTH NOTE & CALORIC INFORMATION

A typical serving of Haemul Pajeon contains approximately 250-300 calories, with a balance of protein from the seafood, carbohydrates from the flours, and moderate amounts of fat from the oil. It is also a source of micronutrients such as selenium and omega-3 fatty acids from the seafood, depending on the varieties used. Keep in mind that dipping sauce and cooking oil can add additional calories.

ARMY STEW

A dish steeped in history, Army Stew, or Budae Jjigae, originated during the Korean War when food was scarce. Resourceful Koreans combined surplus processed meats from U.S. military bases, such as spam and hot dogs, with traditional Korean flavors to create this hearty, spicy stew. It's a comfort food that represents a unique fusion of cultures, still beloved in South Korea today.

INGREDIENTS

- 150g Spam, sliced
- 2 hot dogs, sliced
- 100g ground beef
- 1/2 onion, sliced
- 2 cups Napa cabbage, chopped
- 1/2 cup kimchi, chopped
- 1 tbsp gochujang (Korean red pepper paste)
- 1 tbsp gochugaru (Korean red pepper flakes)
- 1 tbsp soy sauce
- 1 tsp sugar
- 1 tbsp minced garlic
- 4 cups chicken or beef broth
- 200g firm tofu, sliced
- 1 pack instant ramen noodles
- 2 green onions, chopped
- 1 tsp sesame oil
- Salt to taste
- Pepper to taste
- 1 slice American cheese (optional)

DIRECTIONS

1. Prepare all the ingredients by slicing the Spam, hot dogs, tofu, and onion. Chop the Napa cabbage, kimchi, and green onions.
2. In a large pot, brown the ground beef over medium heat, breaking it apart as it cooks. Once browned, remove the ground beef and set aside.
3. Using the same pot, sauté onions until they become translucent. Add minced garlic and cook until fragrant.
4. Add gochujang, gochugaru, soy sauce, and sugar. Stir to create a fragrant base.
5. Pour in the broth and bring the mixture to a boil.
6. Add the Spam, hot dogs, tofu, kimchi, Napa cabbage, and the cooked ground beef to the pot. Season with salt and pepper to taste. Reduce the heat and let it simmer for 20 minutes, allowing the flavors to meld.
7. In the last 5 minutes of cooking, add the instant ramen noodles and allow them to cook until soft.
8. Once the stew is done, stir in the chopped green onions and drizzle with sesame oil.
9. Serve hot in a communal pot or individual bowls. Optionally, top with a slice of American cheese, which will melt into the stew for a creamy texture.

DIETARY MODIFICATIONS

Vegetarian: Substitute the meat with mushrooms, a variety of tofu, and vegetable broth. You can also add sliced cheese or a vegetarian cheese alternative to keep the creamy texture.

Vegan: Follow the vegetarian modifications but ensure all processed items like the instant ramen noodles are vegan. Replace the cheese with nutritional yeast or a vegan cheese to achieve a cheesy flavor.

Gluten-Free: Ensure that the soy sauce is gluten-free, and use gluten-free ramen or rice cakes instead of regular ramen noodles. Additionally, verify all processed meats are gluten-free or use gluten-free alternatives.

INGREDIENT SPOTLIGHT: GOCHUJANG

Gochujang is a deep red, sticky paste made from red chili, glutinous rice, fermented soybeans, and salt. It's a quintessential Korean condiment, infusing dishes with umami, heat, and a slight sweetness. The fermentation process gives gochujang a complex flavor that's essential in creating the authentic taste of dishes like Budae Jjigae. Its history dates back to the Joseon dynasty, where it has been a staple in Korean kitchens for centuries.

CHEF'S TIPS

- For a more intense flavor, let the kimchi and gochujang sauté with the onions and garlic before adding the broth.
- The quality of the broth can make or break this dish. A flavorful chicken or beef broth will serve as a rich base for the stew.
- The stew is traditionally spicy, but you can adjust the level of heat by moderating the amount of gochugaru and gochujang you use.
- American cheese adds a trademark creaminess but can be omitted if preferred. The stew is still delicious without it.
- Enjoy the budae jjigae communal-style, right out of the pot, for an authentic Korean dining experience.

POSSIBLE VARIATIONS OF THE RECIPE

- **Seafood Budae Jjigae:** Add shrimp, mussels, and squid to the stew for a pescatarian version that adds a different flavor profile.
- **Cheese Lover's Budae Jjigae:** Increase the cheese by adding in mozzarella and cheddar, and melt it under the broiler before serving for a gooey, cheesy experience.
- **Spicy Lover's Budae Jjigae:** Add more gochugaru, a few slices of fresh hot chili, and a splash of Korean hot pepper oil for those who crave an extra fiery kick.

HEALTH NOTE & CALORIC INFORMATION

Army Stew is high in protein due to its various meats and tofu. It is also moderately high in sodium, particularly from the processed meats and seasonings. The vegetables and kimchi provide some fiber and vitamins. A typical serving of Budae Jjigae can range from 300 to 500 calories, depending on the ingredients and portion size. Therefore, it's important to consume this dish in moderation if you're watching your caloric intake.

SUNDUBU JJIGAE

Sundubu Jjigae is a popular Korean stew that's as comforting as it is flavorful. By combining silken tofu with a spicy, savory broth and a variety of mix-ins, it creates an enticingly warm and hearty dish. Traditionally served bubbling from its stone pot, it's a staple in Korean households, especially during cold seasons. Its origins are humble, with variations reflecting different regional ingredients throughout Korea. Today, it's celebrated in Korean cuisine for its depth of flavor and versatility.

INGREDIENTS

- 1 tablespoon sesame oil
- 3 cloves garlic, minced
- 1 onion, sliced
- 1/2 zucchini, sliced
- 100g Korean soft tofu (sundubu)
- 1 tablespoon Korean red pepper flakes (gochugaru)
- 1 tablespoon soy sauce
- 1 teaspoon sugar
- 200g seafood mix (shrimp, clams, and squid)
- 4 cups water or anchovy stock
- 1 teaspoon Korean fermented soybean paste (doenjang), optional
- 2 green onions, chopped
- 1 egg
- Salt to taste

DIRECTIONS

1. Preheat the stone pot or a regular pot on medium heat; add sesame oil. Once hot, sauté garlic and onions until translucent.
2. Add the zucchini and continue to sauté for another 2 minutes.
3. Sprinkle the red pepper flakes over the vegetables and stir frequently, cooking for about 1 minute until fragrant.
4. Pour in water or anchovy stock, soy sauce, and sugar. Stir well and bring to a boil.
5. If using, dissolve the Korean fermented soybean paste (doenjang) in a little bit of the stew's liquid, then add it back into the pot.
6. Gently add in the seafood mix and let cook for 2-3 minutes.
7. Now, open the soft tofu container and slide it into the stew. Break it up slightly with a spoon, but be careful not to stir too vigorously to maintain some tofu texture.
8. Allow the stew to come back to a gentle boil and cook for an additional 3-5 minutes for the flavors to meld.
9. Right before serving, crack an egg into the center of the stew and let it poach slightly in the residual heat.
10. Garnish with chopped green onions and a sprinkle of salt to taste.
11. Serve piping hot straight from the pot with a side of steamed rice.

DIETARY MODIFICATIONS

Vegetarian: Substitute seafood with mushrooms (such as shiitake or oyster) for a rich, umami flavor. Use vegetable broth instead of anchovy stock.

Vegan: In addition to the vegetarian substitutions, omit the egg and add extra vegetables like carrots and bell peppers for more substance.

Gluten-Free: Make sure to use gluten-free soy sauce, and check that the gochugaru and doenjang (if used) are certified gluten-free.

INGREDIENT SPOTLIGHT: SOFT TOFU

The spotlight ingredient is the Korean soft tofu, known as sundubu. Sundubu is fresh, unpressed tofu that has a higher water content and silkier texture than regular tofu. Its history in Korea goes back centuries and is particularly famous in the region of Paju. In Sundubu Jjigae, the sundubu is the star, providing a delicately smooth contrast to the robust and spicy broth. It absorbs the flavors around it while contributing a melt-in-your-mouth experience that defines this dish.

CHEF'S TIPS

- Begin with a well-heated pot to build flavors as you sauté the aromatics.
- Adjust the level of heat by increasing or decreasing the amount of gochugaru.
- For the most authentic taste and extra depth, use homemade anchovy stock.
- Break the tofu gently to maintain some texture contrast in the stew.
- Add the egg at the very end and allow it to poach in the broth's heat for a soft-set yolk.

POSSIBLE VARIATIONS OF THE RECIPE

- **Pork Sundubu Jjigae:** Start by cooking thinly sliced pork belly before adding the vegetables for a meatier version.
- **Kimchi Sundubu Jjigae:** Include chopped kimchi for a tangy flavor and additional spice; this is especially good with pork.
- **Cheese Sundubu Jjigae:** Top the stew with shredded mozzarella before serving and let it melt for a creamy, comforting twist.

HEALTH NOTE & CALORIC INFORMATION

A single serving of Sundubu Jjigae is rich in protein from both the seafood and tofu. The stew is also high in vitamins A and C from the vegetables and pepper flakes, with moderate calories. While being low in carbohydrates, it is advisable to eat it with rice for a more balanced meal. The sesame oil and egg contribute healthy fats. A typical bowl might range from 300-400 calories, depending on the additions like meat or cheese.

CLASSIC GIMBAP

Gimbap (also spelled kimbap) is a beloved Korean dish reminiscent of Japanese sushi rolls but with its own unique flavors. Originating in Korea, it is a popular picnic food and can be found in many Korean eateries around the world. Its name combines the words "gim" (dried seaweed) and "bap" (rice), the two main components of the dish. Gimbap includes a variety of fillings, such as vegetables, omelette, and processed meats, showcasing a balance of colors, textures, and flavors wrapped in a sheet of seaweed and sliced into bite-size pieces.

INGREDIENTS

- 4 sheets of gim (dried seaweed sheets)
- 2 cups of short-grain rice, cooked and seasoned with 1 tablespoon of sesame oil and 1 teaspoon of salt
- 1 small carrot, julienned
- 1 cucumber, julienned
- 4 strips of danmuji (yellow pickled radish), often sold as "gimbap radish" in Korean markets
- 2 eggs, beaten and cooked into a thin omelette, then sliced into strips
- 1/2 pound of bulgogi (Korean marinated beef), cooked and thinly sliced (optional)
- Cooking oil for frying
- Bamboo rolling mat (for assembling Gimbap)

DIRECTIONS

1. Wash and cook the rice according to instructions. Once cooked, mix in seasoning of sesame oil and salt while rice is still warm. Allow it to cool to room temperature.
2. Julienne carrot and cucumber into matchstick-sized pieces, then stir-fry the carrot in a pan with a little oil until slightly softened. Let it cool.
3. Prepare the eggs for the omelette by beating them and frying in a flat pan with a little oil. Once cooked, roll the omelette and slice into long strips. Set aside.
4. Slice the pickled radish into long strips similar in width to the cucumber and carrot.
5. If you are using bulgogi, cook it according to your favorite recipe or store-bought marinade instructions.
6. Lay a sheet of gim on the bamboo rolling mat, shiny side down.
7. Spread about a half cup of seasoned rice in an even layer over the gim, leaving about an inch of space at the top.
8. Arrange the carrot, cucumber, omelette strips, pickled radish, and beef across the rice, about a third of the way up from the bottom of the seaweed sheet.
9. Begin rolling the gimbap tightly from the bottom, using the bamboo mat to guide you. Make sure the fillings remain in place.
10. Once you've rolled over the fillings, squeeze the roll gently to compact everything.
11. Continue to roll, using the mat to apply even pressure until you reach the end of the seaweed sheet. Use a dab of water to seal the edge.
12. Lightly coat the blade of a sharp knife with sesame oil or water to prevent sticking.
13. Slice the roll into bite-size pieces, cleaning the knife between cuts if necessary to ensure clean slices.
14. Arrange Gimbap slices on a platter with the cut side facing up.

DIETARY MODIFICATIONS

Vegetarian: Replace bulgogi with tofu or tempeh that has been marinated in soy sauce, sugar, garlic, and sesame oil, then pan-fried until golden brown. Count all ingredients to ensure you have the right amount of filling.

Vegan: Follow the vegetarian modifications and use a vegan egg alternative for the omelette, such as a chickpea flour-based mixture pan-fried like eggs.

Gluten-Free: Ensure that the soy sauce used in any marinades or seasonings is gluten-free. Replace bulgogi with unmarinated tofu, or use a homemade bulgogi sauce made with gluten-free ingredients.

INGREDIENT SPOTLIGHT: GIM

Gim (Dried Seaweed Sheets) - Gim is the cornerstone of gimbap, providing a distinctly oceanic flavor and a crisp texture that contrasts with the soft rice and diverse fillings. It's an edible seaweed that has been pressed into thin sheets and dried. Rich in vitamins and minerals, gim has been a staple in Korean cuisine for centuries, tracing its history back to the period of the Three Kingdoms (57 BC to 668 AD). The gim's umami-rich taste complements the seasoned rice and savory fillings, making it indispensable for the perfect roll.

CHEF'S TIPS

- When spreading the rice on the seaweed, use a rice paddle or spatula moistened with water to prevent sticking.
- Do not overfill the rolls; less is more when it comes to making a tight, neatly shaped gimbap.
- If you have time, letting the cooked rice cool to room temperature will make it easier to handle and prevent the seaweed from getting soggy.
- Always roll the gimbap as tightly as possible without tearing the seaweed to prevent the rolls from falling apart.
- Gimbap can become dry if left out for too long, so it's best to wrap them in plastic wrap if not consuming immediately.

POSSIBLE VARIATIONS OF THE RECIPE

- **Spicy Tuna Gimbap:** Swap the bulgogi for canned tuna mixed with mayonnaise and gochujang (Korean chili paste) for a spicy kick.
- **Cheese Gimbap:** Add a strip of mild cheese, like mozzarella or cheddar, for a gooey texture and a different taste profile.
- **Kimchi Gimbap:** Incorporate finely chopped kimchi for its quintessential Korean flavor and a tangy, spicy element in the gimbap.

HEALTH NOTE & CALORIC INFORMATION

Each serving of Gimbap, depending on the size of the slices and specific ingredients used, typically contains a balance of macronutrients, with carbohydrates from the rice, protein from the eggs and bulgogi, and various vitamins and minerals from the vegetables. The exact calorie content can vary, but an average slice can have approximately 80-100 calories. It's also important to note that Gimbap can be high in sodium due to the pickled ingredients and seasoned rice.

SOONDAE

Soondae, also known as sundae, is a beloved type of Korean blood sausage stuffed with various ingredients including sweet rice, glass noodles, and pork blood. Historically, it is said to date back to the Goryeo Dynasty, where it was a dish for the royals and nobility. Its popularity soared as it spread to the masses, and today, it's a common street food found in markets and stalls throughout Korea, each region boasting its own unique twist to the recipe.

INGREDIENTS

- 1 cup sweet (glutinous) rice
- 2 cups pig's blood
- 8 ounces glass noodles (dangmyeon), soaked in water
- 1/2 cup finely chopped kimchi
- 1/2 pound ground pork
- 1/2 pound pork liver, finely chopped
- 1 onion, finely diced
- 4 garlic cloves, minced
- 2 teaspoons salt
- 1 teaspoon ground black pepper
- Hog casings, thoroughly rinsed and soaked
- Saltwater, for boiling
- Cooking twine, for tying

DIRECTIONS

1. Begin by preparing the sweet rice: rinse it under cold water until it runs clear. Cook the rice according to package instructions, and set aside to cool.
2. While the rice is cooking, prepare the glass noodles by soaking them in warm water until they're soft, then drain and cut into shorter lengths, about 2 inches long.
3. Combine the cooked sweet rice, soaked glass noodles, kimchi, ground pork, pork liver, onion, and garlic in a large mixing bowl. Add salt and pepper and mix thoroughly.
4. Pour the pig's blood into the mixture and stir until everything is evenly incorporated.
5. Prepare the hog casings by rinsing them inside out under cold running water. If they are too long, cut them into manageable lengths, approximately 12-15 inches.
6. Stuff the casings with the blood and rice mixture, being careful not to overfill to prevent bursting. Leave about an inch at both ends to tie them off with cooking twine securely.
7. In a large pot, bring saltwater to a gentle boil. Carefully add the filled sausages to the pot and let them cook for 20-30 minutes or until the sausages are firm to the touch.
8. Remove the soondae from the pot with a slotted spoon and let them rest on a paper towel to drain any excess moisture.
9. To serve, slice the soondae into bite-sized pieces and serve with a side of salted shrimp sauce or a soy sauce-based dipping sauce.

DIETARY MODIFICATIONS

Vegetarian: Replace the pork blood and meat with a pureed mixture of kidney beans for body and beet juice for color. Substitute mushrooms for the pork liver to maintain a meaty texture.

Vegan: Follow the vegetarian modifications and use a vegan kimchi (made without fish sauce). Consider adding more vegetables like carrots and spinach for additional nutrition and flavor.

Gluten-Free: Ensure that the glass noodles (dangmyeon) you purchase are certified gluten-free. Watch out for cross-contamination with other ingredients and check that your kimchi does not contain any gluten-based additives.

INGREDIENT SPOTLIGHT: PIG'S BLOOD

With a history deep-rooted in frugality and sustainability, pig's blood is an ingredient that has allowed many cultures around the world to use every part of the animal. Pig's blood is rich in protein and iron, making it nutritionally valuable. In soondae, the blood acts as a binding agent for the rice and noodles, contributing to the sausage's unique texture and flavor. It's a key ingredient that transforms soondae into an authentic Korean delicacy, distinguishing it from other sausages.

CHEF'S TIPS

- When handling the casings, being gentle to avoid tears is imperative. This will ensure that your sausages do not burst during the cooking process.
- The texture of the soondae filling before cooking should be wet but not too loose. If the mixture is too dry, the soondae can turn out tough, so adjust with a little water or blood if necessary.
- Boil the sausages at a low simmer to prevent the casings from rupturing due to high heat and to cook the filling evenly throughout.
- After boiling, cooling the soondae down quickly will also help firm up the texture. Consider transferring them to an ice bath before draining.

POSSIBLE VARIATIONS OF THE RECIPE

- **Spicy Soondae:** Add gochugaru (Korean red pepper flakes) or finely chopped fresh hot peppers into the filling for a spicy kick that will complement the savory flavors.
- **Seafood Soondae:** Instead of using pork, integrate finely chopped squid or octopus into the mixture for a seafood twist, which is particularly popular in coastal regions of Korea.
- **Herb-Infused Soondae:** Incorporate finely minced Korean herbs like perilla leaves, chives, or parsley for an aromatic version that's both traditional and refreshing.

HEALTH NOTE & CALORIC INFORMATION

Soondae is rich in protein and iron due to the pork blood and meat contents. The sweet rice and glass noodles add a carbohydrate component, making it energy-dense. Typically, one serving of soondae (100g) contains approximately 200-300 calories. However, given its nutritional makeup, it's best enjoyed in moderation, as part of a balanced diet.

DAKGANGJEONG

Dakgangjeong is a popular Korean dish known for its perfect blend of sweetness, crunchiness, and a touch of heat. This street-food favorite, typically found bustling in markets of Seoul, has been enjoyed for decades and has made its international mark, thanks to the worldwide love for Korean cuisine. The dish combines crispy fried chicken with a glossy, sweet, and spicy sauce, showcasing the harmony of textures and flavors quintessential to Korean cooking.

INGREDIENTS

- 500g boneless chicken thigh, cut into bite-sized pieces
- 1/2 cup cornstarch
- 1/4 cup all-purpose flour
- 1/2 teaspoon baking powder
- 1 egg
- Salt, to taste
- Ground black pepper, to taste
- Cooking oil, for frying

For the glaze:
- 1 tablespoon soy sauce
- 3 tablespoons ketchup
- 2 tablespoons honey
- 2 tablespoons brown sugar
- 1 tablespoon rice vinegar
- 3 cloves garlic, minced
- 1 teaspoon grated ginger
- 1 tablespoon gochujang (Korean red chili paste)
- 1 teaspoon sesame oil
- 1 tablespoon water

For garnish:
- Toasted sesame seeds
- Thinly sliced green onions

DIRECTIONS

1. In a large bowl, mix together the cornstarch, all-purpose flour, baking powder, salt, and pepper. Add the egg and chicken pieces, mixing well to coat.
2. Heat the oil in a deep fryer or large pan to 180°C (350°F). In batches, add the coated chicken pieces and fry until golden brown and fully cooked, about 6 to 8 minutes per batch. Use a thermometer to ensure that the internal temperature of the chicken reaches 75°C (165°F).
3. Remove the chicken from the oil and drain on paper towels. Allow the chicken to rest for a few minutes while you prepare the glaze.
4. For the glaze, combine the soy sauce, ketchup, honey, brown sugar, rice vinegar, minced garlic, grated ginger, gochujang, sesame oil, and water in a saucepan over medium heat. Stir continuously until the mixture comes to a boil and starts to thicken, about 5 minutes.
5. Reduce the heat to low and add the fried chicken to the glaze. Toss to coat all the pieces evenly.
6. Sprinkle with toasted sesame seeds and sliced green onions.
7. Serve immediately while hot and enjoy the sweet and crispy Dakgangjeong!

DIETARY MODIFICATIONS

Gluten-free: Replace all-purpose flour with gluten-free flour and use gluten-free soy sauce. Ensure that the gochujang and ketchup you select are certified gluten-free versions to accommodate this dietary need.

Vegetarian: Swap chicken for firm tofu or cauliflower. Press the tofu to remove excess moisture, or cut the cauliflower into bite-sized florets, and follow the same coating and frying steps.

Less sugar: Reduce the amount of honey and brown sugar by half for a less sweet version. Increased use of vinegar can provide additional tanginess to balance out the reduced sweetness.

INGREDIENT SPOTLIGHT: GOCHUJANG

Gochujang is a Korean red chili paste that is a staple in Korean cooking. Made from red chili powder, glutinous rice, fermented soybeans, and salt, this paste is aged over years, resulting in a complex flavor that is spicy, sweet, and deeply savory. Its role in creating the signature flavor of Dakgangjeong is indelible, contributing both heat and a subtle richness. It's also widely used in other Korean dishes, such as bibimbap and bulgogi, underscoring its versatility and importance in the cuisine.

CHEF'S TIPS

- Pat the chicken dry before coating to ensure the batter sticks better and results in a crisper texture.
- Allow the fried chicken to cool slightly before coating with the glaze; this helps retain the crispiness.
- Continuously stir the glaze as it cooks to prevent burning and ensure even thickening.
- To add a deeper flavor to the glaze, slightly caramelize the minced garlic and ginger before adding the other sauce ingredients.
- Serve Dakgangjeong immediately after tossing with the glaze to enjoy the maximum crunch.

POSSIBLE VARIATIONS OF THE RECIPE

- **Extra spicy:** Add more gochujang or a teaspoon of red pepper flakes to the glaze to turn up the heat for those who love a fierier taste.
- **Nutty flavor:** Garnish with chopped peanuts or almonds along with sesame seeds to add an earthy crunch.
- **Citrus twist:** Include a teaspoon of orange zest to the glaze for a fresh, citrusy undertone that pairs wonderfully with the sweet and spicy components.

HEALTH NOTE & CALORIC INFORMATION

Dakgangjeong is a high-calorie dish due to the fried chicken and sweet glaze. The chicken is a good source of protein, while the gochujang offers small amounts of vitamins and minerals. However, it is also high in sugars and fats, especially saturated fats from the frying process. The estimated calorie content for a standard serving size of Dakgangjeong is around 600-700 calories. It's recommended to enjoy this dish in moderation as part of a balanced diet.

NAENGMYEON

Originating from North Korea, Naengmyeon has become a summertime staple across the Korean Peninsula. With its roots in the mountainous regions, this cold dish provided a refreshing and nourishing meal that could offer relief from the oppressive heat. Its popularity soared following the Korean War, where it found its way into the hearts and stomachs of South Koreans.

INGREDIENTS

- 2 servings of naengmyeon noodles (buckwheat noodles)
- 4 cups beef or vegetable broth (chilled)
- 1/2 Asian pear, thinly sliced
- 1/2 cucumber, julienned
- 1 hard-boiled egg, halved
- 2 tablespoons pickled radish, thinly sliced
- 2 teaspoons sesame seeds
- Ice cubes

For the sauce:

- 2 tablespoons Korean hot pepper paste (gochujang)
- 1 tablespoon rice vinegar
- 1 tablespoon sugar
- 1 tablespoon sesame oil
- 1 clove garlic, minced
- 1 teaspoon soy sauce
- 1 teaspoon Korean mustard (gyeoja) or Dijon mustard (optional)

DIRECTIONS

1. Begin by preparing the naengmyeon noodles according to the package instructions. Frequently, this means bringing a large pot of water to a boil, adding the noodles, and cooking for 3-5 minutes until they are soft yet chewy.
2. Once cooked, promptly drain the noodles and rinse them under cold running water to stop the cooking process. This also removes excess starch from the noodles, improving their texture.
3. While the noodles cool, whisk together the ingredients for the sauce in a bowl. This mixture should be tangy, sweet, and slightly spicy. Adjust to taste if needed.
4. Take the chilled broth and pour it into serving bowls. It's important that the broth is cold to maintain the refreshing quality of the dish. Adding a few ice cubes to each bowl can enhance this effect.
5. Divide the rinsed noodles between the bowls, ensuring they are submerged in the broth. Then, artfully arrange the pear, cucumber, pickled radish, and half of a hard-boiled egg on top of the noodles in each bowl. Sprinkle sesame seeds over the ingredients for a nutty crunch.
6. Serve with the sauce on the side or drizzle it over the noodle bowls. Each diner can stir the sauce into their naengmyeon to their preferred taste.

DIETARY MODIFICATIONS

Vegetarian: Use vegetable broth instead of beef broth, and you might want to top with an extra serving of pear or radish for added substance.

Vegan: Follow the vegetarian modifications and substitute the hard-boiled egg with half an avocado for creaminess, or tofu for protein.

Gluten Intolerance: Make sure to use gluten-free noodles or buckwheat noodles that are certified gluten-free, and adjust the sauce ingredients to be gluten-free (many soy sauces contain gluten).

INGREDIENT SPOTLIGHT: NAENGMYEON

Buckwheat noodles, or naengmyeon, are the star of this dish. Despite its name, buckwheat is not a type of wheat but rather a fruit seed related to rhubarb and sorrel. This makes it naturally gluten-free, though it can be mixed with wheat in some products. Buckwheat has been cultivated in Korea for centuries and is celebrated for its high protein, fiber, and nutrient content—including manganese, copper, and magnesium. The chewy texture and subtle nutty flavor of the noodles make them uniquely suited for this cold dish.

CHEF'S TIPS

- Ensure the broth is well-seasoned and flavorful as it forms the base of the dish. Homemade broth is best, but a high-quality store-bought broth can work in a pinch.
- To get a perfectly hard-boiled egg, start with eggs in cold water, bring to a boil, then turn off the heat and let them sit for 10 minutes before cooling in ice water.
- For the best texture, don't overcook the noodles; they should be slightly chewy.
- Placing the cooked noodles in an ice bath after rinsing them can further improve their texture and temperature.
- If you like your naengmyeon spicy, adjust the amount of gochujang according to your taste.

POSSIBLE VARIATIONS OF THE RECIPE

- **Spicy Seafood Naengmyeon:** Top with thinly sliced octopus or shrimp for an ocean-inspired twist, and add a splash of seafood broth into the mix.
- **Kimchi Naengmyeon:** Include some chopped kimchi for a tangy, spicy kick that complements the cold noodles excellently.
- **Fruitier Naengmyeon:** Add slices of apple and bits of pineapple for a sweeter, more fruit-forward version of this classic dish.

HEALTH NOTE & CALORIC INFORMATION

Naengmyeon is a meal that's typically light in calories but satisfying due to the protein from the egg and nutrients from the vegetables. A typical serving with beef broth and added sauce has about 350-450 calories with moderate amounts of protein and low fat. Buckwheat noodles also offer a good source of complex carbohydrates and fibers. However, the sodium content can be high, especially if using a pre-made broth or extra sauce, so those monitoring salt intake should be mindful.

DOENJANG JJIGAE

Doenjang Jjigae is a staple in Korean cuisine, beloved for its deep and robust flavor. This traditional stew is typically made with fermented soybean paste (doenjang), vegetables, and often includes seafood or meat. It's a dish that is rooted in Korean history, with the fermentation methods dating back to the Three Kingdoms period (37 BC–668 AD). Originally, it was a way to preserve food and add nutrition during harsh winters. Today, it's enjoyed all year round and is revered for its comforting umami flavor.

INGREDIENTS

- 2 tablespoons doenjang (Korean soybean paste)
- 4 cups water or anchovy stock
- 200 grams tofu, cubed
- 1/2 zucchini, sliced into half-moons
- 1/2 onion, sliced
- 2 green onions, chopped
- 100 grams of fresh mushrooms (shiitake or oyster), sliced
- 1 hot green chili, sliced (optional)
- 1 hot red chili, sliced (optional)
- 2 cloves garlic, minced
- 1 tablespoon gochugaru (Korean red pepper flakes), optional
- 1 teaspoon sesame oil
- 1 teaspoon Korean fish sauce (optional)
- 100 grams of beef or seafood (such as shrimp or clams), optional

DIRECTIONS

1. If using anchovy stock, prepare it in advance by simmering dried anchovies and kelp in water for about 20 minutes. Strain and set aside.
2. In a large pot, gently dissolve doenjang in water or anchovy stock over medium heat. Avoid boiling to preserve the doenjang's flavor.
3. Add the garlic, onion, zucchini, mushrooms, and optional beef or seafood to the pot. Bring the mixture to a gentle boil, then reduce the heat to simmer.
4. Allow the stew to simmer for about 15 minutes, or until the vegetables are tender and the meat or seafood is fully cooked.
5. Add the tofu, green onions, and optional chili peppers and gochugaru to the pot. Simmer for an additional 5 minutes.
6. Finish the stew by stirring in sesame oil and optional Korean fish sauce for added depth.
7. Serve hot with a bowl of steamed rice and other banchan (side dishes) if desired.

DIETARY MODIFICATIONS

Vegetarian: Replace anchovy stock with vegetable broth and omit the fish sauce and optional meat/seafood. Add more vegetables like spinach or sweet potato.

Vegan: Follow the vegetarian modifications and ensure that the doenjang used does not contain any seafood-based ingredients, as some varieties may.

Gluten-Free: Use a gluten-free soybean paste and check the labels of any additional sauces (like fish sauce) to make sure they do not contain wheat or gluten.

INGREDIENT SPOTLIGHT: DOENJANG

Doenjang, the base ingredient in our recipe, has been a cornerstone in Korean cooking for centuries. This fermented soybean paste is similar to Japanese miso but often contains a mix of grains like wheat and has a distinct, punchy flavor profile that is richer and more complex. The fermentation process involves an age-old technique where soybeans are pounded, then compacted into blocks and aged, sometimes for years. The paste is packed with umami, enhancing the depth of stews, marinades, and sauces. Doenjang is not just a condiment but also a source of probiotics, vitamins, and minerals.

CHEF'S TIPS

- Use aged, high-quality doenjang for a deeper, more complex flavor.
- Gently simmer the stew instead of boiling to prevent the flavors of the doenjang from becoming too harsh.
- Adjust the thickness of the stew with water or stock to suit your taste; some prefer a heartier soup while others like it a bit thinner.
- Try using a stone pot (dolsot) to cook the stew if available, as it can enhance the stew's flavor and keep it hot when served.
- Experiment with additional ingredients such as potatoes, daikon radish, or different types of mushrooms to create variations of this classic dish.

POSSIBLE VARIATIONS OF THE RECIPE

- **Seafood Delight:** Incorporate a variety of seafood such as mussels, clams, squid, and shrimp for a rich ocean flavor.
- **Spicy Upgrade:** For those who enjoy a spicy kick, increase the amount of gochugaru or add slices of Korean hot peppers to the stew.
- **Meaty Twist:** Use chunks of pork belly or beef brisket for a heartier version that will satisfy meat lovers.

HEALTH NOTE & CALORIC INFORMATION

A serving of Doenjang Jjigae is relatively low in calories but high in nutrients. It provides a good amount of protein from tofu and the microbial benefits that come from fermented soybean paste. Depending on whether meat or seafood is added, and the type of stock used, a serving can range from 150-250 calories. The stew is also rich in B-vitamins, particularly B12 in the case of anchovy stock, and provides minerals such as calcium, iron, and potassium.

SSAMJANG

Ssamjang is a flavorful, thick, spicy paste used as a condiment in many Korean dishes, particularly in wraps (ssam). Its name translates to "wrap sauce," and it typically accompanies grilled meats, fresh leafy vegetables, and various side dishes in a Korean BBQ setting. The blend of fermented soybean paste (doenjang) and chili paste (gochujang) results in a savory, umami-rich, and slightly spicy taste that is distinctive to Korean cuisine. It is said that the harmony of these flavors enhances one's dining experience, adding depth to every bite.

INGREDIENTS

- 2 tablespoons doenjang (Korean fermented soybean paste)
- 1 tablespoon gochujang (Korean red chili paste)
- 1 tablespoon honey or brown sugar
- 1 tablespoon sesame oil
- 1 tablespoon rice wine (optional, for added depth)
- 2 cloves garlic, minced
- 2 teaspoons soy sauce
- 1 teaspoon sesame seeds, toasted
- 1 scallion, finely chopped
- 1 tablespoon finely chopped onion (optional, for a sweeter taste)

DIRECTIONS

1. In a small mixing bowl, combine the doenjang and gochujang until well incorporated.
2. Add the honey (or brown sugar) to the mixture and stir thoroughly.
3. Pour in the sesame oil and mix until the consistency becomes smooth and the oil is fully integrated.
4. (Optional) Add rice wine to the mixture and whisk it in for additional complexity in flavor.
5. Mince the garlic cloves finely and chop the scallion. Add both to the paste.
6. Stir in the soy sauce and mix everything until the sauce becomes homogenous.
7. Sprinkle toasted sesame seeds into the sauce and fold them in gently.
8. (Optional) For a touch of sweetness, mix in finely chopped onion.
9. Allow the ssamjang to sit for about 10 minutes to let the flavors meld together.
10. Serve as a condiment with lettuce wraps, grilled meats, or as a dipping sauce for vegetables.

DIETARY MODIFICATIONS

Vegetarian/Vegan: Substitute honey with maple syrup or agave nectar to keep the dish vegan-friendly, ensuring that the sweetener is plant-based.

Gluten-Free: Replace soy sauce with tamari or a certified gluten-free soy sauce to eliminate gluten from the recipe while maintaining the savory profile.

Low-Sodium: Use low-sodium soy sauce and consider making homemade doenjang and gochujang with less salt to control the overall sodium content in the sauce.

INGREDIENT SPOTLIGHT: DOENJANG

The spotlight ingredient for this recipe is doenjang, a quintessential Korean fermented soybean paste. It has been a staple in Korean cooking for centuries, traced back to the Three Kingdoms period (57 BC – 668 AD). Made from soybeans, salt, and water, it undergoes a fermentation process that can last several weeks to several years. The paste offers a deep, earthy flavor and is rich in umami, making it an essential ingredient in ssamjang. Doenjang is not only vital for the taste of ssamjang, but it also contains beneficial bacteria and is touted for its health properties.

CHEF'S TIPS

- For a smoother ssamjang, you can use a food processor to blend the ingredients.
- Letting the ssamjang rest overnight will enhance the flavors as they meld together.
- Gently toasting the sesame seeds before adding them increases their nutty aroma.
- Adjust the spice level by controlling the amount of gochujang added.
- The freshness of the garlic and scallions is key, so use them as fresh as possible for the best flavor.

POSSIBLE VARIATIONS OF THE RECIPE

- **Peanut Ssamjang:** Add a tablespoon of peanut butter for a nuttier version of the sauce. This addition makes for a creamier texture and a subtle sweetness that complements the savory flavors.
- **Seafood Ssamjang:** Mix in a tablespoon of finely minced raw shrimp or a teaspoon of anchovy paste to introduce a briny, seafood depth that's fantastic with grilled fish.
- **Citrusy Ssamjang:** Squeeze in the juice of half a lime or lemon for a refreshing twist on the classic, providing a zesty lift that's particularly good in summer.

HEALTH NOTE & CALORIC INFORMATION

Ssamjang is rich in protein and fiber due to the presence of soybeans in doenjang. With addition of sesame oil and seeds, it's also a good source of healthy fats. Moderation is key since it's a condiment with a high sodium content. One tablespoon of ssamjang typically contains around 25-35 calories, but this can vary based on modifications and serving size.

GLASS NOODLE STIR FRY

Japchae is a classic Korean dish with a history that dates back to the 17th century. It was first introduced to the Korean royal court by a palace chef named Lee Chung. The name "Japchae" literally means "mixed vegetables," but the dish has since evolved to include sweet potato starch noodles, known as dangmyeon, as a key ingredient. Traditionally served on special occasions and during the festive holidays, Japchae is a colorful and flavorful dish that represents the harmony of taste and texture, much beloved in Korean cuisine.

INGREDIENTS

- 150g sweet potato starch noodles (dangmyeon)
- 100g spinach, washed and trimmed
- 1 medium carrot, julienned
- 1 onion, thinly sliced
- 5 shiitake mushrooms, soaked if dried and sliced
- 150g beef (top sirloin or tenderloin), thinly sliced
- 2 garlic cloves, minced
- 3 tablespoons soy sauce
- 2 tablespoons sugar
- 2 tablespoons sesame oil
- Salt to taste
- Pepper to taste
- 1 tablespoon vegetable oil, for stir-frying
- 1 tablespoon toasted sesame seeds, for garnish
- 1 scallion, finely chopped, for garnish

DIRECTIONS

1. Soak the sweet potato starch noodles in warm water for about 20 minutes, until they start to soften. Drain and set aside.
2. Blanch spinach in boiling water for 30 seconds. Immediately refresh in icy water to stop the cooking process and retain the vibrant green color. Squeeze out excess water, season with a pinch of salt, and set aside.
3. Heat a teaspoon of vegetable oil in a pan over medium heat. Stir-fry the beef with half of the minced garlic until browned. Remove and set aside.
4. In the same pan, add another teaspoon of vegetable oil and stir-fry the onions and carrots until they begin to soften. Add the shiitake mushrooms and the remaining garlic, cooking until fragrant.
5. Bring a large pot of water to a boil. Cook the drained noodles for about 7 minutes or until they are soft and chewy. Drain and rinse under cold water.
6. In the empty noodle pot, combine soy sauce, sugar, and 1 tablespoon of sesame oil. Add the noodles and toss to coat them evenly with the sauce. Cook over low heat, stirring until heated through.
7. Add the spinach, beef, and stir-fried vegetables to the noodles, seasoning with salt and pepper to taste. Stir gently to combine all ingredients.
8. Drizzle the remaining sesame oil over the Japchae, toss once more, then transfer to a serving platter.
9. Garnish with toasted sesame seeds and finely chopped scallion before serving.

DIETARY MODIFICATIONS

Vegetarian: Replace beef with firm tofu or additional vegetables like colored bell peppers. Ensure to press the tofu to remove excess water and then slice it into thin strips before stir-frying.

Vegan: Follow the vegetarian modifications and also replace beef with extra veggies or tofu. Make sure your soy sauce is vegan, as some brands may use animal products in the fermentation process.

Gluten-Free: Use tamari or a certified gluten-free soy sauce instead of regular soy sauce to ensure the dish is gluten-free. Also, verify that the noodles are made purely from sweet potato starch, without any wheat additives.

INGREDIENT SPOTLIGHT: DANGMYEON

Sweet potato starch noodles, or dangmyeon, are the hallmark of Japchae. These transparent noodles become chewy and almost glass-like when cooked. They are made from sweet potato starch, offering a unique texture that is much appreciated in Korean cuisine. Originating from China, these noodles have been adapted into Korean gastronomy for centuries and are valued for their ability to absorb flavors while maintaining their springy texture. In Japchae, they provide a delightful contrast to the crunchy vegetables and savory meat.

CHEF'S TIPS

- Do not overcook the noodles; they should retain a slight chewiness.
- Refresh the blanched spinach in ice water immediately to keep a vibrant green color.
- Use a big pot when stir-frying to avoid overcrowding and ensure each ingredient cooks properly.
- If the noodles start to stick while stir-frying, a splash of water can help loosen them.
- Balance the seasoning as you go; the dish should have a harmonious flavor of sweet, savory, and nutty notes.

POSSIBLE VARIATIONS OF THE RECIPE

- **Seafood Japchae:** Add sautéed shrimp or squid instead of beef for a pescatarian version. Ensure seafood is cooked just until done to prevent chewiness.
- **Spicy Japchae:** Introduce a spicy element by adding gochujang (Korean red chili paste) or slices of fresh red chili during the stir-frying process.
- **Cold Japchae Salad:** Serve the Japchae at room temperature or chilled for a refreshing noodle salad; adjust the seasoning accordingly as cold dishes can taste less flavorful.

HEALTH NOTE & CALORIC INFORMATION

Japchae is a balanced dish combining carbohydrates from the noodles, protein from the beef, and nutrients from the assortment of vegetables. A typical serving contains approximately 350-400 calories, with a mix of macronutrients conducive to energy sustenance. However, because of the added sugar and sesame oil, those watching their fat and sugar intake should enjoy this dish in moderation.

HOMEMADE MAKGEOLLI

Makgeolli is a traditional Korean rice wine that dates back to the 10th century Goryeo Dynasty. This milky, off-white, and lightly sparkling alcoholic beverage is made from rice or wheat mixed with nuruk, a Korean fermentation starter. It's a drink often enjoyed during farming seasons and has gained popularity for its unique taste and artisanal brewing processes. Makgeolli is deeply embedded in Korean culture and is making a resurgence as a trendy, craft beverage around the world.

INGREDIENTS

- 2 cups sweet rice (also known as glutinous rice)
- Water, for soaking and steaming rice
- 1 cup of nuruk (Korean fermentation starter)
- 4 cups of filtered water (for mixing)
- 1/2 cup sugar (optional, for sweeter taste)

DIRECTIONS

1. Rinse the sweet rice under cold water until the water runs clear, then soak the rice in water for at least 8 hours, or overnight. This process is essential for achieving the proper texture and ensuring the rice cooks evenly.
2. After soaking, drain the rice and place it in a steamer. Steam the rice for about 40 minutes or until the grains are tender but still chewy.
3. Let the steamed rice cool down to room temperature. It is crucial that the rice is not too hot to prevent killing the fermentation microorganisms.
4. In a large, clean container, mix the nuruk with 4 cups of filtered water, stirring until well combined.
5. Add the cooked rice to the nuruk mixture. Mix thoroughly with clean hands or a wooden spoon to ensure that the rice and nuruk are well combined.
6. Cover the container with a breathable cloth and secure it with a rubber band or string. This will allow airflow while keeping out contaminants.
7. Allow the mixture to ferment at room temperature (around 20°C or 68°F) for about 7 to 10 days. Stir the mixture once a day to prevent mold from forming and to equally distribute yeast and bacteria.
8. After the fermentation period, the makgeolli will separate into a clear liquid on top and rice sediment at the bottom. Stir the mixture and then strain it through a cheesecloth into a clean bottle or container.
9. For a sweeter taste, dissolve the sugar in some makgeolli and add it to the strained brew, adjusting to your preference.
10. Chill the bottled makgeolli in the refrigerator for at least a day before serving. It can be enjoyed cold and shaken, or still, with the clear liquid poured off the sediment.

DIETARY MODIFICATIONS

For those with a diabetic condition: Replace the optional sugar with a diabetic-friendly sweetener and adjust the amount to keep the carbohydrate content in check. Be sure to monitor blood sugar levels as alcohol can affect them.

Gluten-free: Makgeolli is naturally gluten-free as it is made from rice. Ensure the nuruk used does not contain any wheat or barley to avoid cross-contamination.

Low-calorie: Skip adding additional sugar to reduce the calorie count. Makgeolli has a gentle sweetness from the rice itself, which might suffice for someone looking for a low-calorie option.

INGREDIENT SPOTLIGHT: NURUK

The spotlight ingredient for makgeolli is "nuruk," a fermentation starter unique to Korea. Nuruk is a dry, cake-like product made from grains that have been inoculated with wild yeasts and beneficial molds. It's the source of the enzymes needed to break starches into sugars and for fermentation. The biodiversity in nuruk can provide a complex flavor profile and it has been used for centuries in traditional Korean alcohol production. It's key to the recipe because it initiates the fermentation process that transforms rice into the signature, lightly effervescent beverage.

CHEF'S TIPS

- Ensure all equipment is sterilized before use to prevent unwanted bacteria from spoiling your batch.
- The quality of water is important in brewing. Use filtered or bottled water if tap water has a high chlorine content or additives.
- Maintain consistent room temperature during fermentation. Temperature fluctuations can affect the microbes and change the flavor profile.
- Taste the makgeolli at different stages to better understand the fermentation process and decide how sour you prefer your brew.
- When serving, consider leaving the sediment behind for a clearer drink, or shake it up if you prefer a fuller, more robust texture.

POSSIBLE VARIATIONS OF THE RECIPE

- **Fruity Makgeolli:** Infuse the makgeolli with fresh fruit, like strawberries or peaches, during the second fermentation for a refreshing twist.
- **Sparkling Makgeolli:** Bottle the makgeolli with a bit of the rice sediment and a teaspoon of sugar to create more natural carbonation for a bubbly experience.
- **Herbal Makgeolli:** Add traditional Korean medicinal herbs such as ginseng or goji berries to the fermentation process for an earthy, health-enhancing flavor.

HEALTH NOTE & CALORIC INFORMATION

Each serving of homemade makgeolli typically contains about 150-200 calories, with 5-8% alcohol by volume. The calorie count can vary depending on the sugar content and the length of the fermentation, which affects residual sugars. It's also a source of dietary fiber and beneficial bacteria from the fermentation process. However, like all alcoholic beverages, it should be enjoyed in moderation due to its alcohol content.

HAEJANGGUK

Haejangguk, which literally means "soup to chase a hangover," is a staple in Korean cuisine, historically enjoyed in the morning after a night of heavy drinking. With its roots in the Joseon Dynasty, it's said that Korean ancestors concocted this hearty soup to rejuvenate and revitalise oneself. There are many regional variations, but most are united by their rich, meaty broths and restorative properties.

INGREDIENTS

- 500g beef brisket
- 8 cups water
- 2 large scallions, chopped
- 1 piece kombu (dried kelp), approx. 10cm
- 200g napa cabbage kimchi, chopped
- 1 tablespoon gochugaru (Korean red pepper flakes)
- 4 cloves garlic, minced
- 1 tablespoon soy sauce
- 1 teaspoon sesame oil
- 100g bean sprouts
- 100g enoki mushrooms
- 2 tablespoons doenjang (Korean fermented soybean paste)
- 1 tablespoon gochujang (Korean red pepper paste)
- Salt and pepper to taste
- Cooked rice, for serving
- 2 eggs (optional, for serving)
- Seaweed and sesame seeds (optional, for garnish)

DIRECTIONS

1. Begin by placing the beef brisket in a large pot with 8 cups of water. Bring to a boil, then reduce the heat to a simmer, skimming any foam or impurities that rise to the surface.
2. Add the scallions and kombu to the pot. Let the broth simmer gently, covered, for about 1.5 hours or until the meat is tender. Remove the kombu after 15 minutes to prevent the broth from becoming too bitter.
3. Once the brisket is tender, remove it from the broth, let it cool slightly, then slice into bite-sized pieces. Set aside.
4. In the same pot with the broth, add the chopped kimchi, gochugaru, minced garlic, soy sauce, and sesame oil. Stir well to combine.
5. Bring the soup to a gentle boil, then add the bean sprouts and enoki mushrooms. Cook for another 5-10 minutes.
6. Stir in the doenjang and gochujang until fully dissolved and let the soup simmer for an additional 10 minutes, allowing the flavors to meld together. Adjust the seasoning with salt and pepper.
7. If desired, fry or poach eggs to top each serving of the soup.
8. To serve, ladle the soup into bowls, ensuring each has a good portion of meat, vegetables, and broth. Add a serving of cooked rice to each bowl if desired.
9. Garnish with the sliced brisket, cooked egg, seaweed, and sesame seeds.

DIETARY MODIFICATIONS

Vegetarian: Replace the beef brisket with firm tofu sliced into bite-sized pieces and use vegetable broth instead of water. You can skip the kombu or add it as per the original recipe.

Vegan: Along with the vegetarian substitutions, omit the eggs and ensure that the kimchi used is vegan (traditional kimchi contains fish sauce). Use mushroom soy sauce instead of regular soy sauce for an added umami flavor.

Gluten-Free: Ensure the doenjang and gochujang are certified gluten-free. Replace soy sauce with tamari, which is a gluten-free soy sauce alternative.

INGREDIENT SPOTLIGHT: KOMBU

Kombu is a type of kelp and a cornerstone of many Asian broths, imparting a subtle umami flavor essential to the depth of the dish. Korean cooking often makes use of kombu in simmering broths, contributing to the complexity of flavors. It's believed to have been introduced to Korea through Japan, where it's a key ingredient in dashi. Rich in minerals, it's not only a flavor enhancer but also touted for its health benefits. Kombu should be removed after a short simmer to avoid bitterness and to capture its essence without overpowering the broth.

CHEF'S TIPS

- Always skim off the impurities that rise to the top when boiling the meat to ensure a clear broth.
- Incorporate the seasoning pastes gradually, tasting as you go, to find the right balance between spicy, savory, and salty.
- Cooking the eggs separately and adding them just before serving helps keep the yolk runny, providing a rich texture to the soup.
- If the soup is too spicy, add a small amount of sugar to balance the heat.
- For a less fatty soup, cool the broth after the initial boil and skim off the solidified fat before reheating and continuing with the recipe.

POSSIBLE VARIATIONS OF THE RECIPE

- **Seafood Haejangguk:** Switch the beef brisket with seafood such as shrimp, clams, or squid and use a seafood or anchovy broth for a pescatarian-friendly version.
- **Cold Weather Comfort:** Add hearty vegetables like potatoes and carrots, and simmer until tender for an extra comforting winter variation.
- **Spicy Lover's Dream:** Introduce additional heat by adding more gochugaru, fresh hot peppers, or even a dash of Korean chili oil for those who love extra spice.

HEALTH NOTE & CALORIC INFORMATION

A bowl of Haejangguk is a nutritious meal, packed with protein from the beef, probiotics from the kimchi, and a range of vitamins and minerals from the vegetables. The exact caloric content can vary, but a typical serving is around 400-500 calories. This soup is also high in sodium due to the soybean pastes and soy sauce; for those watching their intake, low-sodium alternatives can be used.

SEOLLEONGTANG

Seolleongtang is a milky-white Korean soup made from ox bones, brisket, and various cuts of beef, simmered over a low flame for several hours. The origins of this dish trace back to the Joseon Dynasty when it was part of a royal cuisine. Nowadays, it is a beloved comfort food commonly enjoyed during cold seasons and known for its nourishing qualities.

INGREDIENTS

- 2 kg beef leg bones
- 300 grams beef brisket
- Water, enough to cover the bones
- 2 whole onions, peeled
- 1 whole garlic bulb, halved horizontally
- 10 black peppercorns
- Salt, to taste
- Long green onions, thinly sliced for garnish
- Cooked rice or noodles, optional

DIRECTIONS

1. Soak the beef bones in cold water for 1-2 hours to remove any blood, changing the water a few times.
2. Place the beef bones in a large stockpot and fill it with water until the bones are fully submerged. Bring to a rapid boil for 10 minutes, then drain and rinse the bones to remove any impurities.
3. Refill the pot with fresh water, re-add the bones, beef brisket, whole onions, garlic bulb, and black peppercorns. Bring to a boil, skim off any froth or excess fat that rises to the surface.
4. Reduce the heat to very low, cover with a lid slightly ajar, and simmer the soup for at least 6 hours; the longer, the better. Add water as necessary to keep the bones covered.
5. Remove the meat and strain the broth through a fine-mesh sieve. Discard the solids.
6. When the brisket is cool enough to handle, slice it into thin pieces, and set aside.
7. Season the strained broth with salt to taste. Return the brisket slices to the broth to warm through.
8. Serve the soup hot, garnished with sliced green onions. Optionally, add cooked rice or noodles to the bowl before ladling in the soup.

DIETARY MODIFICATIONS

Vegetarian: Use a rich vegetable stock and include umami-rich ingredients like shiitake mushrooms and seaweed. Replace the beef with tofu or jackfruit for added texture.

Vegan: Follow the vegetarian modifications and ensure all accompaniments like noodles or rice are vegan-friendly. Use soy sauce or tamari to season instead of salt for a deeper flavor.

Low Sodium: Do not add salt to the broth to achieve a lower sodium content. Instead, offer soy sauce or salt on the side for individuals to season their soup according to their dietary needs.

INGREDIENT SPOTLIGHT: BEEF LEG BONES

Beef leg bones are the cornerstone of seolleongtang. They are rich in collagen, which breaks down during the long simmering process to create the soup's characteristic milky consistency. This collagen is also believed to offer health benefits, such as improving skin elasticity and joint health. Cooking the bones for an extended period is what delivers the deep flavor and nutritional benefits that seolleongtang is known for.

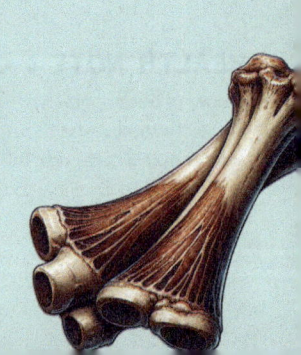

CHEF'S TIPS

- Rinse the leg bones thoroughly after the initial boil to ensure a clear broth.
- Maintain a low and steady simmer to prevent emulsifying the fat into the broth, which can make it cloudy.
- Regularly skim the broth during the initial stages of simmering for a cleaner flavor profile.
- Simmering for an extended period (up to 24 hours) will result in a richer and more gelatinous broth.
- Chill the soup after the first cooking to solidify the fat, making it easier to remove, for those who prefer a less greasy soup.

POSSIBLE VARIATIONS OF THE RECIPE

- **Spicy Version:** Serve with Korean chili flakes or chili oil on the side for diners to spice up their bowl to taste.
- **Herbal Infusion:** Add medicinal herbs like ginseng and jujube during the simmering process to infuse additional flavors believed to boost health.
- **Mild and Creamy:** Stir in a few tablespoons of ground sesame seeds or add a dash of milk to make the broth even creamier and milder in taste.

HEALTH NOTE & CALORIC INFORMATION

Seolleongtang is low in carbohydrates but high in protein. It is rich in collagen and can be a beneficial part of a balanced diet. The exact calorie content can vary, but a typical serving without rice or noodles can contain approximately 150-250 calories per bowl, with the majority of the calories coming from the protein in the beef. The fat content can be controlled by removing the solidified fat after chilling, if preferred.

GAMJATANG

Gamjatang, which means "potato stew," actually focuses on tender pork spine bones rather than potatoes. This iconic Korean dish dates back to the Joseon Dynasty and was particularly popular among laborers due to its hearty and nourishing qualities. The spicy, rich broth is packed with flavors from a variety of unique Korean ingredients and has become a beloved comfort food, often enjoyed late at night or after drinking.

INGREDIENTS

For the Pork Bone Broth:
- 1.5 kg pork neck bones
- 12 cups water
- 1 medium onion
- 4 cloves garlic
- 2 green onions
- 1 thumb-sized piece ginger, sliced

For the Spice Paste:
- 1/4 cup Korean red pepper flakes (gochugaru)
- 1 tablespoon soybean paste (doenjang)
- 1 tablespoon fish sauce
- 1 tablespoon minced garlic
- 1 tablespoon grated ginger
- 1 teaspoon ground black pepper

For the Soup:
- 2 medium potatoes, peeled and cut into large chunks
- 2 perilla leaves, chopped (optional)
- 1/2 napa cabbage, cut into bite-sized pieces
- 2 green onions, chopped
- 1/2 cup Korean wild sesame leaves (perilla/sesame leaves), chopped
- 4 cups of water or use broth from above

Garnish:
- 2 green onions, chopped
- 1 tablespoon wild sesame seeds (deulkkae)

DIRECTIONS

1. Begin by thoroughly rinsing the pork neck bones under cold water. This helps to remove any bone fragments and blood.
2. In a large pot, place the cleaned bones and cover with cold water. Bring to a boil and blanch for about 10 minutes. This will help remove impurities. Afterward, drain and rinse the bones and clean the pot.
3. Return the bones to the pot, add 12 cups of water, onion (halved), 4 cloves of garlic, green onions, and sliced ginger. Bring to a boil, then reduce heat to a simmer. Cover and cook for at least 1 hour to extract a rich, flavorful broth. Alternatively, use a pressure cooker to reduce cooking time.
4. While the broth cooks, prepare the spice paste. In a bowl, mix together Korean red pepper flakes, soybean paste, fish sauce, minced garlic, grated ginger, and ground black pepper.
5. Once the broth has finished simmering, strain it to remove the bones and vegetables. Skim off any excess fat.
6. Return the clear broth to the pot. Add the spice paste and dissolve it into the broth over medium heat.
7. Add the potatoes to the broth and cook until they start to soften.
8. Add the pork bones back into the soup with napa cabbage, chopped perilla leaves, chopped green onions, and Korean wild sesame leaves.
9. Let the soup simmer for an additional 15 to 20 minutes or until the vegetables are tender and the meat is falling off the bones.
10. Taste and adjust seasoning as needed with additional salt, pepper, or fish sauce.
11. Serve hot, garnished with more green onions and a sprinkle of wild sesame seeds.

DIETARY MODIFICATIONS

Vegetarian: Replace pork bones with a variety of mushrooms such as shiitake, enoki, and oyster to mimic the savory depth. Use vegetable broth instead of water and add a tablespoon of miso paste to enhance umami flavor.

Gluten-Free: Ensure that the soybean paste and fish sauce used are certified gluten-free. Alternatively, use tamari or a gluten-free soy sauce as a substitute for the soybean paste.

Low Fat: For a less fatty version, prepare the broth a day ahead and chill. Once chilled, remove the solidified fat on top of the broth before reheating and continuing with the rest of the recipe.

INGREDIENT SPOTLIGHT: GOCHUGARU

Korean red pepper flakes, or gochugaru, are essential to this recipe for their distinctive sweet, smoky heat and vibrant color. Typically sun-dried and made from Korean red chili peppers, gochugaru has a unique flavor profile unlike other chili powders, and it provides the characteristic spice found in many Korean dishes. Originating from the Korean practice of kimchi making, it has become indispensable in the country's culinary landscape.

CHEF'S TIPS

- Soaking the pork bones in cold water before cooking can help to pull out even more impurities for a cleaner broth.
- If you have time, simmer the broth longer than 1 hour, up to 3 hours, for a deeper taste.
- The spice paste's flavors are best when they have time to meld into the broth, so don't rush this step.
- Adjust spiciness to suit your preference by controlling the amount of gochugaru.
- If desired, you can add additional vegetables such as mushrooms or leeks for more layers of flavor.

POSSIBLE VARIATIONS OF THE RECIPE

- **Seafood Gamjatang:** Use seafood stock and add shrimp, mussels, and clams for a pescatarian variation.
- **Spicy Pork Gamjatang:** Substitute beef short ribs for pork and add red beans for a hearty beefy version.
- **Mild Chicken Gamjatang:** Use chicken thighs instead of pork, and reduce the amount of gochugaru for a milder, child-friendly version.

HEALTH NOTE & CALORIC INFORMATION

A serving of Gamjatang is rich in protein due to the pork bones and contains a moderate amount of carbohydrates from the potatoes. The soup is relatively high in sodium, particularly from added condiments like fish sauce and soybean paste, so those watching their sodium intake should temper these ingredients accordingly. An estimated calorie content for a serving would be approximately 400-500 calories, depending on the size of the serving and the amount of meat on the bones.

GOCHUJANG EGGPLANT

Gochujang, a staple of Korean cuisine, is renowned for its complex heat and deep umami flavors. It's traditionally made by fermenting chili, glutinous rice, fermented soybeans, and salt. This recipe transforms the simple eggplant into a global delight, showcasing the versatility of gochujang beyond Korean dishes.

INGREDIENTS

- 2 medium-sized eggplants
- 2 tablespoons gochujang (Korean red chili paste)
- 1 tablespoon soy sauce
- 1 tablespoon honey
- 2 teaspoons sesame oil
- 1 teaspoon rice vinegar
- 3 cloves garlic, minced
- 1 inch piece of ginger, grated
- 2 tablespoons vegetable oil
- 1 teaspoon toasted sesame seeds
- 2 green onions, sliced for garnish
- Salt to taste

DIRECTIONS

1. Preheat the oven to 400°F (200°C).
2. Wash the eggplants and cut them in half lengthwise. Score the flesh in a diamond pattern, being careful not to pierce the skin.
3. In a bowl, mix together gochujang, soy sauce, honey, sesame oil, and rice vinegar. Stir in minced garlic and grated ginger until well combined to form the glaze.
4. Brush the eggplants with vegetable oil and season with a pinch of salt.
5. Place the eggplant halves, cut-side up, on a baking sheet lined with parchment paper.
6. Generously brush the gochujang glaze over the eggplant.
7. Bake in the preheated oven for 25-30 minutes, or until the eggplant is soft and the glaze has caramelized.
8. Remove from the oven and sprinkle with toasted sesame seeds and sliced green onions.
9. Serve warm as a side dish or a main course with rice or noodles.

DIETARY MODIFICATIONS

Vegetarian/Vegan: Swap honey for agave syrup or maple syrup to cater to vegan diets without losing the sweet balance in the glaze.

Gluten-Free: Use tamari or a certified gluten-free soy sauce instead of regular soy sauce to accommodate a gluten-free diet without compromising on the savory aspect of the dish.

Low-Sugar: Reduce the overall sugar content by using a sugar substitute like stevia in place of honey, adjusting the quantity to taste as stevia is sweeter.

INGREDIENT SPOTLIGHT: GOCHUJANG

Gochujang is a bold, fermented condiment that has been a cornerstone in Korean cooking for centuries. The fermentation process gives it a complex flavor profile—spicy, sweet, and savory. Made from chili powder, glutinous rice, fermented soybeans, and salt, gochujang provides a distinct pungency that enhances the taste of any dish it graces. It's often used in marinades, stews, sauces, and tableside condiments. Essential to this recipe, gochujang brings a harmonious balance of flavor and heat that infuses the eggplant with a memorable kick.

CHEF'S TIPS

- Ensure that the eggplant is scored deeply to allow the gochujang glaze to penetrate for maximum flavor.
- For a smokier taste, finish the eggplant by broiling on high for the last 2-3 minutes of cooking.
- If you prefer a less spicy dish, mix the gochujang with a bit more honey and sesame oil.
- Allow the eggplant to rest for a few minutes after coming out of the oven; this helps the glaze to thicken and adhere better.
- Store leftover gochujang in the refrigerator well-sealed; it keeps well for months and can be used in a variety of other recipes.

POSSIBLE VARIATIONS OF THE RECIPE

- **Stir-Fry Twist:** Cube the eggplant and stir-fry with the glaze, adding bell peppers and onions for a quick, savory side dish.
- **Grilled Version:** Slice the eggplant, grill until charred, then brush with the gochujang glaze for a barbeque touch.
- **Meaty Match:** Top the glazed eggplant with stir-fried ground pork or beef for an extra protein-packed dish.

HEALTH NOTE & CALORIC INFORMATION

Eggplant is high in fiber and contains important vitamins and minerals like vitamin C, potassium, and magnesium. Gochujang, while high in flavor, is also high in sodium, so it's best used in moderation, especially for those on sodium-restricted diets. A single serving of this dish (without rice or noodles) contains approximately 200 calories, with the caveat that larger eggplants contain more calories. This recipe is also naturally low in saturated fat, depending on the type of vegetable oil used.

KIMCHI BOKKEUMBAP

Kimchi bokkeumbap, a popular comfort food, is a Korean culinary treasure showcasing the vibrant flavors of fermented vegetables. Dating back to when people sought resourceful ways to use leftover food, this dish transforms day-old rice and the nation's beloved kimchi into a sizzling, satisfying meal. Its ease of preparation has made it a go-to dish for home cooks and a favorite among those looking to experience the essence of Korean flavors.

INGREDIENTS

- 2 cups cooked rice, preferably a day old
- 1 cup kimchi, chopped
- 1/2 cup kimchi juice
- 200g pork belly, diced (optional)
- 2 tablespoons gochujang (Korean red pepper paste)
- 1 tablespoon soy sauce
- 1 tablespoon sesame oil
- 2 tablespoons vegetable oil
- 3 cloves garlic, minced
- 1/2 onion, diced
- 2 green onions, sliced
- 1 teaspoon sugar (optional)
- 1 tablespoon toasted sesame seeds
- 2 eggs (for topping, fried or raw depending on preference)
- Salt and pepper, to taste

DIRECTIONS

1. Heat the vegetable oil in a large pan or wok over medium heat.
2. Add the diced pork belly (if using) and cook until it starts becoming crispy.
3. Add the minced garlic and diced onion to the pan and sauté until the onion turns translucent.
4. Stir in the chopped kimchi and cook for another 2-3 minutes until it is heated through and slightly softened.
5. Add the rice, breaking up any lumps with a spatula, and stir well to combine with the kimchi mixture.
6. Pour in the kimchi juice, gochujang, soy sauce, sugar (if using), and a sprinkle of salt and pepper. Mix thoroughly, ensuring each grain of rice is coated with the seasoning.
7. Cook for another 5-7 minutes, frequently stirring, until the rice has taken on a uniform color and the bottom begins to crisp slightly.
8. Drizzle sesame oil over the rice and add the sliced green onions, stirring them in for a final minute of cooking.
9. Taste and adjust seasoning with salt, pepper, or more soy sauce if needed.
10. Serve hot, topped with a fried or raw egg and a sprinkle of toasted sesame seeds.

DIETARY MODIFICATIONS

Vegetarian: Omit the pork belly and use a substitute like diced tofu or mushrooms to add some protein and texture to the dish. Fry the substitute first to develop a golden crust before proceeding with the recipe.

Vegan: Follow the vegetarian modifications and replace the eggs with pan-fried cubes of firm tofu or a vegan egg substitute. Ensure the kimchi used is vegan, as some varieties contain fish sauce.

Gluten-Free: Substitute the soy sauce with tamari or a gluten-free soy sauce alternative, and ensure the gochujang and kimchi are labeled gluten-free, as they can sometimes contain wheat or barley.

INGREDIENT SPOTLIGHT: KIMCHI

Kimchi, the heart of this recipe, is a Korean staple made from salted and fermented vegetables, most commonly napa cabbage and Korean radishes, with a variety of seasonings, including chili powder, scallions, garlic, and ginger. It dates back to ancient times, providing essential vitamins during the winter months. Its distinct tang and depth of flavor are key components in kimchi fried rice, offering probiotics and a spicy kick. The fermentation process not only develops its unique taste but also enhances its nutritional value, making kimchi a beloved ingredient well beyond Korea's borders.

CHEF'S TIPS

- Use day-old rice that has been refrigerated as it has less moisture, which is essential for achieving the perfect texture in fried rice.
- Adjust the heat level of the dish by adding more or less gochujang and consider adding Korean chili flakes for an extra kick.
- To get the characteristic 'crunch' at the bottom of the fried rice, press the rice firmly into the pan and let it sit undisturbed for a minute before stirring.
- If adding pork belly, render the fat out slowly on low-medium heat for a crispier and more flavorful addition.
- When topping with a raw egg, use fresh, high-quality eggs to minimize the risk of salmonella contamination and ensure the best flavor.

POSSIBLE VARIATIONS OF THE RECIPE

- **Seafood Twist:** Add shrimp, squid, or both when cooking the pork belly (or as a replacement) to introduce a seafood variant that complements the kimchi flavors.
- **Extra Vegetables:** For a more balanced meal, stir-fry vegetables such as carrots, bell peppers, or zucchini with the onion and garlic.
- **Cheese-topped:** Sprinkle grated mozzarella or cheddar cheese over the fried rice just before serving and cover or broil until the cheese melts for a gooey, indulgent finish.

HEALTH NOTE & CALORIC INFORMATION

Kimchi fried rice is a calorie-dense meal, primarily from the rice and added fats like oil and pork belly. A single serving without the optional pork and with one fried egg can contain approximately 400 to 600 calories, depending on portion sizes and specific ingredients used. Kimchi adds vitamins A and C, while the rice provides carbohydrates for energy. The dish can be high in sodium due to kimchi, soy sauce, and added salt; moderation is key to maintain a balanced diet.

KONGGUKSU

Kongguksu is a chilled, refreshing noodle soup perfect for hot summer days, hailing from Korea. The dish consists of wheat noodles in a rich, nutty broth made from ground soybeans. Its origins can be traced back to the Joseon Dynasty, and it's known for its cooling properties and nutritional benefits. Kongguksu captures the simplicity of Korean culinary traditions, focusing on the flavor and wholesomeness of its few but hearty ingredients.

INGREDIENTS

- 200g dried wheat noodles (somyeon)
- 1 cup dried soybeans
- 6 cups water (for boiling soybeans)
- Salt to taste
- 1/2 cucumber, julienned
- 2 tomatoes, sliced (optional)
- 1/2 teaspoon roasted sesame seeds (optional)
- Ice cubes

DIRECTIONS

1. Soak the dried soybeans in water overnight, or for at least 8 hours, to soften them.
2. Drain the soybeans and peel off the skins. This can be time-consuming but contributes to a smoother soup.
3. In a large pot, bring 6 cups of water to a boil and cook the soybeans until they are completely tender, about 10 minutes.
4. Drain the soybeans, reserving the cooking liquid, and let them cool to room temperature.
5. Blend the cooked soybeans with enough reserved liquid to create a milk-like consistency. This may need to be done in batches.
6. Season the soybean milk with salt to taste. Place the milk in the refrigerator to cool while you prepare the other components.
7. Boil water in a large pot and cook the wheat noodles until al dente, usually about 3-5 minutes. Drain and rinse under cold water to stop the cooking process. Make sure to drain the noodles thoroughly.
8. Divide the noodles into serving bowls. Pour the chilled soybean milk over the noodles and add ice cubes to keep the soup cold.
9. Garnish the bowls with julienned cucumbers, tomato slices, and a sprinkle of roasted sesame seeds.

DIETARY MODIFICATIONS

For gluten-free: Use gluten-free noodles made from rice or buckwheat instead of wheat noodles.
For soy allergies: Replace soybeans with soaked and blended almonds or cashews to make a nut milk broth as an alternative, adjusting the salt accordingly.
For added protein (vegan): Include cubed tofu or hemp seeds as garnish to increase protein content without deviating from the vegan nature of the dish.

INGREDIENT SPOTLIGHT: SOYBEANS

Soybeans are the star of kongguksu. They have been a staple in Asian diets for thousands of years, providing an excellent source of protein, fiber, and vitamins. Soybeans can be processed in numerous ways, leading to products like tofu, soy milk, and tempeh. In kongguksu, soybeans are celebrated in their simplest form—blended into a creamy, milk-like consistency that forms the base of this wholesome soup.

CHEF'S TIPS

- When peeling soybeans, gently squeeze the beans between your fingers, and the skins should slip off.
- Ensure the soybean milk is silky smooth by blending for several minutes and straining if necessary.
- Chill the soy milk thoroughly before serving; this soup is best enjoyed when it's cold.
- Keep the noodles and soup separate until just before serving to prevent the noodles from absorbing the soup and becoming soggy.
- Experiment with the thickness of the soy milk to find your preferred consistency—some like it thin and refreshing, others creamy and rich.

POSSIBLE VARIATIONS OF THE RECIPE

- **Spicy version:** Add a drizzle of Korean chili oil or a sprinkle of gochugaru (red chili flakes) for a spicy kick.
- **Flavor twist:** Infuse the soy milk with aromatic ingredients such as ginger or garlic while blending for additional depth.
- **Garnish change-up:** Top with thinly sliced radish, a boiled egg cut in half, or fresh herbs like cilantro for different textures and flavors.

HEALTH NOTE & CALORIC INFORMATION

A typical serving of Kongguksu contains high-quality plant protein from the soybeans, complex carbohydrates from the noodles, and is low in fat. The dish also provides dietary fiber and is rich in various essential vitamins and minerals. It is naturally vegan and cholesterol-free. The calorie content for one serving of kongguksu is approximately 450 kcal.

YAKGWA

Yakgwa, meaning "medicinal confectionery," is a traditional Korean sweet treat often served during special occasions such as Korean Thanksgiving (Chuseok) and weddings. These deep-fried delights date back to the Goryeo Dynasty and carry a history of being offered in ancestral rites. Made with a dough of wheat flour, honey, sesame oil, and ginger juice, Yakgwa are not only scrumptious but were also believed to possess health benefits. Their unique texture — crispy on the outside and tender within — makes them an enduring favorite.

INGREDIENTS

- 2 cups wheat flour
- 1/3 cup sesame oil
- 1/2 cup honey, for the dough
- 1/4 cup ginger juice (from grated and strained fresh ginger)
- 1/2 cup soju or rice wine
- 1/2 cup pine nuts for garnish (optional)
- Vegetable oil for deep frying
- 1 cup honey, for glaze
- 2 tablespoons water, for glaze
- 1 teaspoon cinnamon powder, for garnish

DIRECTIONS

1. In a large mixing bowl, combine the wheat flour and sesame oil, rubbing them between your hands until the mixture is crumbly and well incorporated.
2. In another small bowl, mix the 1/2 cup honey, ginger juice, and soju. Pour this mixture into the flour and sesame oil blend, stirring until a smooth, pliable dough forms.
3. Wrap the dough in plastic wrap and let it rest for 30 minutes at room temperature.
4. Roll out the dough on a floured surface to about 1/4 inch thickness and use a cookie cutter (traditionally flower-shaped) to cut out the cookies.
5. Heat a deep-fryer or a deep skillet with vegetable oil to 350°F (175°C). Carefully add the cookies a few at a time, frying them until they are golden brown, about 2-3 minutes per side.
6. Remove the yakgwa with a slotted spoon and drain on paper towels.
7. In a small saucepan, combine 1 cup honey with water and heat over low heat until thinned slightly. Brush or dip the fried cookies into the honey glaze, ensuring they are well coated.
8. Sprinkle with cinnamon powder and garnish with pine nuts if using. Let the glaze set before serving.

DIETARY MODIFICATIONS

Vegetarian: No modifications needed, as the recipe is inherently vegetarian.
Vegan: Replace honey with agave syrup or another vegan-friendly sweetener for both the dough and glaze. Note that the flavor profile will slightly cha**nge**.
Gluten-Free: Use a gluten-free flour blend in place of wheat flour, but be aware that the texture may be different from traditional yakgwa.

INGREDIENT SPOTLIGHT: SESAME OIL

Sesame oil is the spotlight ingredient here. This essential Korean cooking oil is made from raw, pressed sesame seeds and features a strong, nutty flavor that is key to many Asian dishes. With a history rooted in the ancient civilizations of Asia and the Middle East, sesame oil adds depth and richness to yakgwa, distinguishing its taste from other confections. Beyond sweets, sesame oil is often used in marinades, dressings, and as a finishing oil due to its potent aroma and flavor.

CHEF'S TIPS
- Ensure sesame oil is fresh as it can become rancid quickly; a rancid oil will spoil the flavor.
- Keep the frying oil at a steady temperature to avoid absorbing excessive oil and prevent the cookies from burning.
- If the dough is too sticky, add a little more flour; if too dry, add a bit more sesame oil.
- Thoroughly drain the deep-fried yakgwa on paper towels to remove excess oil before glazing.
- For a more decorative look, use cookie cutters with intricate designs typical to Korean festive traditions.

POSSIBLE VARIATIONS OF THE RECIPE
- **Citrus-Infused:** Add a tablespoon of finely grated orange zest to the dough for a citrus note.
- **Spice-Infused:** Include a teaspoon of ground ginger or a pinch of cardamom in the dough to deepen the warm spice flavor.
- **Nutty:** Mix finely chopped walnuts or almonds into the dough for added texture and nutty taste.

HEALTH NOTE & CALORIC INFORMATION
Yakgwa is a rich, sweet indulgence. The cookies are high in calories, largely from the sesame oil and honey components. Each cookie contains approximately 150-200 calories, depending on the size and the amount of oil absorbed during frying. They contain carbohydrates mainly from the flour and sugars, and there is a moderate amount of fats from sesame oil. However, they also offer traces of minerals such as calcium and magnesium from honey and sesame oil. As part of a balanced diet, enjoy these in moderation.

GUKBAP

Gukbap is a cherished, heartwarming Korean dish that originated during the Joseon Dynasty. Historically, this comforting soup was a simple meal for commoners, made from ingredients they had on hand. Gukbap literally means "soup with rice" in Korean and it remains a popular choice in Korea for its nutritious contents and the ease of preparation. It's particularly favored during cold seasons or as a restorative meal.

INGREDIENTS

- 200g beef brisket, sliced thinly
- 6 cups of beef or anchovy broth
- 1/2 cup cooked rice (short-grain sushi rice)
- 2 cloves garlic, minced
- 1/2 onion, sliced
- 2 green onions, chopped
- 1 tablespoon soy sauce
- 1 tablespoon sesame oil
- 1 teaspoon salt (adjust to taste)
- 1/2 teaspoon black pepper
- 1/2 teaspoon Korean red pepper flakes (gochugaru)
- 1 tablespoon seaweed, cut into strips (optional)
- Kimchi, for serving (optional)
- 2 teaspoons toasted sesame seeds (optional)

DIRECTIONS

1. Begin by heating the sesame oil in a large pot over medium heat. Add the garlic and onions, sautéing until they're transparent and fragrant, about 2-3 minutes.
2. Increase to medium-high heat and add the beef brisket, browning it on all sides.
3. Pour in the beef or anchovy broth and bring the mixture to a boil. Skim off any foam or fat that rises to the surface.
4. Once boiling, reduce heat to a simmer. Add soy sauce, salt, black pepper, and Korean red pepper flakes, and let the soup simmer for 20-25 minutes to allow the flavors to meld together.
5. Add the cooked rice to the pot and simmer for another 5-10 minutes until the rice is heated through and has absorbed some of the soup's flavor.
6. Just before serving, stir in the chopped green onions and seaweed strips, if using, and allow them to warm in the soup for about 1 minute.
7. Serve hot in individual bowls with optional kimchi and a sprinkle of toasted sesame seeds on top.

DIETARY MODIFICATIONS

Vegetarian: Use a hearty mushroom or vegetable broth instead of beef or anchovy broth, and substitute beef with tofu or a blend of mushrooms like shiitake and oyster for a similar umami flavor profile.

Vegan: Follow the vegetarian modifications and also ensure that the soy sauce is vegan (some brands may contain traces of fish sauces). Skip the optional kimchi if it contains fish sauce, or use a vegan kimchi variant.

Gluten-Free: Use tamari instead of regular soy sauce, and check that your gochugaru and other ingredients are certified gluten-free.

INGREDIENT SPOTLIGHT: GOCHUGARU

Gochugaru, or Korean red pepper flakes, is the spotlight ingredient in this recipe. Originating from sun-dried red chili peppers, it is a staple in Korean cuisine, prized for its vibrant red color and smoky, sweet, with moderate heat profile. Whether used in kimchi, soups, or marinades, gochugaru imparts depth and authentic Korean spicy flavor. In this recipe, it balances the rich broth and adds an essential kick that makes Gukbap distinctively Korean.

CHEF'S TIPS

- To achieve a clear broth, it's important to skim off scum as it rises to the top during boiling.
- Slicing the beef brisket thinly ensures that it will cook quickly and soak up the soup's flavor.
- Letting the soup simmer for a proper duration is crucial for a full-bodied taste.
- Adding the rice toward the end of cooking maintains its texture.
- Serve the Gukbap steaming hot to enjoy its full aroma and warmth; it's meant to comfort with both its heat and taste.

POSSIBLE VARIATIONS OF THE RECIPE

- **Seafood Gukbap:** Incorporate seafood such as shrimp, clams, or mussels instead of beef and use a fish-based broth for a different variety of this soup.
- **Spicy Gukbap:** For those who love extra heat, increase the amount of gochugaru or add fresh sliced Korean chilies while cooking.
- **Doenjang Gukbap:** Add a tablespoon of doenjang (Korean fermented soybean paste) to the soup for an earthy, robust flavor.

HEALTH NOTE & CALORIC INFORMATION

A serving of Gukbap provides a good balance of protein, carbohydrates, and fats. Beef brisket is rich in protein and iron, while the rice provides energy-giving carbohydrates. Seasoning ingredients such as garlic, green onions, and seaweed offer vitamins and minerals. A standard serving without kimchi is approximately 300-400 calories, keeping in mind that variations in ingredients and portion sizes can change nutritional content.

JEONBOKJUK

Jeonbokjuk is a luxurious and nutritive Korean porridge that features abalone, a prized seafood delicacy with a subtle sweetness and firm texture. Revered for its health benefits and savory flavor, this porridge is often consumed for recovery during illness or as a hearty breakfast to kickstart the day. Historically, it's also a dish associated with the Korean royal court cuisine, emphasizing its status as a specialty.

INGREDIENTS

- 2 large abalones, cleaned and diced
- 1 cup short-grain rice, rinsed and soaked for 1 hour
- 4 cups water
- 2 cups chicken or anchovy broth
- 2 teaspoons sesame oil
- 1 tablespoon soy sauce
- 3 cloves garlic, minced
- 1 tablespoon finely chopped ginger
- 2 green onions, finely sliced
- Salt to taste
- Freshly ground black pepper to taste
- Roasted seaweed strips for garnish (optional)

DIRECTIONS

1. Begin by gently scrubbing the abalones with a brush to remove any dirt or debris from their shells. Carefully extract the meat using a spoon, and remove the entrails and the hard beak found at the center of the body.
2. Rinse the abalone meat under cold water and pat dry. Cut into small dice, set aside.
3. In a pot, heat sesame oil over medium heat. Add the minced garlic and chopped ginger, sautéing until fragrant—about 1 minute.
4. Drain the soaked rice and add it to the pot, stirring continuously for another 2 minutes to lightly toast the grains.
5. Pour in the water and broth, stirring the mixture. Bring to a gentle simmer and cook, uncovered, for about 1 hour. Stir occasionally to prevent sticking, and adjust the heat as necessary to maintain a low simmer.
6. After the porridge has begun to thicken, add the diced abalone, soy sauce, salt, and pepper. Continue to cook the porridge for an additional 15-20 minutes or until the abalone is fully cooked and the porridge has reached a creamy consistency.
7. Taste and adjust the seasoning if needed. Serve in bowls, garnished with sliced green onions and roasted seaweed strips if desired.

DIETARY MODIFICATIONS

Vegetarian: Skip the abalone and enhance the porridge with a variety of mushrooms, like shiitake or oyster mushrooms, which have a meaty texture. Adjust the broth to a vegetable-based option.

Vegan: Follow the vegetarian modifications and use soy sauce cautiously, as it's also considered non-vegan due to the use of fermented products. You can replace it with tamari or a vegan soy sauce alternative.

Gluten-Free: Ensure that the soy sauce used is labelled gluten-free, as traditional soy sauce contains wheat. Alternatively, tamari can serve as a gluten-free substitute.

INGREDIENT SPOTLIGHT: ABALONE

Abalone is the star ingredient, known scientifically as Haliotis. These sea snails are cultivated in coastal waters and also found wild, with a shell that is a source of mother-of-pearl. Nutritionally rich, abalones are full of protein, omega-3 fatty acids, and essential minerals. They have a mild taste, often compared to scallops, and a tender yet firm texture. In Jeonbokjuk, abalone brings an oceanic depth, elevating the porridge from humble to opulent.

CHEF'S TIPS

- Clean your abalone meticulously. Any residual grit can ruin the smooth texture of your porridge.
- For an even creamier texture, continuously stir the porridge during the last 15 minutes of cooking.
- Reserved abalone liver can be minced and added to the porridge for an extra burst of flavor.
- If using fresh abalone, tenderize the meat with a meat mallet before dicing to ensure a tender bite.
- Gently simmering is key; high heat can cause the rice to burn at the bottom of the pot and may toughen the abalone.

POSSIBLE VARIATIONS OF THE RECIPE

- **Seafood Medley**: Add clams, mussels, and diced shrimp along with the abalone to turn this into a sea bounty porridge.
- **Ginseng Infusion**: Include thinly sliced ginseng while simmering the porridge for an extra health boost, particularly popular for convalescence in Korean tradition.
- **Spiced-Up Version**: Incorporate red pepper flakes or a touch of gochujang (Korean red chili paste) for a spicy kick.

HEALTH NOTE & CALORIC INFORMATION

A serving of Jeonbokjuk is typically rich in protein and low in fat, thanks to the lean nature of abalone. It is also high in complex carbohydrates from the rice, making it an energy-dense meal. The exact calories can vary depending on the size of the serving and any additional ingredients or garnishes used, but a single serving without extra garnishes is generally around 200 to 300 calories. Additionally, it provides essential vitamins and minerals, including B-vitamins, iron, and selenium from the abalone.

DAKDORITANG

Dakdoritang, also known as Dakbokkeumtang, is a hearty and spicy Korean dish that has become a comforting staple during colder months and festive family gatherings. With roots in Korea's culinary traditions, this stew marries the heat of gochugaru (Korean red pepper flakes) with the deep flavors of soy sauce and aromatic vegetables. It's a dish that warms you from the inside out, capturing the essence of Korean comfort food.

INGREDIENTS

- 1.5 lbs (680 g) chicken thighs, cut into chunks
- 2 medium potatoes, peeled and cut into large cubes
- 2 carrots, peeled and cut into thick slices
- 1 large onion, chopped
- 4 cloves of garlic, minced
- 4 green onions, sliced, whites and greens separated
- 2 tablespoons gochugaru (Korean red pepper flakes)
- 1 tablespoon gochujang (Korean red pepper paste)
- 3 tablespoons soy sauce
- 1 tablespoon rice wine (such as mirin)
- 1 tablespoon honey
- 1 teaspoon sesame oil
- 2 cups water or chicken stock
- 1 teaspoon black pepper
- 2 tablespoons vegetable oil
- Sesame seeds, for garnish

DIRECTIONS

1. Heat vegetable oil in a large pot or Dutch oven over medium-high heat.
2. Add the chicken pieces and brown them on all sides, approximately 3-4 minutes per side.
3. Add the minced garlic and white parts of the green onions; sauté with the chicken for 1-2 minutes until aromatic.
4. Mix in the gochugaru, gochujang, soy sauce, rice wine, honey, sesame oil, and black pepper to create the flavor base.
5. Add the water or chicken stock, ensuring it covers the chicken. Bring to a boil.
6. Reduce heat to medium-low, cover, and simmer for 20 minutes.
7. Add the potatoes, carrots, and onions to the pot. Stir to combine and continue to simmer covered for an additional 20 minutes, or until the vegetables are tender.
8. Uncover, increase heat to medium-high, and allow the stew to reduce and thicken for about 10 minutes.
9. Adjust seasoning to taste, and add the green parts of the onions just before serving.
10. Serve hot in bowls, garnished with sesame seeds.

DIETARY MODIFICATIONS

Vegetarian: Replace chicken with firm tofu cubes and use vegetable stock instead of chicken stock. Sear the tofu cubes before adding them to ensure they hold up in the stew.

Vegan: Follow the vegetarian modifications but also use a vegan soy sauce and substitute honey with maple syrup or sugar for sweetness.

Low Sodium: Use low-sodium soy sauce and opt for low-sodium chicken stock or water. Adjust the seasoning cautiously and increase the use of spices to compensate for less salt.

INGREDIENT SPOTLIGHT: GOCHUGARU

Gochugaru (Korean red pepper flakes) is a quintessential Korean spice with a vibrant red color, which is made from dried, ground red peppers. Unlike other red chili flakes, gochugaru has a unique flavor profile that is spicy-sweet with smoky undertones and is essential for authentic Korean spiciness. It's used in kimchi, stews, and marinades. In this recipe, gochugaru brings a complex heat that's fundamental to the dish's identity, infusing it with the right level of warmth and depth of flavor.

CHEF'S TIPS

- Pat the chicken dry before browning to ensure maximum crispness.
- Control the heat level by adjusting the amount of gochugaru used.
- If gochujang is unavailable, a good substitute would be a mix of red chili flakes with a little soy sauce and sugar.
- Allow the stew to cool slightly before serving; this will let the flavors meld together more deeply.
- To achieve the perfect stew consistency, keep an eye on your simmering time and adjust as needed. It should be brothy, but with a slightly thickened sauce.

POSSIBLE VARIATIONS OF THE RECIPE

- **Seafood Twist:** Replace chicken with a mix of seafood such as shrimp, mussels, and squid for a lighter, pescatarian-friendly version.
- **Extra Veggies:** Add mushrooms, zucchini, or bell peppers to increase the vegetable content and add more flavors and textures to the dish.
- **Heat Level Adjustment:** For a less spicy version, reduce gochugaru and gochujang while adding more soy sauce and a touch of sugar to maintain flavor balance.

HEALTH NOTE & CALORIC INFORMATION

Dakdoritang is a hearty meal that provides a balance of protein from chicken, carbohydrates from vegetables, and is rich in vitamins and minerals. A typical serving contains roughly 400-500 calories, with variations in caloric content based on the chosen ingredients and serving sizes. It's high in vitamin A from gochugaru and vitamin C from the vegetables. Keep in mind that despite its nutritional benefits, this dish can be high in sodium, so it's best enjoyed in moderation for those watching their salt intake.

PATBINGSU

Patbingsu, also spelled as "patbingsoo," is a popular Korean shaved ice dessert with sweet toppings that may include chopped fruit, condensed milk, fruit syrup, and red beans. This delightful dessert has evolved from a simple dish of shaved ice and sweetened red beans to an elaborate treat with various mix-ins and toppings. Traditionally enjoyed during the summer to beat the heat, patbingsu has become a year-round favorite in South Korea, spreading its sweet, refreshing charm worldwide.

INGREDIENTS

- 2 cups of ice cubes (or use a block of ice for authentic texture)
- 1 can of sweetened red beans (pat)
- 1/2 cup condensed milk
- 1/4 cup whole milk (optional, for a softer texture)
- 1/2 cup sweet rice cakes (tteok), diced
- 1/2 cup assorted fruits (e.g., strawberries, kiwi, bananas), chopped
- 2 tablespoons roasted soybean powder (injeolmi)
- 2 scoops of vanilla or sweet red bean ice cream
- 1 tablespoon of honey or sugar syrup (optional, for added sweetness)
- Mint leaves (for garnish)

DIRECTIONS

1. Drain and rinse the can of sweetened red beans. Keep a half-cup aside for topping later.
2. Set Up Shaved Ice:
3. If using a shaved ice machine, prepare according to the manufacturer's instructions. If not, wrap the ice cubes in a clean towel and use a rolling pin or meat hammer to crush into fine, fluffy snow-like ice.

Blend the Base:
1. Place the drained red beans in a blender. Add condensed milk and whole milk. Blend until smooth.
2. Assemble the Patbingsu:
3. In serving bowls, layer the blended red bean mixture at the bottom.
4. Pile the shaved ice over the red bean mixture evenly.
5. Drizzle with a little more condensed milk if desired.

Toppings:
1. Artfully arrange the sweet rice cakes, chopped fruits, and the remaining red beans on top of the shaved ice.
2. Final Touches:
3. Add a scoop of vanilla or red bean ice cream to each serving.
4. Dust with soybean powder.
5. Drizzle with honey or sugar syrup if a sweeter dessert is preferred.
6. Garnish with mint leaves.

DIETARY MODIFICATIONS

Vegetarian: This recipe is already suitable for vegetarians.

Vegan: Substitute condensed milk with a vegan condensed milk alternative (soy, almond, or coconut-based). Choose a vegan ice cream instead of the traditional dairy-based version.

Lactose Intolerance: Replace both condensed milk and whole milk with lactose-free versions or non-dairy alternatives such as soy or almond milk. Also, ensure the ice cream selected is lactose-free.

INGREDIENT SPOTLIGHT: PAT

This ingredient is the soul of patbingsu. Originating from East Asia, red beans or azuki beans are often sweetened and turned into a paste, known as 'pat' in Korea. They provide not only a sweet, earthy flavor but also a creamy texture which is a match made in heaven with shaved ice. The use of red beans in desserts is widespread in East Asia and is integral to this particular dish, offering a unique taste that's unlike typical Western sweet treats.

CHEF'S TIPS

- **Ice Consistency:** Take the time to crush or shave the ice to the right consistency—neither too coarse nor too melted—as it's crucial for the perfect patbingsu experience.
- **Fruit Selection:** Use seasonal fruits for the best flavor and freshness. Fruits also add color and make the dessert more eye-catching.
- **Milk Blend:** Adjust the amount of milk to control the softness and creaminess of the ice. Less milk makes a firmer shaved ice.
- **Rice Cake Softness:** Soften the sweet rice cakes (tteok) by steaming them for a few minutes if they aren't fresh, to ensure they're chewy and not hard.
- **Serving Immediately:** Assemble the patbingsu just before serving to prevent the ice from melting and turning the dessert into a soup.

POSSIBLE VARIATIONS OF THE RECIPE

- **Mocha Patbingsu:** For a coffee twist, mix in a shot of espresso with the condensed milk before pouring it over the ice. Top with chocolate shavings.
- **Matcha Patbingsu:** Incorporate matcha powder into the milk mixture and dust the final dessert with extra matcha. Use mochi pieces instead of sweet rice cakes for a Japanese take.
- **Tropical Patbingsu:** Use coconut milk in place of condensed milk and whole milk, and top with tropical fruits such as mango, pineapple, and lychee.

HEALTH NOTE & CALORIC INFORMATION

A serving of patbingsu typically contains a mix of carbs from the fruits and red beans, sugar from the condensed milk and toppings, and small amounts of protein from the red beans and dairy. It's a high-calorie treat, especially with the addition of ice cream and sweeteners. For those concerned with sugar intake, reduce or eliminate the honey/syrup and use fruits with lower sugar content.

AGUJJIM

Agujjim, also known as Agwi-jjim, is a Korean dish that features braised monkfish with soybean sprouts in a spicy sauce. Hailing from the coastal cities of Korea, like Busan, this dish traditionally utilized the freshly caught monkfish by local fishermen. The dish became widely popular for its robust flavors and substantial texture. The harmony of spices and seafood celebrates Korea's love for piquant and hearty stews, perfect for sharing at the table with loved ones.

INGREDIENTS

- 1 kg monkfish, cleaned and cut into bite-sized pieces
- 300 g soybean sprouts
- 2 stalks of green onions, chopped
- 1 small white onion, thinly sliced
- 4 cloves of garlic, minced
- 2 tablespoons of gochugaru (Korean red pepper flakes)
- 1 tablespoon gochujang (Korean red pepper paste)
- 2 tablespoons soy sauce
- 1 tablespoon fish sauce
- 1 tablespoon rice wine (mirin or sake)
- 1 teaspoon sesame oil
- 1 teaspoon ginger, grated
- 1 teaspoon sugar
- 1 cup water
- Sesame seeds (for garnish)
- 1 small carrot, julienned (optional for garnish)
- Vegetable oil

DIRECTIONS

1. Begin by rinsing the monkfish pieces in cold water and pat them dry with paper towels.
2. In a small bowl, mix together the gochugaru, gochujang, soy sauce, fish sauce, rice wine, minced garlic, grated ginger, sesame oil, and sugar to create the sauce.
3. Heat a tablespoon of vegetable oil in a large, deep skillet or pot over medium heat.
4. Sauté the sliced onions until they become translucent.
5. Add the monkfish pieces to the skillet and sear them until they're lightly browned on all sides.
6. Pour the sauce over the monkfish and gently toss to coat the pieces evenly.
7. Add the soybean sprouts and water to the skillet, then bring the liquid to a simmer.
8. Cover and let it cook for about 10 minutes, or until the monkfish is cooked through and the sprouts are tender.
9. Uncover and sprinkle the chopped green onions over the stew, letting them wilt slightly.
10. Serve the agujjim hot, garnished with sesame seeds and julienned carrots for a colorful presentation.

DIETARY MODIFICATIONS

Vegetarian: Substitute monkfish with firm tofu or king oyster mushrooms. Adjust cooking time as these will cook faster than fish.
Vegan: Follow the vegetarian substitutes and ensure that the soy sauce is vegan. Also, replace fish sauce with a vegan fish sauce alternative or more soy sauce to taste.
Gluten-Free: Make sure that the gochujang, soy sauce, and fish sauce are all certified gluten-free. The rest of the ingredients are naturally gluten-free.

INGREDIENT SPOTLIGHT: GOCHUGARU

Gochugaru, Korean red pepper flakes, is an essential ingredient in Korean cuisine known for its distinct flavor that is both spicy and slightly sweet. Made from sun-dried Korean red chili peppers, it varies in spiciness and is used in making kimchi, stews, sauces, and marinades. Gochugaru adds a deep red color and smoky heat to dishes, which is integral to the unique taste of Korean food. For Agujjim, it brings the fiery red hue and imparts a warmth that balances with the fresh, oceanic taste of the monkfish.

CHEF'S TIPS

- Pat the monkfish dry to ensure it browns nicely when seared.
- For an authentic Korean taste, use Korean soy sauce and gochujang for the right balance of flavors and fermentation.
- Adjust the spiciness by increasing or decreasing the amount of gochugaru and gochujang to suit your heat preference.
- When braising, maintain a gentle simmer to keep the fish tender and avoid overcooking the sprouts.
- Always taste and adjust the seasoning before serving - the saltiness and spiciness can vary based on the brands of sauces used.

POSSIBLE VARIATIONS OF THE RECIPE

- **Seafood Medley Agujjim:** Incorporate shrimp, mussels, and scallops along with monkfish for a seafood feast.
- **Mild Agujjim:** For those who enjoy less heat, reduce the gochugaru by half and add a sweet bell pepper for flavor without the spice.
- **Green Agujjim:** Add bok choy, zucchini, and other green vegetables for additional color and nutrition.

HEALTH NOTE & CALORIC INFORMATION

Monkfish, the star of Agujjim, is low in fat and high in protein. A serving of this stew is rich in vitamins from the vegetables and provides a moderate number of calories, making it a wholesome and hearty meal. The soybean sprouts add crunch and are an excellent source of fiber. The seasonings contribute sodium, so it's recommended to consume this dish in moderation if watching salt intake. The exact calorie content can vary, but a standard serving of Agujjim is approximately 200-300 calories.

GODEUNGEO GUI

Godeungeo Gui is a simple yet beloved dish in Korean cuisine, heralding from a culinary tradition that treasures the natural flavors of fresh ingredients, particularly seafood. Mackerel, known as 'godeungeo' in Korean, is a fish rich in omega-3 fatty acids and is often enjoyed for its savory and robust flavor. This dish is a staple in Korean households, often served with a side of steaming rice and kimchi. Grilled to perfection, the mackerel's crispy skin and moist interior encapsulate the essence of homely Korean comfort food.

INGREDIENTS

- 2 whole mackerel, gutted and cleaned
- 1 tablespoon of coarse sea salt
- 2 teaspoons of vegetable oil
- 2 cloves of garlic, thinly sliced (optional for garnishing)
- 1 lemon, sliced for serving (optional)
- Freshly ground black pepper (optional)

DIRECTIONS

1. Begin by rinsing the mackerel under cold water and patting them dry with paper towels.
2. Score the mackerel on both sides with diagonal cuts about an inch apart, this allows heat to penetrate the flesh more evenly and seasoning to infuse the fish.
3. Rub the entire surface of each fish, including the cavity and scores, with coarse sea salt.
4. Preheat your grill or grill pan over medium-high heat. Once hot, brush it with vegetable oil to prevent sticking.
5. Place the mackerel on the grill, skin side down, and let it cook undisturbed for 5-7 minutes until the skin is crispy and golden brown.
6. Carefully flip the mackerel and cook for another 5-7 minutes on the other side.
7. The mackerel is done when the flesh flakes easily with a fork. Optionally, garnish with thinly sliced garlic and a squeeze of lemon juice just before serving.
8. Serve hot, alongside steamed rice and kimchi for a traditional Korean meal.

DIETARY MODIFICATIONS

Gluten-Free: This recipe is already gluten-free; just ensure that all the ingredients, especially the garnishes like kimchi, are certified gluten-free.
Low-Sodium: Reduce the sea salt by half to lower the sodium content, or use a sodium-free seasoning option.
Pescatarian: No modifications are needed; this meal is perfect for pescatarians as it highlights the natural flavors of the sea.

INGREDIENT SPOTLIGHT: COARSE SEA SALT

Coarse sea salt is a fundamental seasoning in many cuisines globally. Unlike refined table salt, coarse sea salt contains minerals and trace elements that add a subtle complexity to its flavor profile. Sourced from the evaporation of seawater, it can also add textural contrast to dishes. In Godeungeo Gui, coarse sea salt does more than season the fish; it helps to draw out moisture, enabling the skin to crisp up beautifully when grilled.

CHEF'S TIPS
- Ensure your grill or grill pan is very hot before adding the fish to achieve the perfect crispy skin.
- Do not move the fish around once it's on the grill; letting it cook undisturbed will prevent sticking and allow for even charring.
- To check if the fish is done, insert a fork into the thickest part of the flesh and gently twist. The fish should flake easily.
- For an additional layer of flavor, try adding a small piece of ginger inside the cavity of the fish before grilling.
- Leftovers can be refrigerated and used to make other dishes like fish tacos or salads.

POSSIBLE VARIATIONS OF THE RECIPE
- **Herbed Mackerel: Stuff the cavity with fresh herbs like dill, parsley, or cilantro before grilling for an aromatic twist.**
- **Spicy Godeungeo Gui: Add a glaze made from gochujang (Korean red pepper paste), soy sauce, and honey during the last few minutes of grilling for a sweet and spicy kick.**
- **Soy-Glazed Mackerel: Combine soy sauce, mirin, and garlic as a basting sauce to apply while grilling, developing a savory glaze with a Japanese-influenced flavor.**

HEALTH NOTE & CALORIC INFORMATION
Mackerel is an excellent source of protein and contains high levels of omega-3 fatty acids, which are beneficial for heart health. It is also rich in vitamins D and B12. A serving of grilled mackerel (about half a fish) contains approximately:
- Calories: 230
- Protein: 21g
- Fat: 15g (with low levels of saturated fat)
- Carbohydrates: 0g Keep in mind that the seasoning and additional garnishes will alter the nutritional content slightly.

ANDONG JJIMDAK

Andong Jjimdak is a hearty Korean dish hailing from the city of Andong. This dish became popular in the 1980s and is renowned for its savory and slightly sweet flavor profile. It combines tender chicken with vegetables and glass noodles in a soy sauce-based broth, making it an ideal family meal. The dish reflects the culinary emphasis on balance and depth of flavor that is essential to Korean cooking.

INGREDIENTS

- 1 kg chicken thighs, cut into pieces
- 2 medium potatoes, peeled and cut into large chunks
- 2 carrots, sliced into thick discs
- 1 large onion, roughly chopped
- 2 green onions, chopped into 2-inch pieces
- 5 cloves garlic, minced
- 1 thumb-sized piece of ginger, thinly sliced
- 2 jalapeño peppers, sliced (optional for heat)
- 1 cup dried Korean glass noodles (dangmyeon)
- 4 cups water
- 5 tbsp soy sauce
- 2 tbsp oyster sauce
- 1 tbsp sugar
- 1 tbsp rice wine (or mirin)
- 1 tsp black pepper
- 2 tbsp vegetable oil
- 1 tbsp sesame oil
- 1 tbsp sesame seeds for garnishing
- 1/2 cup of mushrooms (shiitake or button), optional

DIRECTIONS

1. Begin by soaking the glass noodles in warm water for at least 20 minutes to soften them.
2. In a large pot or deep pan, heat the vegetable oil over medium heat.
3. Add the chicken pieces to the pot and brown them on all sides, then remove and set aside.
4. In the same pot, add a touch more oil if needed, and sauté the garlic, ginger, onions, and jalapeño peppers (if using) until the onions are translucent.
5. Pour in the water, soy sauce, oyster sauce, rice wine, and sugar. Stir until the sugar is dissolved.
6. Add the chicken back into the pot along with the potatoes and carrots. Bring the mixture to a boil, then lower to a simmer and cover the pot.
7. Let it cook for about 20 minutes, then add the pre-soaked glass noodles and mushrooms (if using), stirring gently to mix them in.
8. Continue to cook for another 10-15 minutes until the chicken is thoroughly cooked and the noodles are soft.
9. Drizzle sesame oil over the dish and add black pepper to taste. Let it simmer for an additional 5 minutes.
10. Garnish with chopped green onions and sesame seeds before serving.

DIETARY MODIFICATIONS

For a **vegetarian** version, substitute chicken with firm tofu and use a vegetarian oyster sauce or simply add more soy sauce. Include more mushrooms to provide a meaty texture.

To make this dish **vegan**, follow the vegetarian modifications and make sure to use sugar that doesn't involve bone char in its processing.

For a **gluten-free** option, use tamari or certified gluten-free soy sauce and gluten-free oyster sauce. Ensure that the noodles used are also gluten-free.

INGREDIENT SPOTLIGHT: GLASS NOODLES

Korean glass noodles, known as dangmyeon, are made from sweet potato starch and water. These noodles are not only gluten-free but also known for their pleasantly chewy texture. They play a pivotal role in many Korean dishes such as Japchae and various types of Jjimdak. Originating from China, these noodles were introduced to Korea, where they have been widely embraced and are now an integral part of the cuisine.

CHEF'S TIPS

- Pat the chicken dry before browning to ensure a nice sear.
- If using bone-in chicken, increase the cooking time by 10-15 minutes to ensure the meat is tender.
- Adjust the amount of jalapeño pepper to control the heat level according to your preference.
- To prevent the glass noodles from sticking together, stir them occasionally as they cook.
- For a richer flavor, consider adding a splash of Korean soy sauce for soup (guk-ganjang) during the seasoning process.

POSSIBLE VARIATIONS OF THE RECIPE

- Include a variety of mushrooms, such as wood ear or oyster mushrooms, for different textures and an earthy flavor.
- Add a sweet and spicy element by including Korean green and red chili peppers and a tablespoon of gochujang (Korean chili paste).
- Consider using boneless skinless chicken breasts for a leaner version; just reduce the cooking time to avoid drying out the meat.

HEALTH NOTE & CALORIC INFORMATION

This recipe is high in protein due to the chicken and provides a moderate amount of carbohydrates from the glass noodles and the vegetables. It contains a mix of vitamins and minerals from the vegetables and is relatively low in fat, especially if skinless chicken is used. The exact calorie content can vary based on the specific ingredients and portion sizes used, but a typical serving may range from 400-600 calories. Keep an eye on sodium intake with this dish due to the soy and oyster sauces; you can use low-sodium options if needed.

DOTORIMUK MUCHIM

Dotorimuk Muchim is a traditional Korean dish which showcases the humble yet unique ingredient - acorn starch. Originally, it was a survival food during times of scarcity, but it has since become a beloved and healthful aspect of Korean cuisine. Acorn jelly, known as "dotorimuk," is valued for its subtle, soft texture and its ability to take on the bold flavors of accompanying seasonings and vegetables.

INGREDIENTS

For the Acorn Jelly:
- 2 cups of acorn starch
- 5 cups of water
- A pinch of salt

For the Salad:
- 1 medium cucumber, julienned
- 1 medium carrot, julienned
- 1/2 a medium red onion, thinly sliced
- 2 scallions, chopped
- 1/2 cup of perilla leaves, thinly sliced (optional)

For the Sauce:
- 3 tablespoons soy sauce
- 1 1/2 tablespoons Korean red pepper flakes (gochugaru)
- 1 tablespoon sesame oil
- 2 teaspoons rice vinegar
- 1 tablespoon sugar
- 1 clove of garlic, minced
- 1 teaspoon of grated ginger
- 1 teaspoon toasted sesame seeds

DIRECTIONS

1. Begin by making the acorn jelly. In a large bowl, stir the acorn starch and salt into the cold water until fully dissolved.
2. Pour the mixture into a pot and heat over a medium flame, constantly stirring to prevent any lumps from forming.
3. Once the mixture starts to thicken and bubbles, lower the heat and continue stirring until it becomes a thick, smooth paste.
4. Transfer the acorn jelly paste into a square mold or a flat dish. Allow it to cool to room temperature, then refrigerate it for 2 hours until firm.
5. While the jelly sets, prepare the vegetables. Clean and julienne the cucumber and carrot, thinly slice the onion, chop the scallions, and slice the perilla leaves.
6. For the sauce, combine soy sauce, red pepper flakes, sesame oil, rice vinegar, sugar, minced garlic, and grated ginger in a bowl. Mix well until the sugar is dissolved, then stir in the toasted sesame seeds.
7. Once the jelly has set, unmold it and cut it into bite-sized cubes.
8. In a large mixing bowl, combine the acorn jelly cubes with the prepared vegetables.
9. Drizzle the sauce over the jelly and vegetables, gently toss to coat evenly.
10. Chill the salad for about 30 minutes before serving to allow the flavors to meld.
11. Serve chilled, garnished with more sesame seeds and chopped scallions.

DIETARY MODIFICATIONS

Vegetarian: This recipe is naturally vegetarian. Ensure that the soy sauce used is free of any animal products, as some brands may include fish or other animal derivatives.

Vegan: Similar to the vegetarian consideration, check the soy sauce. Additionally, confirm that sugar is vegan as some processing methods involve animal products.

Gluten-Free: Substitute the soy sauce with tamari or a gluten-free soy sauce alternative to accommodate a gluten-free diet without compromising the dish's flavor profile.

INGREDIENT SPOTLIGHT: ACORN STARCH

Acorn starch is the star here, derived from oak trees' nuts. Historically, acorns have been a significant food source for many cultures. In Korea, they are leached to remove tannins, then ground and dried to form a starch used for jelly, soups, and pancakes. Its use dates back centuries and is a testament to Korean innovation in creating sustenance from available resources. Acorn starch provides an earthy flavor and a signature jello-like consistency which is essential to this recipe as it absorbs the spicy, tangy flavors of the accompanying sauce.

CHEF'S TIPS

- Patience is key while cooking the acorn jelly; a continuous stir and vigilant eye prevent lumps and ensure a smooth texture.
- Use a vegetable peeler for efficient and uniform julienne cuts for the carrot and cucumber.
- Adjust the level of Korean red pepper flakes to your spice preference, but remember it's meant to be a bit fiery.
- Letting the salad chill after mixing allows the flavors to intensify and the jelly to maintain its firmness.
- To achieve an authentic taste, use Korean soy sauce and red pepper flakes, as they can differ in flavor intensity and color from other variations.

POSSIBLE VARIATIONS OF THE RECIPE

- **Seafood Twist:** Top the salad with thinly sliced seafood such as squid or baby octopus for a Korean banchan (side dish) experience.
- **Sweet and Sour:** For a tangier salad, increase the rice vinegar and reduce the sugar by half. Add a splash of fresh lemon juice for added zing.
- **Herbaceous Lift:** Include a variety of fresh herbs like mint, cilantro, or dill alongside the perilla for a more aromatic and refreshing take on the salad.

HEALTH NOTE & CALORIC INFORMATION

Acorn jelly is low in calories but high in fiber, making it a satiating yet light choice. The vegetables contribute vitamins and minerals with minimal caloric addition. The sesame oil and seeds offer healthy fats. A serving of Dotorimuk Muchim is roughly 150-200 calories, varying with portion size and additional toppings. It is also a dish low in cholesterol and saturated fats, supporting heart health.

JOKBAL

Jokbal is a beloved Korean dish made from pig's trotters cooked with soy sauce and spices until tender. Its history dates back to the Joseon Dynasty where it was considered a gourmet delicacy. A harmonious blend of flavors—savory, sweet, and slightly spicy—makes it a popular choice for family gatherings and festive occasions. This dish is not only savored for its taste but also appreciated for its collagen content, believed to promote youthful skin.

INGREDIENTS

- 2 pig's feet (approximately 2-3 pounds)
- 1 cup soy sauce
- 1/2 cup dark brown sugar
- 1 medium onion, peeled and quartered
- 10 cloves garlic, peeled
- 2 leeks, only the white parts, cleaned and cut in half
- 4 slices ginger (about ¼ inch thick each)
- 1 Asian pear, peeled and quartered
- 2 tbsp rice wine
- 1 cinnamon stick
- 2 star anise
- 2 liters water, or enough to cover the feet
- 1 tbsp whole black peppercorns
- 1 chili pepper (optional, for heat)

DIRECTIONS

1. Begin by thoroughly cleaning the pig's feet with cold water. Using a brush, scrub the skin to remove any remaining hair or debris.
2. Place the cleaned pig's feet in a large pot, and cover with water. Bring to a boil for about 10 minutes to blanch and remove any impurities. Drain and rinse the feet with cold water, then wipe them dry.
3. In the same pot, combine the soy sauce, dark brown sugar, onion, garlic, leeks, ginger, Asian pear, rice wine, cinnamon stick, star anise, black peppercorns, and chili pepper (if using). Add the pig's feet back to the pot then pour in enough water to cover everything.
4. Bring the pot to a boil over high heat, then reduce to a simmer. Cover and let it cook for at least 2-3 hours, or until the meat is tender and easily pulls away from the bones.
5. Carefully remove the pig's feet from the pot and set aside to cool slightly. In the meantime, strain the cooking liquid into a saucepan and bring to a simmer to reduce into a glaze.
6. Once the glaze has thickened slightly, brush it over the pig's feet before serving.
7. To serve, cut the pig's feet into thin slices and enjoy with the reduced glaze, along with steamed rice and kimchi.

DIETARY MODIFICATIONS

For **Gluten Sensitivity**: Replace the soy sauce with tamari or a gluten-free soy sauce to avoid gluten while keeping the savory flavor of the jokbal.

For **Reduced Sugar**: Cut the sugar by half and add an additional pear to naturally sweeten the broth without relying on added sugars.

For a **Spicier Version**: Add more chili peppers to the broth, or serve with a side of spicy Korean chili paste, such as gochujang, for those who like extra heat.

INGREDIENT SPOTLIGHT: ASIAN PEAR

The Asian pear is a spotlight in this recipe - a fruit indigenous to East Asia, revered for its juicy, crisp texture and gentle sweetness. Used in Korean cooking both as a sweet flavoring and a meat tenderizer due to its natural enzymes, the Asian pear balances the savory depth of soy sauce and the aromatic spices in jokbal. Essential to the dish, it offers a subtle fruitiness that complements the rich, umami-laden trotters.

CHEF'S TIPS

- To ensure the pig's feet are completely clean, consider using a torch or lighter to singe off any remaining hairs before the initial scrub.
- The initial blanching is crucial as it helps to remove unwanted impurities that can affect the final taste.
- Simmering the feet for an extended time is key to achieving the perfect texture. The longer they cook, the more tender they become.
- For a clearer glaze, consider clarifying the reduced liquid using a fine-mesh strainer or cheesecloth to remove any bits and pieces.
- Traditional jokbal can be garnished with finely sliced green onions, sesame seeds, and a light drizzle of sesame oil for an extra hit of flavor.

POSSIBLE VARIATIONS OF THE RECIPE

- **Spicy Jokbal:** Introduce a spicy sauce blend with gochujang, soy sauce, a touch of vinegar, and honey, then glaze the pig's feet after slicing for a fiery kick.
- **Jokbal Bossam:** Serve the sliced pig's feet with fermented shrimp sauce (saeujeot), garlic, chilies, and Napa cabbage leaves for wrapping, turning the jokbal into a hands-on communal meal.
- **Soy and Honey Glazed Jokbal:** Substitute the sugar with honey for a different sweet profile and a glaze with a richer, more complex flavor.

HEALTH NOTE & CALORIC INFORMATION

Jokbal is high in protein and also contains a good amount of collagen, which is beneficial for skin and joint health. However, it is also rich in fat, so moderation is key. On average, a serving size of 100 grams of jokbal will contain around 350 calories, of which 25 grams are from protein, 25 grams from fat, and a minimal amount from carbohydrates. The inclusion of Asian pear adds a modest amount of dietary fiber. To maintain a balanced diet, enjoy jokbal with a variety of side dishes like fresh vegetables and rice.

SANNAKJI

Sannakji is a controversial and thrilling dish hailing from Korea. It's a type of hoe, or raw dish, typically served immediately after the octopus is killed, sometimes even while the pieces are still moving. Eaten primarily for its unique texture and fresh taste, it is often accompanied by a dip of sesame oil seasoned with salt. Adventurous food lovers seek out Sannakji for the experience as much as for the flavor.

INGREDIENTS

- 1 small live octopus
- 2 tablespoons sesame oil
- 1 teaspoon roasted sesame seeds
- 1 tablespoon Korean chili powder (gochugaru)
- Sea salt, to taste

DIRECTIONS

1. Purchase a small live octopus from a reputable seafood market, ensuring it has been humanely treated.
2. In the kitchen, quickly and humanely kill the octopus by severing the brain. If you're uncomfortable with this step, ask for assistance from a professional.
3. Clean the octopus under cold running water, making sure to remove the beak and any internal parts.
4. Cut the tentacles from the octopus. The pieces may continue to move due to nervous reactions.
5. Prepare the dipping sauce by mixing sesame oil, a pinch of sea salt, sesame seeds, and Korean chili powder in a small bowl.
6. Arrange the tentacles on a plate and serve immediately with the dip.

DIETARY MODIFICATIONS

Vegetarian/Vegan: Sannakji is distinctly non-vegetarian due to its use of octopus. Instead, a vegetarian/vegan option could be Korean seasoned kelp (Dasima) that mimics the texture with a chewy appeal. Prepare in a similar fashion with sesame seasoning.

Lactose Intolerance: This recipe is naturally lactose-free and requires no modifications.

Gluten Sensitivity: Ensure that any added ingredients such as Korean chili powder or sesame oil are gluten-free, as some products may have additives containing gluten.

INGREDIENT SPOTLIGHT: SESAME OIL

Sesame oil is an essential condiment in Korean cuisine, valued for its nutty aroma and flavor. It is made from pressed sesame seeds and varies from light to golden for cooking or toasty dark for finishing dishes. Rich in antioxidants and healthy fats, it has been a staple since the Three Kingdoms period (57 BC – 668 AD) and is key in this recipe, providing a velvety counterbalance to the ocean-fresh zing of the octopus.

CHEF'S TIPS

- Always source the octopus from reputable vendors that adhere to ethical and sustainable practices.
- The freshness of the octopus is paramount; it should be prepared the same day it's purchased.
- When severing the brain, be swift and sure to prevent needless suffering.
- Ensure the tentacles have completely stopped moving before consuming to avoid choking hazards.
- Keep the dipping sauce simple to let the unique texture and flavor of the octopus be the star.

POSSIBLE VARIATIONS OF THE RECIPE

- **Spicy Sesame Dip:** Enhance the dipping sauce with a teaspoon of gochujang (Korean chili paste) for an extra kick.
- **Soy Sauce Dip:** Swap out the sesame oil dip for a light soy sauce, mixed with a drop of rice vinegar and a sprinkle of scallions.
- **Citrusy Twist:** Add a hint of yuzu or lemon juice to the dipping sauce for a refreshing, citrusy note that complements the sea flavors.

HEALTH NOTE & CALORIC INFORMATION

A serving of sannakji is low in calories but rich in protein and omega-3 fatty acids. It also provides essential nutrients such as vitamin B12 and minerals like zinc and iron. The sesame oil adds healthy unsaturated fats to the dish. As for the calorie content, it varies depending on the size of the octopus but generally, a 100-gram serving of raw octopus coupled with the dipping sauce would be approximately 200-250 calories.

HWAJEON

Hwajeon is a traditional Korean pancake that translates to "flower cake" in English. This delightful treat combines simple ingredients to create a visually stunning and subtly sweet snack. Historically, Hwajeon was often made during Samjinnal, a Korean festival celebrated in early spring. Women would gather, picking seasonal edible flowers and incorporating them into these delicate pancakes, representing the beauty of spring and the joy of gathering together. Today, Hwajeon endures as a beloved example of Korean aesthetics in cuisine, heralding the fresh beauty of the season.

INGREDIENTS

- 1 cup of sweet rice flour (also known as glutinous rice flour or mochiko)
- 3/4 cup of warm water
- A pinch of salt
- Edible flowers (such as azaleas, chrysanthemums, or violets), thoroughly washed and petals separated
- Neutral-flavored oil (such as vegetable or canola), for frying
- A small amount of honey or rice syrup, for glazing

DIRECTIONS

1. In a mixing bowl, combine the sweet rice flour and salt together. Gradually add the warm water to the flour mixture while stirring, until the dough forms a smooth, pliable ball that does not stick to your hands. You may need slightly more or less water depending on the flour's absorbency.
2. Pinch off a piece of the dough, roughly the size of a walnut, and roll it into a ball. Then, flatten the ball into a round disc approximately 1/4 inch thick. Repeat with the remaining dough.
3. Heat a nonstick skillet over medium-low heat and lightly coat it with the neutral oil.
4. Place a few dough pancakes in the skillet, ensuring they do not touch each other.
5. Gently press a selection of edible flower petals onto the top of each pancake.
6. Fry the pancakes for about 1–2 minutes or until the bottoms become golden brown, then carefully flip them, frying the flower side just until set, about 30 seconds to 1 minute.
7. Transfer the pancakes to a serving plate and while still warm, brush the top with a light coating of honey or rice syrup, giving them a nice shine and a sweet flavor.
8. Serve your Hwajeon warm or at room temperature, ideally with a cup of green tea.

DIETARY MODIFICATIONS

Gluten-Sensitive: A natural gluten-free delight since sweet rice flour lacks gluten. No modifications are required.
Vegan: Substitute honey with a plant-based syrup like agave or maple to keep the dish vegan-friendly.
Low Sugar: For a less sweet variant, omit the honey or syrup glaze. The natural subtlety of the rice pancake combined with the flowers' flavor will still shine through.

INGREDIENT SPOTLIGHT: SWEET RICE FLOUR

Sweet rice flour, also known as glutinous rice flour or mochiko, is the spotlight ingredient for Hwajeon. Despite its name, it contains no gluten; rather, "glutinous" refers to the sticky, chewy texture it imparts. Made from short-grain glutinous rice, this flour is foundational in East Asian cuisine, forming the base for various sweets and dumplings. Its ability to create a delightfully chewy texture is crucial for Hwajeon, allowing the pancake to maintain its shape and capture the delicate imprint of the edible flowers.

CHEF'S TIPS

- For the ideal texture, the water used to form the dough should be warm—not hot—to encourage the dough to be smooth and pliable.
- Use a gentle touch when pressing flowers into the dough to avoid them getting submerged.
- Ensure the skillet is properly heated to prevent sticking, but not too hot, or the pancakes will brown too quickly without cooking through.
- For a more ceremonial or seasonal touch, choose flowers that are indicative of the current season or occasion.
- To keep Hwajeon soft when stored, place a damp paper towel over them before sealing in an airtight container. This helps them retain moisture.

POSSIBLE VARIATIONS OF THE RECIPE

- **Nutty Hwajeon:** Add finely chopped nuts such as walnuts or almonds into the dough for a delightful crunch and additional layer of flavor.
- **Colorful Batter:** Mix natural food colorings such as beet juice, matcha powder, or butterfly pea flower into separate portions of dough before shaping to create a vibrant assortment of Hwajeon.
- **Savory Spin:** Instead of sweetening with honey, sprinkle a little soy sauce and sesame seeds over your Hwajeon for a savory version that pairs wonderfully with tea or as a unique appetizer.

HEALTH NOTE & CALORIC INFORMATION

A typical sweet Hwajeon pancake is relatively low in calories, with each small pancake containing approximately 60-70 calories, mostly from carbs, with a negligible amount of protein and fat. The calories may vary slightly depending on the size of the pancakes and the amount of honey or syrup used. The edible flowers add minimal caloric value but can offer various vitamins and antioxidants, depending on the flower type used.

DEODEOK GUI

Originating from the mountainous terrains of Korea, Deodeok Gui has been a delicacy savored for its medicinal and nutritional properties. Deodeok, a native Korean root vegetable, has a unique woody fragrance and a bittersweet taste. It is often considered a mountain herb and is believed to promote vitality and health. Deodeok Gui embraces the essence of Korean barbecue—marinating and grilling to elicit sweet, smoky flavors. This dish is loved for its ability to bring the taste of the wild Korean landscape to the dinner table.

INGREDIENTS

- 500g deodeok root, cleaned and cut into 1/4-inch slices
- 3 tablespoons soy sauce
- 2 tablespoons brown sugar
- 2 tablespoons sesame oil
- 1 tablespoon minced garlic
- 1 tablespoon gochujang (Korean red pepper paste)
- 1 teaspoon grated ginger
- 2 green onions, finely chopped
- 1 tablespoon sesame seeds
- 1 teaspoon ground black pepper
- Vegetable oil, for grilling

DIRECTIONS

1. In a large bowl, whisk together the soy sauce, brown sugar, sesame oil, minced garlic, gochujang, grated ginger, chopped green onions, sesame seeds, and ground black pepper to create the marinade.
2. Submerge the deodeok slices in the marinade, ensuring each piece is well coated. Cover the bowl with plastic wrap and let it marinate in the refrigerator for at least 30 minutes, or up to 2 hours for a deeper flavor.
3. Preheat your grill or grill pan over medium-high heat. Lightly brush the grill with vegetable oil to prevent sticking.
4. Remove the deodeok slices from the marinade, allowing any excess to drip off. Reserve the leftover marinade for basting.
5. Place the deodeok slices onto the hot grill and cook for about 3 to 4 minutes on each side, basting occasionally with the reserved marinade, until the slices have nice grill marks and are tender.
6. Once grilled to perfection, transfer the deodeok to a serving platter.
7. Garnish with additional chopped green onions and sesame seeds if desired.
8. Serve immediately as a standalone dish or as a companion to rice and other Korean side dishes.

DIETARY MODIFICATIONS

Vegetarian/Vegan: Substitute soy sauce with tamari or a vegan soy sauce alternative to ensure no animal products are used.

Gluten-Free: Use gluten-free tamari instead of regular soy sauce to make it suitable for those with gluten intolerances.

Low-Carb/Sugar-Free: Replace the brown sugar with a sugar-free sweetener like stevia or erythritol and choose a low-carb gochujang alternative or omit it for a less sweet but still flavorful dish.

INGREDIENT SPOTLIGHT: GOCHUJANG

Gochujang is a fermented red chili paste and a staple in Korean cooking. Made from gochu (Korean red chili pepper), glutinous rice, fermented soybeans, and salt, it is aged over years in earthen pots outdoors. This process gives gochujang its complex sweetness, heat, and umami flavor. Integral to the marinade for Deodeok Gui, it imparts a deep, savory spice that complements the earthiness of the root vegetable.

CHEF'S TIPS

- When cleaning deodeok, use a brush to remove the dirt from its grooves without stripping the skin, preserving its natural flavor and nutrients.
- Score the deodeok slices lightly to help them absorb more of the marinade.
- Always let the grill heat up adequately before starting to ensure the best sear and to prevent sticking.
- Don't discard the marinade. Use it for basting to add an extra layer of flavor while grilling.
- Let the cooked deodeok rest for a couple of minutes after grilling to redistribute its juices and enhance its taste.

POSSIBLE VARIATIONS OF THE RECIPE

- **Spicy Deodeok Gui:** Add more gochujang to the marinade or sprinkle with sliced hot peppers before serving for an extra kick.
- **Citrusy Twist:** Include a dash of lemon juice or orange zest in the marinade for a refreshing citrus undertone.
- **Herbal Fusion:** Incorporate fresh herbs such as thyme or rosemary into the marinade to introduce a different aromatic profile.

HEALTH NOTE & CALORIC INFORMATION

Deodeok is rich in vitamins and minerals, contributing to its status as a health food in Korean cuisine. This dish is relatively low in calories, with a single serving containing approximately 150-200 calories, depending on the size of the portions and the specifics of the marinade ingredients. It is high in fiber and contains beneficial compounds that are said to aid in digestion and the immune system.

BOSSAM

Bossam is a beloved Korean dish that is often enjoyed at gatherings and special occasions. The dish consists of tender, flavorful pork that has been boiled in a rich broth and is served alongside a variety of accompaniments. It is traditionally wrapped in salted napa cabbage leaves and can be embellished with kimchi, garlic, peppers, and a savory, spicy sauce. The practice of wrapping food in leaves dates back to the Joseon Dynasty and was a method to enjoy foods in a neat, communal manner. Bossam brings the table together, encouraging diners to interact as they build their own wraps, making it a social and engaging meal.

INGREDIENTS

- 1.5 kg boneless pork belly (skin-on)
- 2 liters of water
- 1/2 onion
- 1 whole garlic bulb, halved horizontally
- 4 scallions, white parts only
- 1 knob ginger, approx. 50 g, sliced
- 1 apple, quartered
- 1 onion, quartered
- 1 cup of coffee milk (milk with coffee grounds)
- 1 tablespoon peppercorns
- 2 bay leaves
- 1 tablespoon doenjang (Korean soybean paste)
- Salted napa cabbage leaves (enough to serve)
- Kimchi, for serving
- Sliced garlic, for serving
- Sliced green chili peppers, for serving
- Ssamjang (Korean dipping sauce), for serving

DIRECTIONS

1. Rinse the pork belly in cold water and pat dry with paper towels.
2. In a large pot, combine 2 liters of water, half onion, halved garlic bulb, white parts of scallions, sliced ginger, quartered apple, quartered onion, and coffee milk. Bring to a boil over high heat.
3. Once the water boils, add the pork belly into the pot. Ensure it is fully submerged.
4. Add in the peppercorns, bay leaves, and Korean soybean paste (doenjang). Stir to combine the ingredients.
5. Lower the heat to a simmer and cook for about 1.5 to 2 hours, or until the pork is tender.
6. While the pork is cooking, prepare the salted napa cabbage leaves by washing them and trimming any excess thick stems. Set aside.
7. Once the pork is tender, remove it from the broth and let it rest for about 15 minutes, then slice it into bite-sized pieces.
8. Serve the pork with salted napa cabbage leaves, kimchi, sliced garlic, sliced green chili peppers, and ssamjang on the side for diners to wrap their own bossam.

DIETARY MODIFICATIONS

Gluten-Free: To make this bossam recipe gluten-free, ensure that the doenjang and ssamjang used are certified gluten-free. These ingredients can contain wheat, which is a source of gluten.

Low-Fat: For a lower-fat version, opt for a leaner cut of pork such as pork loin or tenderloin, and trim any excess fat. Boil the meat using the same method, which will still impart deep flavor with less fat content.

Low-Sodium: To accommodate a low-sodium diet, reduce the amount of doenjang or use a low-sodium alternative. You can also opt for low-sodium ssamjang or make a homemade version with reduced salt.

INGREDIENT SPOTLIGHT: DOENJANG

The spotlight ingredient of this recipe is doenjang, a fermented soybean paste that is fundamental in Korean cuisine. It's made by fermenting soybeans with salt and water, forming a rich, savory paste that can be quite pungent and earthy in flavor. Doenjang's origins can be traced back to the Three Kingdoms period of Korea over 1,500 years ago, a testament to its enduring popularity. This paste is not only pivotal as a flavor enhancer in soups, stews, and marinades, but it also contributes essential umami notes to the bossam's broth, marrying beautifully with the pork's natural richness.

CHEF'S TIPS

- Score the pork belly skin before cooking to help it absorb more flavors.
- If the pork belly is not fully submerged, rotate it every 30 minutes for even cooking.
- Adding coffee milk to the broth helps neutralize the pork's odor and tenderizes the meat.
- Allow the meat to rest before slicing to keep it tender and juicy.
- Traditional bossam is all about balance in flavor, texture, and heat — don't skimp on the accouterments, and encourage diners to play with combinations.

POSSIBLE VARIATIONS OF THE RECIPE

- **Spicy Bossam:** To add some heat to the dish, include a teaspoon of Korean red pepper flakes (gochugaru) into the broth and serve with extra spicy kimchi.
- **Citrus-Scented Bossam:** Substitute the apple in the broth with an orange or a lemon for a subtle citrus aroma that will infuse the pork.
- **Herb-Infused Bossam:** Add aromatic herbs such as star anise, cinnamon sticks, or cloves to the broth for a unique, fragrant twist on the classic recipe.

HEALTH NOTE & CALORIC INFORMATION

Bossam is rich in protein from the pork belly but is also high in fat and sodium, particularly because of the soybean paste and the salting process. A single serving can have approximately 600-700 calories, with significant variation depending on the size of the portion and the accompaniments. To lower the calorie and sodium content, serve smaller portions and use less doenjang or a low-sodium alternative.

GALBITANG

Galbitang is a traditional Korean soup made with beef short ribs, daikon radish, and glass noodles, simmered in a clear, savory broth. With its origins dating back to the Joseon Dynasty, this dish was initially prepared for Korean royalty and noble families. Galbitang is praised for its hearty flavors and its ability to showcase the rich taste of the beef. It is now widely enjoyed across Korea, especially during the cold months or for special occasions as a comforting, nourishing meal.

INGREDIENTS

- 1.5 lbs of beef short ribs
- 10 cups of water
- 1/2 medium-sized daikon radish, peeled and cut into large chunks
- 2 scallions, sliced
- 4 cloves of garlic, minced
- 2 tbsp of soy sauce
- 1 tbsp of sesame oil
- Salt and pepper, to taste
- 100 g of soaked glass noodles (dangmyeon)
- 1 egg, lightly beaten
- 1 small carrot, julienned (for garnish)
- Chopped fresh cilantro, for garnish (optional)
- 1 tbsp of rice wine (optional)

DIRECTIONS

1. Begin by preparing the short ribs. Rinse the ribs under cold water to remove bone fragments. Soak the ribs in cold water for 20 minutes to draw out blood, which helps create a clearer broth.
2. While the ribs are soaking, fill a large pot with 10 cups of water and bring it to a boil.
3. After soaking, drain the ribs and add them to the boiling water. Allow them to boil vigorously for 10 minutes to remove impurities.
4. Carefully remove the ribs from the pot, discard the water, and rinse the ribs and pot to remove any residues.
5. Refill the pot with 10 cups of fresh water and add the ribs back in. Bring to a boil, then reduce the heat to a low simmer.
6. Add the daikon radish chunks, soy sauce, rice wine (if using), and half of the minced garlic to the pot. Cover and simmer the soup for 1.5 to 2 hours or until the beef is tender.
7. About 30 minutes before the end of cooking time, soak the glass noodles in warm water to soften.
8. In a separate pan, sauté the remaining garlic in sesame oil until fragrant, then set aside.
9. Remove the beef ribs from the pot and let them cool slightly. When cool enough to handle, remove the meat from the bones and slice it into bite-sized pieces.
10. Strain the broth to remove solids and return the clear broth to the pot. Add the cooked beef, sautéed garlic, and salt and pepper to taste. Bring to a gentle simmer.
11. Drain the glass noodles and add them to the soup, cooking until tender—about 6-8 minutes.
12. Add the lightly beaten egg to the soup in a thin stream while stirring slowly to create thin ribbons of cooked egg.
13. Serve the Galbitang hot, garnished with sliced scallions, julienned carrot, and cilantro if desired.

DIETARY MODIFICATIONS

For **Vegetarian**: Swap the beef short ribs with hearty mushrooms like shiitake or portobello, and use vegetable stock instead of water. Soy sauce and sesame oil give depth to the broth.

For **Vegan**: Follow the vegetarian modifications and omit the egg. Add additional vegetables like bok choy or spinach, and enrich the broth with a piece of kombu (dried kelp) during simmering for umami.

For **Gluten-Free**: Ensure that the soy sauce is gluten-free and the glass noodles are made from 100% sweet potato starch, as some brands may contain wheat.

INGREDIENT SPOTLIGHT: DAIKON

Daikon radish is a mild-flavored, large white radish that plays a critical role in many Asian cuisines. In Galbitang, daikon contributes a subtle sweetness and a pleasing texture as it softens in the simmering broth. Its history dates back thousands of years in East Asia, and it has since become a global ingredient cherished for its versatility. In this recipe, it helps to balance the richness of the beef and rounds out the flavor profile of the soup.

CHEF'S TIPS

- Blanche the short ribs vigorously to achieve a clean, clear broth, which is essential for an authentic Galbitang.
- Adjust the cooking time based on the size of your short ribs; larger pieces may require more time to become tender.
- Use a fine-mesh strainer to ensure the broth is free of impurities when serving.
- Do not boil the soup after adding the glass noodles to prevent them from becoming too soft.
- Personalize the soup to your taste by adjusting the amount of soy sauce, garlic, and sesame oil used.

POSSIBLE VARIATIONS OF THE RECIPE

- **Spicy Galbitang:** Add sliced Korean red chili peppers or a spoonful of gochujang (red chili paste) to the broth for a spicy kick.
- **Galbitang Jjigae:** For a stew-like version, reduce the amount of water used, resulting in a thicker, more concentrated flavor.
- **Seafood Galbitang:** Replace beef ribs with seafood such as shrimp, clams, and mussels for a lighter yet equally satisfying soup.

HEALTH NOTE & CALORIC INFORMATION

Galbitang is a high-protein, low-carbohydrate dish due to the beef and minimal use of starchy vegetables. The beef short ribs provide essential amino acids, but also contribute saturated fat; removing excess fat from the broth can reduce this. The soup is quite low in calories, with an estimated 300-400 calories per serving, depending on portion size and specific ingredients used. It also contains vitamins and minerals from the vegetables, including vitamin A from the carrots and vitamin C from the daikon radish.

KIMCHI TACOS

Kimchi, a staple in Korean cuisine, is a traditional side dish of salted and fermented vegetables. Tacos, on the other hand, are a beloved Mexican classic. Fusion dishes bring together the best of different culinary traditions to create something new and exciting. The Kimchi Taco is a perfect example of this, merging the tangy and spicy flavors of Korean kimchi with the fresh and hearty components of a Mexican taco. This dish symbolizes a culinary handshake between two cultures, offering a delicious adventure for the palate.

INGREDIENTS

- 8 small corn or flour tortillas
- 1 lb (450g) thinly sliced beef (such as sirloin or ribeye) or pork belly
- 1 cup kimchi, roughly chopped
- 1 tbsp soy sauce
- 1 tbsp sesame oil
- 1 tbsp brown sugar
- 2 cloves garlic, minced
- 1 tsp ginger, grated
- 1/4 cup green onions, sliced
- 1 tsp Korean red pepper flakes (gochugaru) or to taste
- Vegetable oil, for frying
- 1 cup shredded lettuce
- 1/2 cup thinly sliced red onion
- Fresh cilantro leaves, for garnish
- Sesame seeds, for garnish
- Optional: Korean hot sauce (gochujang) or Mexican hot sauce

DIRECTIONS

1. In a bowl, combine the soy sauce, sesame oil, brown sugar, garlic, and ginger to create the marinade. Add the beef or pork to the marinade and ensure it's fully coated. Cover and let it marinate in the refrigerator for at least 30 minutes to an hour.
2. While the meat is marinating, prepare the garnishes. Wash and shred the lettuce, thinly slice the red onion, chop the kimchi (if not already pre-chopped), and slice the green onions.
3. Heat a pan over medium-high heat and add a little vegetable oil. Once hot, add the marinated meat in batches to avoid overcrowding, cooking it until nicely browned and caramelized. This should take about 2-3 minutes on each side for beef, slightly longer for pork belly.
4. Warm the tortillas by placing them in a dry pan over medium heat for about 30 seconds on each side or until they have some color.
5. To assemble, place some shredded lettuce on the center of each tortilla, followed by a serving of the cooked meat.
6. Top with the chopped kimchi, sliced red onions, and green onions.
7. Garnish with cilantro leaves, sesame seeds, and a drizzle of hot sauce if desired.
8. Serve the tacos immediately, allowing guests to construct their own or presenting them pre-assembled.

DIETARY MODIFICATIONS

Vegetarian: Replace the beef or pork with thick slices of firm tofu or tempeh. Marinate and cook in the same manner as the meat.

Vegan: In addition to the vegetarian swap, omit sesame seeds if desired and use a vegan hot sauce. Ensure that the kimchi is also vegan, as traditional kimchi is made with fish sauce.

Gluten-Free: Use gluten-free soy sauce in the marinade and ensure the tortillas are gluten-free as well. Always check labels to confirm.

INGREDIENT SPOTLIGHT: KIMCHI

Kimchi is more than just a side dish; it's a vital part of Korean heritage. Made from a mix of vegetables, primarily napa cabbage and Korean radishes, with a variety of seasonings like chili pepper, garlic, ginger, and jeotgal (salted seafood), every family has its unique recipe, passed down through generations. The fermentation process not only provides its distinctive tang but also nurtures beneficial lactobacilli, making kimchi a probiotic powerhouse. It brings a balance of umami, sweetness, and acidity that's central to the flavor profile of these tacos.

CHEF'S TIPS

- For best flavor, marinate the meat overnight. This allows the flavors to fully penetrate the meat, making it more tender and flavorful.
- When slicing beef or pork for the tacos, freeze the meat slightly to make it easier to cut into thin strips.
- Double the fresh factor by topping your tacos with a quick slaw made from additional fresh veggies like carrots and radishes.
- When warming tortillas, stack them wrapped in a damp cloth or paper towel and microwave for a few seconds for pliability with less risk of drying out or burning.
- Adjust the level of spiciness by adding more or less Korean red pepper flakes to the marinade to suit your taste.

POSSIBLE VARIATIONS OF THE RECIPE

- **Bulgogi Tacos:** Marinate the meat in a traditional bulgogi marinade before cooking, adding a sweeter profile to the taco.
- **Fish Tacos with Kimchi Slaw:** Replace the meat with a mild white fish such as tilapia or cod. Serve with a slaw made by mixing kimchi and coleslaw for a tangy crunch.
- **Tofu Kimchi Tacos with a Sesame-Maple Glaze:** For a sweet and nutty flavor, glaze the tofu with a mixture of sesame oil and maple syrup after marinating and before frying.

HEALTH NOTE & CALORIC INFORMATION

One serving (2 tacos) typically contains approximately 350-450 calories. The dish is high in protein due to the meat or alternative protein source. By including kimchi, you're also getting a dose of probiotics and potentially beneficial fermentation byproducts. Calories will vary based on exact ingredients used and portion sizes. Always consult with a nutritionist or use a calorie tracking app for precise nutritional information.

BULGOGI FUSION PIZZA

This recipe combines the timeless appeal of Italian pizza with the bold flavors of Korean cuisine. Bulgogi, which means "fire meat" in Korean, is a marinated meat dish renowned for its tenderness and savory profile. By adding it atop a classic pizza base, we create a culinary crossover that's as unique as it is delicious. This dish represents a merge of culinary traditions, bringing a new twist to pizza night that's sure to intrigue and delight.

INGREDIENTS

- 500g pizza dough (store-bought or homemade)
- 250g thinly sliced beef (sirloin or ribeye)
- 1 cup shredded mozzarella cheese
- 1 small onion, thinly sliced
- 1/2 red bell pepper, thinly sliced
- 1/2 yellow bell pepper, thinly sliced
- 2 green onions, chopped
- 2 tablespoons sesame seeds for garnish
- Olive oil for brushing
- Salt and pepper to taste

For the Bulgogi Marinade:

- 1/4 cup soy sauce
- 1 tablespoon sesame oil
- 2 tablespoons brown sugar
- 3 cloves garlic, minced
- 1 inch piece of ginger, minced
- 1 pear or apple, grated
- 1 tablespoon rice wine or mirin
- 1/2 tablespoon ground black pepper
- 1 tablespoon gochujang (Korean red pepper paste)

For the Pizza Sauce:

- 1 can (15 oz) tomato sauce
- 2 teaspoons Italian seasoning
- 1 clove garlic, minced
- Salt to taste

DIRECTIONS

1. Start by preparing the bulgogi marinade. In a bowl, mix together the soy sauce, sesame oil, brown sugar, minced garlic, minced ginger, grated pear or apple, rice wine, black pepper, and gochujang. Whisk until the sugar has dissolved and the ingredients are well combined.
2. Place the thinly sliced beef in the marinade making sure each piece is well coated. Cover and let it marinate in the refrigerator for at least 1 hour, preferably overnight.
3. Preheat your oven to the highest setting, usually between 475°F to 500°F (245°C to 260°C). If you have a pizza stone, place it in the oven to heat as well.
4. Prepare the pizza sauce by combining tomato sauce, Italian seasoning, minced garlic, and salt in a saucepan over medium heat. Simmer for about 10 minutes, until the sauce thickens slightly. Set aside to cool.
5. Roll out your pizza dough on a floured surface to your desired thickness. Transfer the dough to a piece of parchment paper or a preheated pizza stone dusted with flour.
6. Lightly brush the surface of the dough with olive oil. Spread a thin layer of the prepared pizza sauce, leaving a small border around the edges.
7. Sprinkle half of the shredded mozzarella cheese over the sauce.
8. In a pan over medium-high heat, cook the marinated beef slices until they are just cooked through, about 2-3 minutes per side.
9. Distribute the cooked bulgogi, onion, and bell peppers evenly over the cheese.
10. Top with the remaining mozzarella cheese and a sprinkle of green onions.
11. Transfer the pizza to the oven and bake for 10-15 minutes, or until the crust is golden and the cheese is bubbly.
12. Remove from the oven and let it rest for a few minutes. Sprinkle with sesame seeds before slicing and serving.

DIETARY MODIFICATIONS

Vegetarian: Substitute the beef with a mix of shiitake and button mushrooms sliced thinly and marinated in the bulgogi-style sauce. Mushrooms provide a meaty texture and can absorb the flavors well.

Vegan: Alongside the vegetarian substitution for beef, use a vegan cheese or nutritional yeast as a cheese alternative to maintain the creamy texture and umami flavor of the melted mozzarella.

Gluten-Free: Ensure the soy sauce used in the bulgogi marinade is gluten-free (tamari) and use a gluten-free pizza dough. Confirm all other ingredients are gluten-free as well, including the gochujang.

INGREDIENT SPOTLIGHT: GOCHUJANG

Gochujang is a savory, sweet, and spicy fermented condiment popular in Korean cooking. Made from red chili, glutinous rice, fermented soybeans, and salt, it has been a staple in Korea since the late 18th century. Its umami-rich flavor adds depth to dishes, and it's key in this recipe not only for the bulgogi marinade but also for delivering that authentic Korean heat that contrasts beautifully with the cheesy, savory pizza base.

CHEF'S TIPS

- Rest your pizza dough at room temperature for at least 30 minutes before rolling it out, to relax the gluten and ensure it doesn't shrink back.
- Use a pizza stone if available, as it mimics the cooking condition of a pizza oven and helps achieve a crispier crust.
- Slice beef against the grain for the most tender bites.
- When cooking bulgogi, ensure the pan is hot enough to sear the beef quickly without overcooking it.
- Let the pizza cool for a couple of minutes after baking to allow the cheese to set, making it easier to slice.

POSSIBLE VARIATIONS OF THE RECIPE

- **Spicy Bulgogi Pizza:** For those who love heat, increase the amount of gochujang in the bulgogi marinade and add spicy pickled jalapenos on top before baking.
- **Bulgogi Calzone:** Instead of making a traditional pizza, encase the bulgogi and cheese filling in pizza dough and bake to create a bulgogi calzone. Don't forget to cut a slit on top to let steam escape.
- **Korean BBQ Party Pizza:** Top the pizza with a variety of traditional Korean BBQ meats like pork belly or chicken alongside the bulgogi and add kimchi for an extra punch of flavor.

HEALTH NOTE & CALORIC INFORMATION

A single slice of Bulgogi Fusion Pizza (1/8 of the pizza) typically contains about 300-400 calories, depending on the amounts of cheese, meat, and dough used. This dish is high in protein from the meat and cheese, and can be high in carbohydrates due to the pizza base and sugar in the marinade. The nutritional content can vary based on the recipe alterations for diet modifications. It is advisable for those tracking their intake to adjust portions and ingredients as necessary.

DOENJANG CARBONARA

Carbonara is a beloved Italian pasta dish traditionally made with eggs, hard cheese, cured pork, and black pepper. Meanwhile, Doenjang, a fermented soybean paste, is a staple of Korean cuisine known for its rich umami flavor. In this fusion dish, we marry the creamy, indulgent nature of Carbonara with the deep, savory taste of Doenjang to create a cross-cultural culinary delight. This recipe is a testament to the versatility of Italian pasta and the flavorful power of Korean condiments.

INGREDIENTS

- 400g spaghetti or your choice of long pasta
- 2 large eggs plus 1 egg yolk
- 100g Pecorino Romano cheese, finely grated
- 4 tablespoons Doenjang (Korean soybean paste)
- 150g pancetta or thick-cut bacon, diced
- 4 cloves garlic, minced
- 1 tablespoons olive oil
- Freshly ground black pepper to taste
- 2 green onions, thinly sliced for garnish (optional)
- 1 teaspoon sesame seeds for garnish (optional)

DIRECTIONS

1. Bring a large pot of salted water to a boil, then add the pasta and cook according to package instructions until al dente. Reserve 1 cup of pasta water before draining.
2. While the pasta is cooking, whisk together the eggs, egg yolk, and grated Pecorino Romano cheese in a bowl until well combined. Set aside.
3. In a large skillet, heat the olive oil over medium heat. Add the diced pancetta or bacon and cook until crisp, about 4-5 minutes. Reduce the heat to low and add the garlic, cooking for an additional minute until fragrant.
4. Stir in the Doenjang and mix well with the pancetta and garlic. Cook over low heat for about 2 minutes, allowing the flavors to meld. If the mixture is too thick, add a splash of the reserved pasta water to loosen it.
5. Add the cooked pasta to the skillet, tossing it with the Doenjang mixture until well coated.
6. Remove the skillet from the heat. Quickly pour the egg and cheese mixture over the pasta, tossing vigorously with tongs or forks to coat the pasta without cooking the eggs. The residual heat will cook the sauce gently, creating a creamy texture.
7. If the sauce is too thick, slowly add more reserved pasta water, a tablespoon at a time, until reaching the desired consistency.
8. Season with freshly ground black pepper and taste for seasoning, adjusting if necessary.
9. Serve immediately, garnished with green onions and sesame seeds if using.

DIETARY MODIFICATIONS

Vegetarian: Replace the pancetta with a vegetarian bacon substitute or shiitake mushrooms for a similar umami depth. The mushrooms impart a savory note that complements the Doenjang.

Vegan: Use vegan pasta, eliminate the eggs, and use a vegan cheese substitute or nutritional yeast to mimic the cheesy flavor. Replace the pancetta with a smoky tofu or tempeh to retain some of the dish's original character.

Lactose Intolerance: Omit the Pecorino cheese and use lactose-free cheese or additional nutritional yeast for the cheesy flavor. Ensure that the pancetta or bacon used does not contain lactose.

INGREDIENT SPOTLIGHT: DOENJANG

Doenjang is traditionally made by fermenting soybeans with salt and water, sometimes with grains like rice. This process can take several months to years. Originating from Korean gastronomy, Doenjang is popular in a variety of dishes, such as stews and sauces. Its earthy, intense flavor lends a distinctive taste to any dish, perfectly enhancing the creaminess of a Carbonara. Employing it in this recipe brings an unexpected but harmonious twist to the Italian classic.

CHEF'S TIPS

- Use the highest quality Doenjang you can find for the best flavor—preferably from a Korean market or specialty store.
- Ensure the skillet is off the heat when adding the egg and cheese mixture to prevent curdling and achieve a silky sauce.
- Continuously toss the pasta while adding the egg and cheese mixture to evenly distribute the heat and the sauce.
- Reserve more pasta water than needed. It's better to have extra for adjusting the sauce consistency.
- When using Pecorino Romano, it's saltier than other cheeses, so be cautious when seasoning the dish.

POSSIBLE VARIATIONS OF THE RECIPE

- **Seafood Twist:** For an oceanic take, add sautéed shrimp or scallops to the Doenjang mixture before tossing with the pasta.
- **Spicy Adventure:** Introduce a teaspoon or so of Gochujang (Korean chili paste) along with the Doenjang for a spicy kick that complements the creamy sauce.
- **Mushroom Medley:** Skip the meat and sauté a variety of mushrooms like shiitake, oyster, and cremini with the garlic to infuse the dish with earthy flavors.

HEALTH NOTE & CALORIC INFORMATION

This dish is high in protein and carbohydrates. Pecorino Romano cheese provides calcium but also contributes to the saturated fat content.

Doenjang is a good source of probiotics due to the fermentation process.

A single serving—assuming the dish serves 4—approximately contains 650 to 700 calories, though this can vary with portion size and specific ingredients used.

BIBIMBAP BURGER

Bibimbap, meaning "mixed rice," is a beloved Korean dish that showcases a vibrant array of vegetables, meat, and gochujang (spicy fermented sauce), all atop a bowl of warm white rice. Our Bibimbap Burger is an innovative take on this classic, marrying the harmony of traditional bibimbap ingredients with the western staple, the hamburger. It represents a delicious fusion that offers a culinary adventure, blending the familiar form of a burger with the exotic flavors of Korea.

INGREDIENTS

- 1 lb (450g) ground beef (preferably sirloin)
- 4 brioche burger buns
- 1/2 cup fresh spinach leaves
- 1/2 cup julienned carrots
- 1/2 cup bean sprouts
- 1/2 cup shiitake mushrooms, sliced
- 1 small zucchini, julienned
- 4 eggs
- 1/4 cup gochujang (Korean chili paste)
- 2 tablespoons soy sauce
- 1 tablespoon sesame oil
- 1 tablespoon honey
- 2 cloves garlic, minced
- 1 teaspoon ginger, grated
- Salt and pepper to taste
- Cooking oil (for frying)
- Sesame seeds (for garnish)
- Green onions, chopped (for garnish)

DIRECTIONS

1. **Patties Preparation:** In a large bowl, combine ground beef, 1 tablespoon soy sauce, 1 clove minced garlic, 1/2 teaspoon grated ginger, salt, and pepper. Mix well but avoid overworking the meat. Form into four even patties about 3/4 inch thick. Set aside to marinate for about 15 minutes.
2. **Vegetable Preparation:** Blanch spinach and bean sprouts separately in boiling water for 1 minute each, then plunge into ice water to stop the cooking process. Drain and set aside. In a small pan over medium heat, sauté carrots, mushrooms, and zucchini with a dash of salt until tender. Remove from heat and keep warm.
3. **Burger Assembly:** Lightly toast the brioche buns and set aside. In a non-stick pan over medium heat, add a little cooking oil and cook each patty to your desired doneness, approximately 3-4 minutes per side for medium. Set the cooked patties aside and keep warm. In the same pan, fry the eggs sunny-side up or over easy, according to preference.
4. **Gochujang Sauce:** Whisk together gochujang, remaining soy sauce, sesame oil, honey, remaining garlic, and remaining ginger in a small bowl. Adjust the seasoning if necessary.
5. **Plating:** To assemble the Bibimbap Burger, spread some of the gochujang sauce on the bottom bun, place a warm beef patty on top, add a generous amount of sautéed vegetables, carefully place a fried egg atop the vegetables, and garnish with sesame seeds and chopped green onions. Drizzle with additional gochujang sauce if desired, and cover with the top bun.

DIETARY MODIFICATIONS

Vegetarian: Replace ground beef with a grilled portobello mushroom cap marinated in the same seasoning as the beef. Ensure the mushroom cap is well-cooked and has released most of its moisture before assembling the burger.

Vegan: Alongside the portobello mushroom substitution, use a vegan-friendly bun and skip the egg. Instead, top the burger with an extra layer of seasoned avocado slices for creaminess. Prepare the gochujang sauce with vegan alternatives to honey, such as agave syrup.

Gluten-Free: Use a high-quality gluten-free bun and ensure that the gochujang and soy sauce are gluten-free varieties. Be cautious of cross-contamination if preparing this in an environment where gluten products are also handled.

INGREDIENT SPOTLIGHT: GOCHUJANG

Gochujang, a deep-red, spicy, and slightly sweet Korean condiment, has been a cornerstone of Korean cuisine for centuries. It's made from red chili, glutinous rice, fermented soybeans, and salt. This fermentation process allows the flavors to develop and deepen, giving gochujang its unique taste. It's used in numerous Korean dishes to add depth, heat, and rich umami flavor. In the Bibimbap Burger, gochujang acts as both a marinade for the patty and a sauce, infusing the dish with authentic Korean zest.

CHEF'S TIPS

- Avoid pressing down on the burgers while cooking, as this can release the juices and result in a drier patty.
- For the gochujang sauce, start with a small amount and continually taste as you add more ingredients to balance the flavors according to your preference.
- Preparing the vegetables while the meat marinates will streamline the cooking process and ensure all components are ready at the same time.
- Rest the cooked patties for a few minutes before assembling to ensure the juices redistribute for a moist burger.
- If you're sensitive to spice, you can control the heat level by reducing the amount of gochujang in the sauce.

POSSIBLE VARIATIONS OF THE RECIPE

- **Low-Carb Bibimbap Burger Bowl:** Forgo the bun entirely and serve the patty and toppings over a bed of cauliflower rice for a low-carb alternative.
- **Turkey Bibimbap Burger:** Substitute ground beef with ground turkey for a leaner burger. Adjust seasonings if necessary, as turkey can handle a more robust spice mix.
- **Seafood Delight:** Replace the beef patty with a seasoned grilled salmon fillet for a pescatarian twist that adds omega-3 fatty acids to your meal.

HEALTH NOTE & CALORIC INFORMATION

A single serving of a Bibimbap Burger (one burger) is approximately 650-750 calories, depending on the size of the bun and amount of gochujang sauce used. It provides a good balance of protein from the beef and egg, carbohydrates from the bun and vegetables, and healthy fats from the sesame oil and beef. The variation of this burger can add valuable fiber if additional vegetables are selected, and calories can be managed by opting for leaner meats or vegetarian options.

KIMCHI SANDWICH

This dish is a cross-cultural marvel that marries the beloved comfort food of a traditional American grilled cheese sandwich with the punchy, fermented flavors of Korean kimchi. The dish symbolizes a fusion of cuisines where East meets West, offering a delicious twist to each culture's staple. Perfect for those who yearn for a touch of adventure in their everyday meals.

INGREDIENTS

- 4 slices of sourdough bread
- 1 cup of grated sharp cheddar cheese
- 1 cup of grated mozzarella cheese
- 1/2 cup of kimchi, chopped
- 2 tablespoons of unsalted butter, room temperature
- 1 tablespoon of mayonnaise (optional for spreading on the bread)
- Freshly ground black pepper (to taste)

DIRECTIONS

1. Preheat a non-stick skillet or griddle over medium heat.
2. If using, spread a thin layer of mayonnaise on one side of each slice of bread. This is an optional step, but it can help create a crisper crust.
3. Place two slices of bread, mayonnaise side down, onto the preheated skillet.
4. Sprinkle each with half of the cheddar and mozzarella cheeses, covering the surface evenly.
5. Add the chopped kimchi on top of the cheese, distributing it equally between the two slices. Season with black pepper to taste.
6. Add the remaining cheese on top of the kimchi, creating a cheese-kimchi-cheese layer.
7. Place the remaining slices of bread on top, mayonnaise side up.
8. Cook the sandwiches for about 3-4 minutes on the first side or until the bread is golden brown and crispy.
9. Carefully flip the sandwiches with a spatula, pressing them down slightly, and cook for another 3-4 minutes or until the second side is golden brown and the cheese has melted.
10. Once cooked, remove from the skillet, let them rest for a minute before cutting in half, and serve hot.

DIETARY MODIFICATIONS

Vegetarian: The recipe is already vegetarian-friendly. Ensure that the kimchi used does not contain fish sauce, which is common in some traditional kimchi recipes.

Vegan: Substitute the cheddar and mozzarella with your favorite vegan cheese alternatives that melt well. Use a dairy-free butter substitute or olive oil for buttering (or mayonnaise alternative for spreading).

Gluten-Free: Use gluten-free bread in place of sourdough. Be sure to check that the kimchi used is free of gluten-containing ingredients like soy sauce.

INGREDIENT SPOTLIGHT: KIMCHI

Kimchi is the heart of this fusion sandwich. A staple in Korean cuisine, kimchi is a traditional side dish made from fermented vegetables, most commonly napa cabbage and Korean radishes, with a variety of seasonings, including chili powder, garlic, ginger, and often fish sauce. Fermentation not only extends the shelf life of the vegetables but also creates a unique tangy, spicy, and umami-packed taste. Kimchi has a rich history dating back to ancient Korea, where it evolved through centuries. It's key to this recipe as it provides the characteristic bold flavor that juxtaposes the mellowness of the melted cheeses.

CHEF'S TIPS

- Remove excess moisture from the kimchi by pressing it between paper towels; this helps to prevent soggy sandwiches.
- Shred your own cheese if possible; pre-shredded cheese often has anti-caking agents that can hinder melting.
- Cook the sandwich slowly on medium heat to ensure the cheese melts completely without burning the bread.
- Using a cast-iron skillet can provide the best heat distribution for a perfectly grilled sandwich.
- Letting the sandwich cool for a minute allows the cheese to set, making it easier to cut and eat without all the cheese oozing out.

POSSIBLE VARIATIONS OF THE RECIPE

- **Spicy Kimchi Grilled Cheese:** Add a spread of gochujang (Korean chili paste) to the bread before adding the cheese for an extra layer of heat.
- **Kimchi Grilled Cheese with Bacon:** For a non-vegetarian twist, add a layer of cooked bacon between the cheese and kimchi layers.
- **Kimchi Grilled Cheese 'Deluxe':** Introduce thinly sliced green onions, a fried egg, or a slice of ham to the sandwich for added flavor and texture.

HEALTH NOTE & CALORIC INFORMATION

A standard serving of the Kimchi Grilled Cheese Sandwich contains approximately 600-700 calories, with high levels of calcium from the cheese and vitamins from the kimchi. The fermented kimchi delivers probiotics beneficial for digestive health, though the dish is also high in sodium, saturated fats, and can be high in cholesterol depending on the cheeses used. For those monitoring their intake, be mindful of portion sizes and cheese selection.

GOCHUJANG SPAGHETTI

Fusing Italian pasta with Korean flavors, this dish is an embodiment of culinary cultural exchange. Gochujang, a staple in Korean cooking, lends a deep, savory spice to the classic comfort of spaghetti. With the addition of crispy tofu, the recipe adapts to various dietary needs while providing a satisfying protein component that soaks up the flavors. It's a modern, flavorful dish that bows to tradition while embracing innovation.

INGREDIENTS

- 400g spaghetti
- 3 tablespoons gochujang (Korean chili paste)
- 2 tablespoons soy sauce
- 1 tablespoon sesame oil
- 2 teaspoons sugar
- 2 garlic cloves, minced
- 300g firm tofu, pressed and cubed
- 2 tablespoons cornstarch
- Vegetable oil, for frying
- 1 bell pepper, thinly sliced
- 4 green onions, sliced into 1-inch segments
- 1 tablespoon toasted sesame seeds
- Salt, to taste

DIRECTIONS

1. Boil a large pot of salted water and cook the spaghetti according to package instructions until al dente. Drain and set aside.
2. In a small bowl, whisk together gochujang, soy sauce, sesame oil, sugar, and minced garlic. Adjust to taste; the sauce should be a harmonious blend of sweet, savory, and spicy.
3. Pat the tofu dry and toss the cubes with cornstarch until evenly coated.
4. Heat a generous amount of vegetable oil in a pan over medium-high heat. Fry the tofu in batches until all sides are golden brown and crispy. Drain on paper towels and sprinkle with a pinch of salt.
5. In the same pan, sauté the bell pepper and half of the green onions until slightly softened, about 2-3 minutes.
6. Reduce the heat to low, add the cooked spaghetti and gochujang sauce to the vegetables, and toss until the pasta is evenly coated.
7. Add the crispy tofu to the pan, gently incorporating it with the spaghetti.
8. Serve the gochujang spaghetti garnished with the remaining green onions and toasted sesame seeds.

DIETARY MODIFICATIONS

Vegetarian: The recipe is already vegetarian-friendly.

Vegan: Substitute the sugar with maple syrup or agave nectar to ensure it's vegan, as some sugar is processed using bone char.

Gluten-Free: Use gluten-free spaghetti and ensure the soy sauce is a gluten-free tamari to accommodate those with gluten sensitivities.

INGREDIENT SPOTLIGHT: GOCHUJANG

Gochujang is a beloved Korean condiment made from red chili, glutinous rice, fermented soybeans, and salt. It dates back to the 18th century and has become integral to the Korean palate. Gochujang offers a complex flavor profile—spicy, umami-rich, slightly sweet—and it's the soul of this dish. Its depth transforms the neutral canvas of spaghetti into a vibrant and nuanced delight.

CHEF'S TIPS

- Ensure the tofu is well-pressed to remove excess moisture; this is key to achieving a crispy texture when fried.
- Do not overcook the spaghetti. Al dente pasta will hold up better when tossed with the sauce and vegetables.
- Adjust the gochujang according to your preference for spice. Start with less and add more as desired.
- You can save the tofu frying oil to use in other dishes; it will have picked up some of the sesame and gochujang flavor.
- Prepare the gochujang sauce ahead of time to let the flavors meld for a richer taste.

POSSIBLE VARIATIONS OF THE RECIPE

- **Seafood Twist:** Add sautéed shrimp or squid with the tofu for a pescatarian option, imbuing the dish with a taste of the sea.
- **Mushroom Medley:** Use a mix of sautéed mushrooms in place of tofu for an earthy flavor and meaty texture.
- **Kale Crunch:** Incorporate sautéed kale for a nutritious punch and to add a crispy texture contrast.

HEALTH NOTE & CALORIC INFORMATION

This dish is high in protein due to tofu and provides complex carbohydrates from the pasta, offering a sustained energy release. Gochujang is calorie-dense, so portion control is advisable for calorie-conscious eaters. A single serving may contain approximately 500 to 600 calories, depending on preparation methods and portion sizes.

FRIED CAULIFLOWER

Fusing the age-old tradition of Korean street food with contemporary tastes, Korean Fried Cauliflower "Kkochi" (meaning skewer) takes inspiration from the popular Korean fried chicken, reimagined for vegetarians and health-conscious eaters. Historically, street foods like tteok-kkochi (rice cake skewers) are devoured by bustling crowds. Here, cauliflower florets replace meat, coated in a crispy batter and slathered with a savory, sweet, and spicy sauce, reminiscent of the buzzing streets of Seoul.

INGREDIENTS

- 1 large cauliflower, cut into bite-sized florets
- 1 cup all-purpose flour
- 1/2 cup cornstarch
- 1 teaspoon baking powder
- 2 teaspoons Korean chili flakes (gochugaru)
- 1 teaspoon garlic powder
- 1 teaspoon ginger powder
- 1 1/2 cups cold water
- Salt, to taste
- Vegetable oil, for frying

Sauce:
- 1/4 cup gochujang (Korean red chili paste)
- 3 tablespoons honey
- 2 tablespoons soy sauce
- 1 tablespoon rice vinegar
- 1 tablespoon sesame oil
- 2 cloves garlic, minced
- 1 teaspoon grated ginger
- 1 tablespoon brown sugar
- 1 tablespoon water

Garnish:
- Sesame seeds
- Sliced green onions

DIRECTIONS

1. Begin by preparing the cauliflower. Wash the florets thoroughly and pat them dry with a paper towel.
2. In a large mixing bowl, whisk together the flour, cornstarch, baking powder, gochugaru, garlic powder, ginger powder, and salt.
3. Slowly add the cold water to the dry ingredients, stirring continuously to form a smooth batter. The consistency should be similar to pancake batter; it should coat the back of a spoon but not be overly thick.
4. Heat vegetable oil in a deep fryer or a large pot to 350°F (175°C). Use a candy thermometer to ensure accurate temperature.
5. Dip each cauliflower floret into the batter, allowing excess to drip off. Carefully lower the battered florets into the hot oil. Do not overcrowd the pot; work in batches.
6. Fry for 3-4 minutes, or until golden and crispy. Remove with a slotted spoon and place on a wire rack or a plate lined with paper towels to drain excess oil.
7. For the sauce, combine gochujang, honey, soy sauce, rice vinegar, sesame oil, minced garlic, grated ginger, brown sugar, and water in a small saucepan. Stir well and simmer over medium heat for about 5 minutes until thickened.
8. Toss the fried cauliflower in the sauce or drizzle it over the top, according to preference.
9. Garnish with sesame seeds and sliced green onions before serving.

DIETARY MODIFICATIONS

Gluten-Free: Replace all-purpose flour with a gluten-free flour blend and ensure that the soy sauce is a gluten-free brand such as Tamari.

Vegan: Substitute honey with maple syrup or agave nectar to retain the sweet and sticky consistency essential to the sauce.

Low-Carb: Swap out all-purpose flour and cornstarch for almond flour and omit brown sugar from the sauce. You may need to adjust water to achieve the right batter consistency.

INGREDIENT SPOTLIGHT: GOCHUJANG

Gochujang is a savory, spicy, and pungent fermented Korean condiment made from red chili, glutinous rice, fermented soybeans, and salt. It's a staple in Korean cuisine, known for its depth of flavor that comes from the fermentation process. The paste is traditionally used in dishes like bibimbap and dakgalbi. In this recipe, gochujang is key for imbuing the sauce with a unique heat and a rich umami kick that is characteristically Korean.

CHEF'S TIPS

- Ensure your cauliflower florets are thoroughly dried to prevent the batter from becoming too runny and to guarantee a crisp coating.
- Cold water in the batter helps prevent gluten formation, keeping the batter light and crispy.
- Double frying the cauliflower will give you an extra crunch. Let them cool slightly after the first fry and then dip them back in the hot oil for one more minute.
- Allow the sauce to cool somewhat before tossing with the cauliflower to prevent the coating from becoming soggy.
- When tossing the cauliflower with the sauce, use a large bowl and a folding motion to coat each piece evenly without knocking off the batter.

POSSIBLE VARIATIONS OF THE RECIPE

- **Spicy Mango:** Add 1/4 cup of pureed mango and a squirt of lime juice to the sauce for a tropical twist with a hint of heat.
- **Soy Garlic:** Forgo the gochujang and mix soy sauce with garlic, a little honey, and a sprinkle of toasted sesame seeds for a milder but equally delicious sauce.
- **Peanut Crunch:** Skip the sauce entirely and toss the fried cauliflower in a mixture of crushed peanuts, a drizzle of honey, and a pinch of salt for a savoury snack with a nutty crunch.

HEALTH NOTE & CALORIC INFORMATION

The Korean Fried Cauliflower is relatively low in calories compared to its chicken counterpart, with an estimated 150-200 calories per serving (without considering oil absorption). This dish is high in vitamin C and K, due to the cauliflower, and offers moderate amounts of iron and fiber. The sauce, however, adds sugar and sodium, so it should be consumed in moderation for a balanced diet.

TTEOKBOKKI FONDUE

Tteokbokki, a well-loved Korean street food, traditionally consists of chewy rice cakes smothered in a spicy, sweet red chili sauce known as gochujang. This recipe elevates the classic dish to an interactive dining experience by transforming it into a fondue. Tteokbokki Fondue marries the communal aspect of Swiss fondue with the unmistakable flavors of Korean cuisine, making it perfect for a social gathering or a fun family meal.

INGREDIENTS

- 2 cups of Korean rice cakes (tteok), cylindrical or sliced
- 4 cups of low-sodium chicken or vegetable broth
- 3 tbsp of gochujang (Korean red chili paste)
- 1 tbsp of soy sauce
- 1 tbsp of honey or sugar (adjust to taste)
- 2 cloves of garlic, minced
- 1 tbsp of sesame oil
- 1 tsp of ground black pepper
- 200g of mozzarella cheese, shredded
- 1 scallion, finely sliced for garnish
- 1 tbsp of sesame seeds for garnish
- Assorted vegetables such as carrot sticks, bell pepper strips, and broccoli florets
- Additional dippers like cooked shrimp or beef slices (optional)

DIRECTIONS

1. If using frozen rice cakes, soak them in warm water for 20 minutes, or until they become soft. Drain and set aside.
2. In a fondue pot or a deep saucepan, heat the sesame oil over medium heat. Add the minced garlic and sauté until fragrant.
3. Pour in the chicken or vegetable broth and bring to a gentle simmer.
4. Stir in the gochujang, soy sauce, and honey or sugar until well combined.
5. Gradually add the shredded mozzarella cheese to the simmering broth, constantly stirring to prevent any cheese from sticking to the bottom and to help it melt evenly.
6. Once the cheese has completely melted into a smooth consistency, add the prepared rice cakes.
7. Let the mixture cook for another 5-7 minutes, or until the rice cakes are fully cooked and have absorbed some of the sauce.
8. Sprinkle in the ground black pepper and adjust seasoning if necessary.
9. Serve hot with the sliced scallion and sesame seeds sprinkled on top.
10. Arrange the assorted vegetables and optional dippers on a platter around the fondue pot.
11. Provide fondue forks or skewers for your guests to dip and enjoy the Tteokbokki Fondue.

DIETARY MODIFICATIONS

Vegetarian: Substitute chicken broth with vegetable broth and use plant-based soy cheese or any meltable vegetarian cheese instead of mozzarella.

Vegan: Alongside the vegetarian substitutions, use agave syrup or maple syrup in place of honey, and ensure that the gochujang is vegan-friendly (some brands may contain fish sauce).

Lactose Intolerance: Opt for lactose-free cheese options that still melt well, such as certain varieties of lactose-free mozzarella or cheddar.

INGREDIENT SPOTLIGHT: GOCHUJANG

Gochujang is the spotlight ingredient of this fusion dish. This quintessentially Korean condiment dates back to the 18th century and is made from red chili powder, glutinous rice, fermented soybeans, and salt. This thick, savory paste imparts a robust umami flavor with a balance of sweetness and heat. Gochujang is key to Tteokbokki Fondue as it provides the foundational flavor profile that makes this dish authentically Korean.

CHEF'S TIPS

- When adding the cheese, do so slowly and on low heat to avoid the sauce from splitting and becoming grainy.
- For an extra kick, you can add a teaspoon of Korean red pepper flakes (gochugaru) alongside the gochujang.
- Avoid overcooking the rice cakes; they should be tender but still have a chewy bite to them.
- Keep the fondue on a low flame or candle to maintain the right temperature and texture when serving.
- If the fondue begins to thicken too much as it cools, add a splash of broth to thin it out, ensuring that it remains dippable.

POSSIBLE VARIATIONS OF THE RECIPE

- **Seafood Delight:** Incorporate seafood such as shrimp, squid, and mussels into the fondue for a pescatarian version.
- **Fiery Challenge:** Add more gochujang and a few dashes of Korean hot sauce for those who love an intense heat.
- **Cheese Trio:** Blend different types of cheese such as cheddar, gruyere, and gouda for a more complex cheese flavor.

HEALTH NOTE & CALORIC INFORMATION

While this dish is a delightful indulgence, it's important to be mindful that it's high in carbohydrates and calories due to the rice cakes and cheese. Gochujang also contains sugars, though it offers the benefit of capsaicin from the red chili, which can boost metabolism. Sharing this dish amongst friends can help moderate individual portion sizes. The estimated calorie content for a serving size of approximately one cup (including a serving of vegetables) is around 450 calories.

MAKGEOLLI SORBET

Makgeolli, a traditional Korean rice wine, has graced tables for centuries, offering a milky, sweet, and tangy flavor. A staple in Korean culture, it is often enjoyed at the end of a meal or during a leisurely afternoon. In this modern twist, we transform the ancient beverage into a refreshing sorbet, perfect for a palate cleanser or a unique dessert. This fusion recipe brings a piece of Korean tradition into the realm of contemporary cuisine, offering a delightful taste experience to the adventurous palate.

INGREDIENTS

- 2 cups makgeolli (Korean rice wine)
- 3/4 cup granulated sugar
- 1 tablespoon honey
- 2 tablespoons lemon juice
- 1 teaspoon lemon zest
- Pinch of salt
- Fresh mint leaves (for garnish)

DIRECTIONS

1. Combine makgeolli, sugar, and honey in a saucepan. Place it over medium heat and stir until the sugar completely dissolves.
2. Remove the saucepan from heat and allow the mixture to cool to room temperature.
3. Stir in lemon juice, lemon zest, and a pinch of salt into the cooled makgeolli mixture.
4. Pour the mixture into a shallow dish and place it in the freezer for about 1 hour or until the edges start to set.
5. Stir the icy edges into the middle every 30 minutes, repeat this process for about 2-3 hours, until the mixture is evenly frozen and has a slushy consistency.
6. For a smoother sorbet, you can blend the semi-frozen mixture in a blender or food processor until smooth, then refreeze until set.
7. Serve the sorbet in chilled bowls or glasses and garnish with fresh mint leaves.

DIETARY MODIFICATIONS

For a **Non-Alcoholic Version:** Replace makgeolli with a non-alcoholic fermented rice drink or rice milk. Adjust sweetness as non-alcoholic substitutions may lack the natural sweetness of makgeolli.

For **Vegans**: Ensure that the makgeolli used is vegan-friendly as some brands may use animal derivatives in the brewing process. The rest of the ingredients are already vegan-friendly.

For **Low-Sugar Diet:** Substitute granulated sugar for a sugar alternative like stevia or use a smaller amount. Adjust to taste as these substitutes vary in sweetness compared to sugar.

INGREDIENT SPOTLIGHT: MAKGEOLLI

Makgeolli is a Korean traditional alcoholic beverage made from fermented rice. Its milky, off-white color characterizes it and is lightly sparkling. As one of the oldest alcoholic drinks in Korea, makgeolli is thought to date back to the 10th century. This drink is enjoyed for its flavor and nutritional benefits, including a rich content of probiotics, vitamins, and amino acids. In our recipe, makgeolli adds a unique depth of flavor that's tangy, slightly sweet, and beautifully complements the zesty lemon notes of the sorbet.

CHEF'S TIPS

- Keep all your utensils and the container for freezing cold by placing them in the fridge before using them.
- To prevent ice crystals from forming, add a tablespoon of alcohol, such as vodka, to the mixture—it lowers the freezing point.
- For an ultra-smooth texture, consider using an ice cream maker if you have one, following its specific instructions for sorbets.
- Drizzle a small amount of extra makgeolli over the sorbet just before serving to enhance the rice wine flavor.
- Lemon zest can be overpowering; make sure to use just enough to add a hint of citrus without overwhelming the makgeolli.

POSSIBLE VARIATIONS OF THE RECIPE

- **Berry Makgeolli Sorbet:** Add 1/2 cup of pureed strawberries or raspberries to the mix before freezing for a fruity twist.
- **Ginger Makgeolli Sorbet:** Infuse the makgeolli with fresh ginger slices while heating it. Strain before cooling for a spicy kick.
- **Cinnamon-Makgeolli Sorbet:** Include a stick of cinnamon during the heating process for a warm, autumnal flavor, then remove before freezing.

HEALTH NOTE & CALORIC INFORMATION

Makgeolli sorbet is relatively low in calories due to its high water content. However, it does contain alcohol and sugars, contributing to its caloric value. A standard serving of this dessert (about half a cup) would typically have approximately 150-200 calories, with traces of vitamins and amino acids from the makgeolli. Keep in mind that nutritional content can vary based on the exact ingredients used and portion sizes.

SAMGYEOPSAL WRAPS

Samgyeopsal, a beloved Korean grilled pork belly dish, meets the refreshing crispness of salad wraps in this fusion of flavors. Traditionally, samgyeopsal is enjoyed with soju, wrapped in lettuce with a dab of ssamjang (a spicy-sweet sauce). This dish takes the communal fun of Korean barbeque and pairs it with the health-conscious focus of salad wraps. The Samgyeopsal Salad Wraps offer a lighter take on the classic while preserving its essence and interactive dining experience.

INGREDIENTS

- 500g pork belly, thinly sliced
- Salt and freshly ground black pepper, to taste
- 1 tablespoon sesame oil
- 1 garlic clove, minced
- 1 teaspoon ginger, minced
- 1 head of butter lettuce, leaves separated
- 1 carrot, julienned
- 1 cucumber, julienned
- 1 red pepper, julienned
- Fresh mint leaves
- Fresh cilantro leaves
- For the sauce (Ssamjang):
- 2 tablespoons doenjang (fermented soybean paste)
- 1 tablespoon gochujang (Korean red chili paste)
- 1 tablespoon sesame oil
- 1 tablespoon honey
- 1 garlic clove, finely minced
- 1 green onion, chopped

DIRECTIONS

1. Start by preheating a grill or a heavy skillet over medium-high heat.
2. Season the pork belly slices generously with salt and pepper.
3. In a small bowl, combine sesame oil, minced garlic, and ginger. Brush this mixture onto both sides of the pork belly slices.
4. Place the seasoned pork belly on the grill or skillet and cook for about 2-3 minutes per side, or until the meat is golden brown and slightly crispy. Ensure proper ventilation during cooking as it can get smoky.
5. While the pork is cooking, wash and dry the butter lettuce leaves and prepare the carrot, cucumber, and red pepper by julienning them into thin strips.
6. To make the ssamjang sauce, combine the doenjang, gochujang, sesame oil, honey, minced garlic, and green onion in a bowl and mix well.
7. Once the pork belly is cooked, transfer it to a plate and let it rest for a couple of minutes before slicing it into pieces that will fit comfortably in a lettuce wrap.
8. To assemble a wrap, take a lettuce leaf and place a few pieces of pork belly in the center, add a few strips of carrot, cucumber, and red pepper, and a few leaves of mint and cilantro.
9. Drizzle with the ssamjang sauce, fold in the edges of the lettuce, and roll it up to create a wrap.
10. Continue with the remaining ingredients until all of the pork belly is used.
11. Serve the wraps immediately.

DIETARY MODIFICATIONS

Vegetarian: Replace the pork belly with thick slices of grilled king oyster mushrooms seasoned with the same sesame oil, garlic, and ginger mix. Mushrooms have a meaty texture that can replicate the pork belly's bite.

Vegan: In addition to substituting mushrooms for pork belly, use maple syrup instead of honey in the ssamjang sauce for a vegan-friendly sweetener.

Gluten-Free: Ensure that the doenjang and gochujang are gluten-free varieties. Some traditional Korean pastes may contain wheat, so checking labels is crucial.

INGREDIENT SPOTLIGHT: DOENJANG

Doenjang is a robust fermented soybean paste that anchors the flavor profile of Korean cuisine. Its origins stretch back to the Three Kingdoms period of Korea (57 BC to 668 AD), making it a time-honored staple. What sets doenjang apart is its rich umami kick and its health benefits coming from probiotics due to the fermentation process. This pungent paste is key to our ssamjang sauce which gives our Samgyeopsal Salad Wraps an authentic depth of flavor that's distinctly Korean.

CHEF'S TIPS

- When grilling the pork belly, don't overcrowd the grill or skillet; it may steam instead of searing.
- Letting the cooked pork belly rest before slicing helps retain its juices, making it more succulent.
- For a crispier pork belly, increase the cooking time slightly but watch carefully to avoid burning.
- When handling the lettuce leaves, be gentle to avoid tearing. They need to be flexible enough to wrap around the filling.
- Personalize the ssamjang sauce to your taste. Adjust the gochujang if you prefer a spicier sauce or the honey for more sweetness.

POSSIBLE VARIATIONS OF THE RECIPE

- **Fish Lover's Delight:** Swap the pork belly for grilled fish like mackerel or salmon for an omega-rich alternative.
- **Spicy Kimchi Wrap:** Add a spoonful of chopped kimchi to each wrap for a tangy and spicy kick.
- **Beef Bulgogi Bites:** Replace pork belly with thinly sliced beef bulgogi, another beloved Korean barbeque staple, and cook similarly.

HEALTH NOTE & CALORIC INFORMATION

Each serving (2 wraps) typically contains about 300-350 calories, with a good balance of protein from the pork belly and a range of vitamins and minerals from the fresh vegetables. However, the calorie count can vary depending on the size of the wraps and the amount of pork belly used. The dish is low in carbs but high in fat due to the pork belly; opt for leaner cuts or alternative proteins for a lower fat option. Additionally, the ssamjang sauce, while flavorful, is relatively high in sodium, so those watching their salt intake should enjoy in moderation.

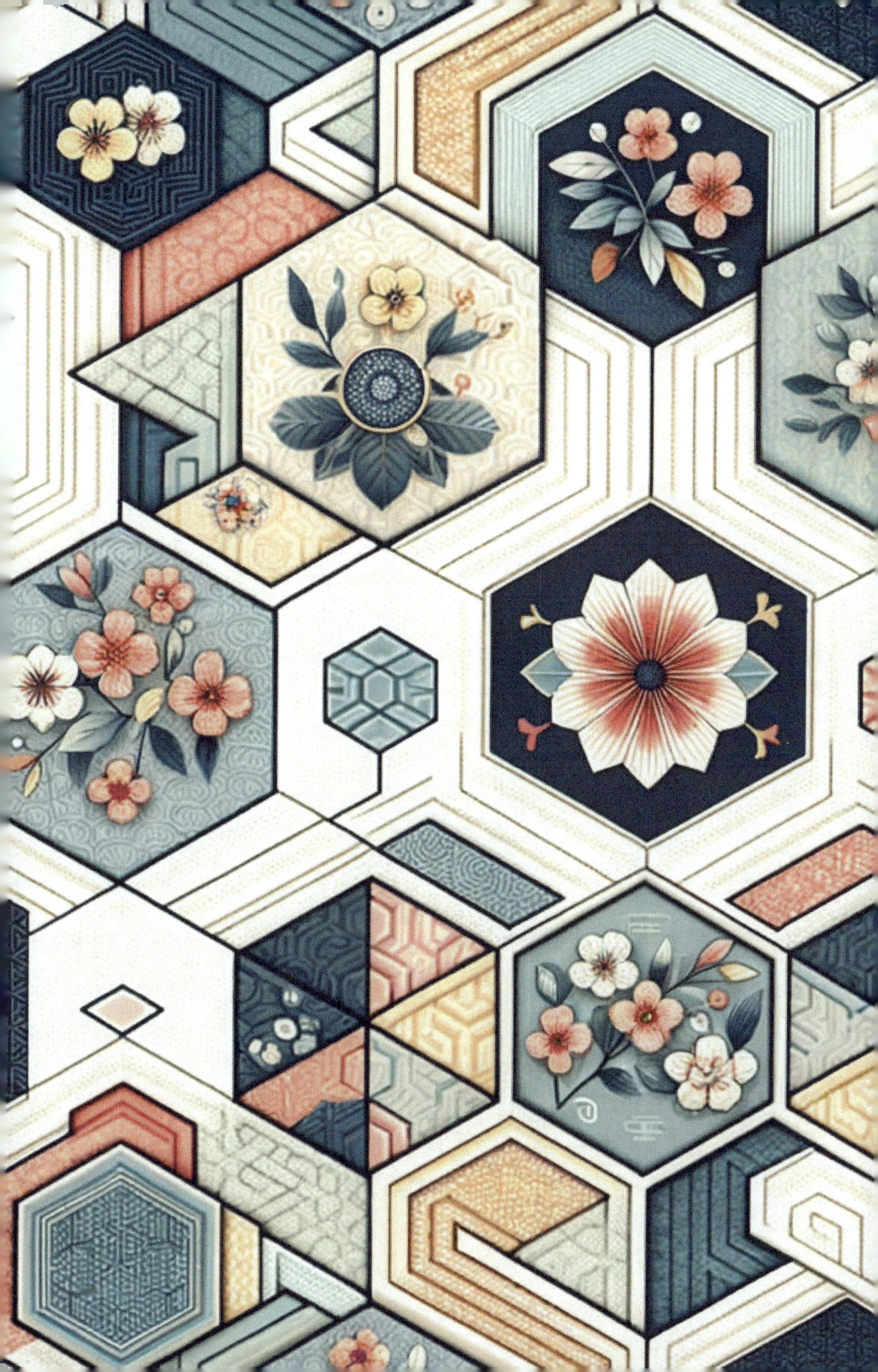

Made in the USA
Las Vegas, NV
09 May 2025